Practical Load Balancing

Ride the Performance Tiger

Peter Membrey
David Hows
Eelco Plugge

Apress®

Practical Load Balancing

ISBN-13 (pbk): 978-1-4302-3680-1

ISBN-13 (electronic): 978-1-3681-8

Trademarked names, logos, and images may appear in this book. Rather than use a trademark symbol with every occurrence of a trademarked name, logo, or image we use the names, logos, and images only in an editorial fashion and to the benefit of the trademark owner, with no intention of infringement of the trademark.

The use in this publication of trade names, trademarks, service marks, and similar terms, even if they are not identified as such, is not to be taken as an expression of opinion as to whether or not they are subject to proprietary rights.

While the advice and information in this book are believed to be true and accurate at the date of publication, neither the authors nor the editors nor the publisher can accept any legal responsibility for any errors or omissions that may be made. The publisher makes no warranty, express or implied, with respect to the material contained herein.

President and Publisher: Paul Manning
Lead Editor: Tom Welsh
Technical Reviewers: Brendan Horan, Richard Pereira, Wouter Thielen
Editorial Board: Steve Anglin, Ewan Buckingham, Gary Cornell, Louise Corrigan, Morgan Ertel,
    Jonathan Gennick, Jonathan Hassell, Robert Hutchinson, Michelle Lowman, James Markham,
    Matthew Moodie, Jeff Olson, Jeffrey Pepper, Douglas Pundick, Ben Renow-Clarke,
    Dominic Shakeshaft, Gwenan Spearing, Matt Wade, Tom Welsh
Coordinating Editor: Corbin Collins
Copy Editor: Mary Behr
Production Support: Patrick Cunningham
Indexer: SPi Global
Artist: SPi Global
Cover Designer: Anna Ishchenko

Distributed to the book trade worldwide by Springer Science+Business Media New York, 233 Spring Street, 6th Floor, New York, NY 10013. Phone 1-800-SPRINGER, fax (201) 348-4505, e-mail orders-ny@springer-sbm.com, or visit www.springeronline.com.

For information on translations, please e-mail rights@apress.com, or visit www.apress.com.

Apress and friends of ED books may be purchased in bulk for academic, corporate, or promotional use. eBook versions and licenses are also available for most titles. For more information, reference our Special Bulk Sales–eBook Licensing web page at www.apress.com/bulk-sales.

Any source code or other supplementary materials referenced by the author in this text is available to readers at www.apress.com. For detailed information about how to locate your book's source code, go to www.apress.com/source-code/.

For Professor Keith Chan and Doctor Yuri Demchenko whose unwavering support, guidance, and understanding have made so many things possible.

–Peter Membrey

For my son Jesse and the one who will soon be calling him "grote broer."

–Eelco Plugge

To Jacqui for her support, her patience, and most of all her love.

–David Hows

Contents at a Glance

Contents

About the Authors

Peter Membrey is a chartered IT professional with nearly 15 years experience using Linux and open source solutions to solve problems in the real world. An RHCE since the age of 17, he has also had the honor of working for Red Hat and writing several books covering open source solutions. He is currently a PhD student at the Hong Kong Polytechnic University where his research interests include trusted cloud computing and cloud security. He lives in Hong Kong with his wonderful wife, Sarah, and his son, Kaydyn. Alas, he still sucks at Cantonese.

Eelco Plugge is a young BSC professional with a great interest in the field of IT security. He started working as a Data Encryption Specialist for McAfee at the tender age of 21 and is currently pursuing his MSc in IT Security at the University of Liverpool while sporadically writing a book. He holds several professional certifications and has a passion for Linux, network security, and encryption. Eelco lives in the Netherlands with his young family. Loves sushi, hates complicated matters.

David Hows is an Honours graduate in Information and Communications Technology from Australia. He started working with performance technologies to find ways to boost the performance of his home PC without boosting his spending. This led him to a university degree and then to a job as a technology consultant in Accenture's Performance Engineering discipline working for governments and telecommunications companies. David has a passion for both system performance and system security, and he is at peace with the irony involved there. David currently lives and works in Sydney.

About the Technical Reviewers

Brendan Horan has an extensive background in server infrastructure technology; he has designed, built, and delivered solutions for many sectors, with a focus on telecommunications and financial. Specializing in system performance and reliability, he has an instinctive grasp of storage, network, backup, and other fascinating (to him) technologies. While he is at home poking around Linux kernel drivers to bend them to his will, he considers his real strength to be HP-UX and enterprise hardware. Currently based in Hong Kong, Brendan spends his time looking for new and more interesting places to eat and is seldom disappointed.

Richard Pereira is an IT professional with more than 24 years of experience building production-quality software and managing projects. Richard has a Masters from the University of Liverpool and is a member of the British Computing Society. He has most recently worked as Application Development Supervisor at McDermott International, a leading engineering and construction company. Outside of work, Richard spends as much time as he can with his family.

Wouter Thielen is originally from the Netherlands and now lives in Tokyo, Japan. He graduated from the University of Applied Sciences in Rotterdam with a Bachelor's degree in Information Technology. He worked at an IT solutions company as a Technical Project Manager for e-commerce projects. Currently he works in Tokyo as a Senior Developer and is also responsible for a number of mission-critical Linux servers. Being deaf, he is often invited by local deaf communities in Japan to talk about his home country. In his free time, he enjoys learning Japanese, reading, and socializing with his friends.

Special Thanks to serverlove

We'd like to offer special thanks to Daniel Keighron-Foster and the team behind serverlove for graciously allowing us to run rampant across their cloud platform during the development of this book.

We've been fans of Melbourne Server Hosting for many years due to their excellent support, awesome infrastructure, and true customer focus. After all, how often do you find a Managing Director helping a customer heft a 2U server into a rack in the middle of the night or support guys who seem to care more about your problem than you do? Whenever we called, we always hung up the phone happy.

So when they started offering a cloud solution, we jumped on board with both feet! We now host several production web sites and applications on the serverlove platform, so it's really no surprise that they were the first people we called when we were looking for somewhere to build and test all the solutions in this book.

If you haven't already guessed, serverlove is highly recommended by us. If you're interested in finding out more about the platform, please check out their site at www.serverlove.com. We would also like to point out that no authors were bribed, coerced, or harmed in the making of this acknowledgement. Any unusual exuberance is due solely to happily running servers and incredibly large uptimes.

Acknowledgments

Without question this book would not exist without the love, support, and understanding of my dear wife. I cannot recall the number of times a hot coffee has appeared on my desk or the quiet company she has given me through the long nights staring at my screen wondering why the server suddenly won't talk to me. For all the success and all that I have achieved, the credit lies solely with her.

There is also no doubt in my mind that this book would never have made it had Eelco and Dave not stepped up to the challenge. The energy and passion they poured into the book puts me to shame. Thank you both for making this possible!

A stupendous amount of effort goes into writing a book and a huge amount of work happens behind the scenes. I would be completely amiss if I did not thank Brendan, Richard, and Wouter for providing their expertise and the team at Apress for their saintly patience and understanding.

Lastly, a big thank you to Dan Keighron-Foster at serverlove and everyone else who has in some way great or small contributed to making this book a reality.

–Peter Membrey

A big thanks to caffeine and sugar for pulling me through, Pete and Dave for their hard work and dedication, and to the authors of the many manpages and documentation who made my nights a little longer.

–Eelco Plugge

This book would not exist were it not for the insights of Mr. Kappallan Nallasami who unwittingly provided some great context for this book.

It would also not exist without the work of Joshua Ryan and Alexey Chernyak who both imparted their knowledge on system performance and who both continue to work in the field.

And finally to Peter Membrey who dragged us into this mess and out the other side.

–David Hows

Preface

Load balancing, caching, and performance remain in very high demand, but the perception that they are either extremely expensive, difficult, or both has managed to persist. It is perhaps not all that surprising, as not so long ago only a few large or specialist companies really needed to take such things seriously. Today, though, even a personal blog can get so much traffic that the server can't cope, and company web sites simply have to be up and running all day, every day—no matter what. If you have a site that has to be fast and reliable all the time but you're not sure where to start or you don't have a multimillion-dollar budget (or even if you do!), this book can help!

Target Audience

This book is for anyone who has ever built a web site and wondered how to make it scale to many thousands of users. The holy grail of performance and reliability need not be restricted to large companies with huge budgets; anyone can use this book to give their applications a severe kick in the pants!

It is also for people who are hoping to build the next great thing and want to be sure that whatever they build can cope with the eventual strain of countless users.

Book Structure

This book is divided into the traditional three parts. First, we start off by introducing the key ideas behind load balancing and caching—and why you should pay attention to them. In part one, we cover the basics. We take a look at the mechanics of a web site: we take each of the pieces apart one by one so you can see how they interact and the importance of their place in the puzzle. Next up is a bumper chapter on caching. We look at its past, the huge variety of caching techniques, and how to get started with a couple of the core technologies. We then look at how DNS can be used as a simple load balancing system, followed by a hands-on tutorial on getting up and running with a content delivery network (as well as what one of those is and why you want one). We round off part one with a look at project management and backups, and how you can often plan your way into excellent performance.

Part two is where you start to get your hands really dirty. You learn the essential concepts you need to attempt the challenges in Chapter 7. In Chapter 8, we show you how to load balance your web servers. Chapter 9 follows in the same vein by giving your database the load balancing treatment. Chapter 10 demonstrates how to load balance the network itself, and Chapter 11 covers how to load balance your SSL connections.

In part three, we go beyond the usual suspects. Chapter 12 shows how to set up your systems for high availability. Chapter 13 discusses the cloud and the way it will change the game as far as performance is concerned. Chapter 14 looks at IPv6 and how you can apply the techniques you've learned to this platform. Finally, in Chapter 15 we review what you've learned so far and cover some related topics such as security, planning, and improving performance in the operating system.

Downloading the Code

A source code link is available on the book's page at www.apress.com in the Source Code/Downloads tab. This tab is located underneath the Related Titles section of the page. To locate your book's information page, enter the title or the 13-digit ISBN in the Search bar.

## CHAPTER 1

Introduction

The Internet, and in particular the World Wide Web, have effectively leveled the playing field for businesses and individuals around the world. Do you have a great idea for a web site or a service? Even the more advanced ideas can be relatively easily and cheaply realized without much in the way of initial outlay. You can get shared hosting for a few pennies each month, and dedicated servers (virtual or otherwise) are getting to the point where they are cheaper now than managed web hosting was just a few years ago.

This is all well and good, and being able to start out despite having just a few coins to rub together is certainly a great achievement. But what do you do when you want to take your application to the next step? What if it really starts to take off and you find you have the new Facebook or Amazon on your hands. What do you do then?

The Problem

Imagine you've come up with the next big thing. It's so awesome and awe-inspiring that people are going to be talking about it for years. You're pretty certain that you'll be *Time* magazine's Person of the Year. No doubt you'll soon be on a first name basis will Bill Gates and Mark Zuckerberg. The future is bright!

You've spent months getting things ready for launch. You've tested and retested. You've had friends and family visit the site and even run a few beta tests. You received rave reviews from all of them. The web site looks gorgeous, it's simple to use, and everybody loves it. You know there is nothing more that you can do to improve the site so you decide that the time is right. You reach over and press the magic button: your web site is live and you sit back and wait for the acclaim that is rightfully yours!

At first, all goes well. You've had some feedback and people are happy. They're telling their friends; more people are signing up. Now would be an appropriate time to start rubbing your hands in glee!

But something goes wrong. Someone just posted your web site's address to Slashdot. All of a sudden everyone wants to see your site. You were serving a good 10 pages per second previously, but now your server is being hammered for ten thousand! You weren't expecting this! Not only is the server not specced to support this sort of load, but you notice that previously fast requests are starting to back up as the database takes a hammering. People are starting to get error pages, some are getting timeouts, and some can't even get that far!

Within 30 minutes it's all over. Slashdot has now recorded that your site can't take the load and everyone is saying how bad the site is. "It's not stable," they say. "Half the time it doesn't load!" they complain. "What a complete waste of time!" they whine.

It's so unfair! Everything was going so well! This can't be happening! All that time, effort, and money for nothing!

■ **Note** The terms *slashdotted* and *slashdotting* have become synonymous with massive demand that no one is able to counter. The full force of Slashdot has been able to shutter the web sites of even the biggest and best funded companies. Although you might not be able to withstand such an onslaught, you can prepare your site for a potential spike in traffic without having to break the bank. Your web site will be more robust and snappier for your visitors. And if you are lucky enough to capture the attention of Slashdot, you will be in a much better position to weather the storm!

The Solution

Okay, that example is somewhat contrived, but hey, it was fun to write and it's based on fact. Don't forget that WWW stands for World Wide Web and there are millions of people using it all day, every day. If you attract just infinitesimally tiny fraction of those people at the same time, you can expect an awful lot of visitors. Most web sites respond well when one or two people visit them, but have you ever tried simulating 100,000 visitors and then tried to look at your site? These sorts of things do happen, and most of the time people get caught out.

(Peter here: For example, I was consulting for a large company that sells various types of fluffy toys online. Now, I'm not entirely sure how you become a large company by selling fluffy toys but I guess they know something that I don't! Anyway, the problem was that like most businesses they had busy and quiet periods. On average they would take around 2,000 orders per week. However, at certain times, such as Christmas and Valentine's Day, their orders would go through the roof, often to 2,000 per day! When they were really busy, they were hitting five orders per second!)

Well, their server couldn't really handle this much load. With that many orders, you can imagine how many web pages and graphics needed to be generated and sent back to customers. For every order that was placed, dozens of people could have been browsing the web site. During the normal periods, their server really had no problem coping with the load. However, during the high periods, the server would start to have problems.

The upshot? Abandoned orders. People who were simply browsing found the site so slow that they gave up and went elsewhere. Those that got through the order process only to get a timeout on the payment page (and we all know how annoying that is) simply gave up and closed the browser.

The obvious solution would be to upgrade the system so it could handle this much load. However, they looked into the pricing and found that such a machine would be many times the price of their current server. It was decided that rather than buy one big machine, they would buy two machines of a similar specification as the existing server and then use a load balancing solution.

This solution had quite a few benefits. First, it was significantly cheaper to buy two more reasonable specced machines than it would have been to buy a much higher specced server that could handle the load all by itself. It also meant more capacity for handling future growth because generally speaking, two servers provide more resources than a single server. If a single server failed, they could still fall back to using one server. This also meant that they could take a server down for maintenance without having to take down the web site.

These sorts of solutions are quite common and are a very effective way for deploying critical web sites where performance and reliability are key. This book will get you up to speed on the basics and will give you all you need to know in order to get your web sites riding the performance tiger!

What Is Load Balancing?

Ok, you've seen what load balancing can do, but what actually is it? The term has been around for many years and chances are that anyone who hasn't kept up with development of the Web will think it has to do with electricity and power stations. Before you laugh, they're quite correct, so this is a great place for you to start your load-balancing journey! No really, it is!

Load Balancing, Old Style

Most things in the home use electricity and that electricity comes from the power grid. To generate electricity, we need power stations of some form or another. That much is fairly obvious and straightforward.

However, at different times of the day the requirement for power changes. In the morning, when people are getting up and getting ready for work, there is a large demand. People are turning on kettles, toasters, ovens, and other high usage appliances. The grid needs to make sure that there is enough power available for everyone to do this.

But what happens when people go to work? Suddenly not so much power is needed, but you can't just turn off a power station. It's also quite possible that when everyone starts making breakfast, the load placed on the grid is higher than what the individual power stations can supply.

Fortunately, it's load balancing to the rescue. By storing power when it's not being used during the off-peak times, the grid is able to provide higher amounts of power during the on-peak times.

So, how is this like load balancing in the computing world? Well, it all comes down to having finite resources and trying to make the best possible use of them. You have the goal of making your web sites fast and stable; to do that you need to route your requests to the machines best capable of handling them.

Load Balancing, New Style

In computing terms, you're going to be doing something similar. People put load on your web site by making lots of requests to it. This is a normal state of affairs and is, after all, why you have a web site in the first place. No one wants a web site that nobody looks at.

But what happens when people turn on their appliances and start stressing your server? At this point things can go bad; if the load is too high (because too many people are visiting), your web site is going to take a performance hit. It's going to slow down, and with more and more users, it will get slower and slower until it fails completely. Not what you want.

To get around this, you need more resources. You can either buy a bigger machine to replace your current server (scale up) or you can buy another small machine to work alongside your existing server (scale out).

Scaling Up

Scaling up is quite common for applications that just need more power. Maybe the database has grown so large that it won't fit in memory like it used to. Perhaps the disks are getting full or the database needs to handle more requests than it used to and needs more processing power.

Databases are generally a good example for scaling up because traditionally they had severe problems when run on more than one machine. This is because many of the things you can take for granted on a single machine simply break when you try to make them work on more than one. For example, how do you share tables across the machines efficiently? It's a really hard problem to solve, which is why several new databases, such as MongoDB and CouchDB, have been designed to work in a very different way.

Scaling up can be pretty expensive, though. Usually when you get above a certain specification, servers suddenly leap in price. Now the machine comes with a high spec RAID controller, enterprise grade disks, and a new type of processor (that mysteriously looks and performs like the previous one but has a much higher price tag). If you're just upgrading components, it might be cheaper to scale up rather than out, but you will most likely find that you will get less bang for your buck this way. That said, if all you need is an extra couple of gigabytes of RAM or some more disk space, or you just need to boost the performance of a particular application, this might be your best solution.

Scaling Out

This is where things start to get interesting and the reason why you actually picked up this book. Scaling out is when you have two or three machines rather than a single machine. An issue with scaling up is that at some point you hit a limit that you can't cross. There is only so much processing power and memory a single machine can hold. What happens if you need more than that?

Many people will tell you you're in an envious position if you have so many visitors that a single machine just can't take the load. This is a nice problem to have, believe it or not! The great thing about scaling out is that you can simply keep adding machines. Sure, at some point you will start to hit space and power issues, but you will certainly have more compute power by scaling out than you could get by scaling up.

In addition, when you scale out, you have more machines. So if one machine were to fail, you still have other machines that can take on the load. When you scale up, if that one machine fails, then everything fails.

Scaling out does have one problem and it's a big one. The scenario is this: you operate a single cohesive web site or web application and you have three machines. How do you make all those three machines operate together so that they give the impression of a single machine? Load balancing!

Load Balancing, Finally

Yes, you're on page four and we haven't as yet really talked about load balancing, which might seem somewhat odd considering that's what this book is all about. But fear not, we're getting into the juicy stuff now! And you're also going to look at caching, which (honestly) goes hand in hand with load balancing and can give you an insanely big performance boost!

But first, back to load balancing. As mentioned, the biggest challenge in load balancing is trying to make many resources appear as one. Specifically, how do you make three servers look and feel like a single web site to your customer?

What Makes the Web Tick?

The first stop in this journey is to look at how the Web holds together. When you click the Go button on your browser, what happens under the covers? This book will go into quite a bit of detail, even looking briefly at the TCP (Transmission Control Protocol, the protocol that powers the web) layer. It has been our experience that while someone might be able to produce the most awe-inspiring web applications, they're not necessarily very clued up on the lower level things that make it all possible. In reality this isn't an issue because, by design, you don't need to know the innards of the Internet in order to write kickass software. However, if you want to make your software scream past the competition at high speed, you need a much better appreciation of how it all hangs together.

Not interested? Don't worry. If you really can't bring yourself to read Chapter 2, you can still get a great deal out of the book. You will be able to make your web sites go faster and you will be able to make them more resilient and reliable. But you risk not knowing exactly why this is happening and that means you might end up creating web sites that have the same problems over and over again.

Caching: Warp Drive for Your Web Site

Chapter 3 gets you started on caching and shows how even the simplest of techniques can make your web site simply scream. If you don't get the sci-fi reference in the subtitle, it just means that your web application is going to be very very fast indeed!

We start with the basics: getting your application to tell the world what it can and can't cache, why this is important, and why you need to be somewhat careful with this approach as you might end up caching things that you hadn't intended.

Next, you look at how you can get more control over what you're caching and how. This is where the power really starts, but amazingly enough it's really easy to do. In our experience, it is this part of caching that pays out in spades. There is a reason web sites like Facebook and Twitter use these techniques, and now you'll be joining them!

Make it so!

Load Balancing with DNS

Chapter 4 takes on the most under-appreciated form of load balancing around. Load balancing with DNS (Domain Name System, the phonebook of the Internet) lacks some of the finesse and power of the other techniques but it's far and away the easiest solution to set up. In seconds you can have load balancing up and running. Not too shabby!

We'll also introduce some of the problems you're likely to walk into when you do any form of load balancing, not necessarily specific to using DNS. We'll show you some potential solutions for the problems and where to start looking if you are doing something a bit different.

You'll get to appreciate how DNS works and why it does what it does, and then you'll take a look at any-cast DNS, a technique used for content delivery networks and a very powerful tool indeed for load balancing across entire countries!

Content Delivery Networks

Following on from the last chapter, Chapter 5 looks at content delivery networks (CDN) and how they can help you boost performance. This isn't something you can build yourself; fortunately, such networks already exist, and you can take advantage of them.

Want to get your downloads as close to your customers as possible? Want to serve your static resources (such as images, JavaScript, and CSS files) without putting load on your already stressed servers? A CDN could be just what you're looking for!

We cover Rackspace Cloud as we have been really impressed with their cloud offerings. However, the principles can be applied with any CDN provider so you are in no way restricted to one provider. In fact, since we've been using Rackspace Cloud, they've changed their CDN provider at least twice without affecting how the system is used by developers and end users. How cool is that?

CDNs are big business and they are becoming critical to web sites that specialize in moving content around the world. If you ever see "CDN" in a web site name (take a look at your status bar next time you load a page from Facebook) you will know that they are leveraging this technology to give their sites a big performance boost. Now you can do the same!

Proper Planning Prevents Pretty Poor Performance

There is a reason why the 6P principle is taught to military officers around the world. If you have a plan, even if it's not a great one, you stand a much greater chance of success than if you just sat down and tried to wing it.

Chapter 6 looks at some basic principles that you can follow to make sure your web applications are nicely layered, easy to scale, and grow with demand. There are no magic tricks here, just good old-fashioned advice from people who have sometimes forgotten it and dug themselves into a nice deep hole. It's dark down there and it's often not easy to get out without a lot of hard work and effort. If you follow our advice (or just some of it) you'll be going a long way towards avoiding that particular pit…

The Essentials

Before we get into heavy-duty load balancing techniques, we provide a quick look at some essential ideas that you need to know before delving in. Chapter 7 is a short chapter—just a primer that will make your journey through the remaining chapters that much easier. We also look at some of the more exotic concepts of load balancing and even though we won't go into those in a great deal of depth, the information will prevent you tripping up if you come across some content on the Web that mentions them.

HTTP Load Balancing

Chapter 8 is where the fun really starts. At this stage your site is so busy it needs at least two servers to keep things running smoothly. Don't worry; we've got you covered!

First, though, we'll look at how you can optimize your individual web servers to get the most out of them before you load balance them. We compare Apache, the most common web server on the planet, with Nginx, one of the fastest, meanest web servers around. Can Nginx really give your site a performance boost? If so, when is it best to use one or the other? This chapter bares all!

We also look at some of the features that improve performance such as enabling compression, disabling DNS lookups for logging, removing unneeded modules, and much more!

Load Balancing Your Database

The database is historically the slowest component of any web application. It doesn't matter how fast you make the machine or how much tuning you do, when compared to the speed you can serve dynamic HTML, databases just can't keep up.

When you need more speed or can't tolerate database failure (and who can?) you need to do some database clustering. This chapter covers how to create a MySQL cluster and how to load balance across it.

Load Balancing Your Network Connection

What do you do when 1GB/sec of network bandwidth isn't enough and you don't want to take out a mortgage to pay for a 10GB-capable network? You take two 1GB connections and use them as one!

Do you want redundancy? Do you want to double your throughput? This chapter will take you through how to get the most out of your network infrastructure. We show you the various ways that the network can be configured to give you the fastest and most reliable connection to the network possible!

SSL Load Balancing

Secure web pages are the core of e-commerce and all modern interactive web applications. These days if the padlock isn't golden, people won't be using your web site. The problem is that handling 10,000 SSL connections can be somewhat intensive for an application server. In fact, you may well find that you're spending more time handling the SSL connections than executing your application!

Chapter 11 starts off by giving an overview of how PKI encryption works and why it's so important (and resource intensive) to use it. We show you how to generate your own keys and certificate requests so that you can easily get your hands on a trusted certificate from one of the many certificate authorities out there today. We will also show you how to generate and sign your own certificates so you can begin testing immediately without having to pay for a trusted certificate.

We'll then show you how to handle SSL termination with Nginx and how to spread the load across more than one machine. We also touch on some security issues and how you can use some simple settings to help improve the security of your web application.

Clustering for High Availability

It's all well and good having a load balancer to spread the load but now you have introduced a single point of failure. If your load balancing goes down, it doesn't matter that the 10 servers behind it are healthy; nothing will be able to get to them.

In Chapter 12 we discuss solutions to make sure that this doesn't happen by building a cluster. If one load balancer fails, the other will take over the load.

Load Balancing in the Cloud

The cloud is the next big thing; with it a whole host of new challenges will be joining the current list that you have to deal with. Chapter 13 will introduce the cloud, what makes it tick, and the things you need to know when looking at the performance of your application. We discuss why not all cloud providers were born equal and why what works well for one web site might not be the best solution for another.

IPv6: Implementation and Concepts

The Web is predominantly IPv4-based but unfortunately we've pretty much run out of available IP addresses. Depending on who you ask, we have already run out. IPv6 is the replacement and it's already being rolled out across the world. How does IPv6 work and how will it affect you? You will learn some of the benefits and problems you can expect to deal with when IPv6 becomes mainstream. For many uses, IPv6 is not significantly or noticeably different from IPv4, but there are some gotchas, especially in the applications discussed throughout the book. This chapter will get you up to speed on applying what you've learned in the other chapters to the world of IPv6.

Where To Go Next

You'll be able to seriously boost the performance of your web applications with just the knowledge contained in these pages. But the Web doesn't sit still. Things are always changing. Chapter 14 looks at some of the cool things sneaking up on the horizon that you should probably be keeping an eye on.

Summary

So what will this book do for you? Well, it assumes you know nothing about how the Internet operates under the covers or how load balancing works in general. It will teach you the basics of how the Internet hangs together and what browsing the Web actually entails. We'll show you how to speed up your web application using caching, how to use various types of load balancing, and the key concepts (and more importantly how to apply them) to make your applications easy to scale. We'll also show you how to cluster your load balancers for high availability, terminate your SSL sessions for higher throughput, and build robust solutions. Finally, we'll look at new technologies that you need to watch, such as IPv6 and cloud computing.

In short, this book will take you from being curious about making your web site faster and more reliable to being someone who can easily set up such a solution, confident that they know why and how it works.

We all hope you enjoy reading this book as much as we enjoyed writing it!

## CHAPTER 2

How Web Sites Work

Why is it that the simplest of questions have hideously complicated answers? On the surface, the Web is quite simple—at least in how it is actually used. Under the covers, though, the systems that work together to make the World Wide Web possible are complex and they interact in various interesting (and often frustrating) ways. We're not kidding when we say that it took about six drafts of this chapter before we had something we were reasonably confident addressed this question sufficiently!

In most cases, we can get away with saying that the Web is simply a collection of documents that link to each other. If pressed further, we might mention web servers, dynamic and static content, HTML and JSON, and other things; this level tends to satisfy most people. For you, dear reader, we need to dig deeper. You need to understand where these beasts came from and what makes them work. Only then can you really get an instinctive feel for web performance.

We can hear the stifled groans already, but yes, we are going to talk about how the Web works and why. Yes, you've probably heard it all before or accidentally read about it during a Wikipedia marathon. For those of you hoping we have some insider information about the birth of the Web, we're afraid we're going to disappoint you. We promise, however, that it is important to revisit this stuff, and we'll tell you why.

The *Guide to Assembly Language Programming in Linux* (by Sivarama P. Dandamudi; Springer, 2005) is a very good book. Although it teaches assembly, you won't see any mention of assembly until you're nearly a third of the way through. The first thing it teaches you is the concept of Boolean logic, and from there, how you can implement the most simple logic gates (such as AND, OR, and NOT) using transistors. It takes around 5 nanoseconds for a transistor to "react" to a change in input. That sounds fast, but when you have millions of them working together, all of a sudden you can see a performance hit. You learn how memory is constructed from 1 bit to a multi-gigabyte array and how the processor addresses it. Why is any of that important? It's important because when you start looking at writing in assembly you know precisely what each command you execute involves, how long it will take, and why. It means you can pick the best commands for a given situation, and you can optimize your code to leverage your chosen architecture. You wouldn't have been able to do any of this if you hadn't first learned about logic gates.

In this chapter, we hope to take a leaf from that book and take you back to the beginning. We3 won't spend too much time in the past, certainly not a third of a book, but we will look at how we got to where we are today. We will look at what the Web was created to solve and some of the challenges we've seen since. We will then look at the network protocols that support the Web and some of the hot spots for performance issues.

Let the Games Commence!

When you view a web page, a surprising number of things need to happen before you get to see the page in all its glory. The good news is that from a user's point of view all they have to do is type in the proper address—and thanks to Google even that isn't really important any more. However, you shouldn't confuse *simple* with *simplistic.* The web as you see it today is made possible because of myriad systems that all work nicely together in order to create the appearance of a single system. If any one of these systems were to fail, it would significantly impact your ability to browse the web—and in many cases would stop it all together.

Coming from a Non-IT Background

Many people have come to building and managing web sites from backgrounds other than the traditional IT route. In fact, some of the best web designers we know have very little in the way of computer science knowledge; it's really their creative side that has made them successful at what they do. The technicalities of making a web site work and the infrastructure to run them is often just a cost of doing business; it's a necessary evil and not something they have a particular interest in. Unfortunately, these folks may be unaware of certain technical issues that they really should address, such as SQL injection attacks and cross-site scripting. (Of course, not everyone falls into this category; many people who develop web sites not only have a grasp of the underlying technology but actively develop and enhance it to the point where they are redefining some of the basic concepts of the Web itself.)

Before I can talk about how to make web sites fast, I need to talk about what makes web sites slow. Some of this information may be obvious but a lot of it is hidden in plain sight; it isn't until you actually think about it that you start to realize the significance of some of things that you take for granted.

Kicking Off the Process

Loading a web page starts on the user's computer with their browser. She enters the address for your web site and hit the Enter button. Already there are several pieces at work here. First, the browser has an impact on the way the web site is loaded, including the order files are requested, the way the page is rendered, and much more. The browser is also impacted by the operating system and the computer that it's running on. Older operating systems may not take full advantage of available system memory (such as any 32-bit version of Linux or Windows) or be able to efficiently use the multi-core CPUs that have been become standard in recent years. Operating systems are, of course, limited to the resources made available by the computer they're running on. Even today's low-cost computer would seem simply incredible to any computer scientist 10 years ago; today, though, it may already seem sluggish and far from high performance. Moreover, computers have moved far beyond the tower sitting under your desk. Every day more and more people browse the web from their phones and tablet devices. These devices have very different performance profiles than desktop computers and usually support a smaller range of features (though not always).

This is just the first stage of browsing the web and already I've identified several significant issues that affect how to deliver high-performing web sites. Clearly it's not simply a case of bigger and faster servers; it doesn't matter how fast your servers are if the browser blows up when it tries to access your page.

Finding the Site with DNS

So the user has pressed the Enter button and is eagerly awaiting your web page. First, her computer needs to look up the IP address of your web site. Computers can't use the URL directly; it must be converted to the numerical address that is used on the network itself. All computers attached to the Internet have been configured with at least one (and usually two) DNS servers. This is normally part of the automatic configuration done when the computer requests an IP address either from your router or your ISP. So, before the browser can even think of connecting to your site, it needs to wait for the OS to contact the ISP's DNS server to ask for the right address. Because there are so many computers on the Internet, no one computer can know all the answers. In other words, unless your web site is the next Facebook or Google, it's pretty unlikely that the user's ISP will have any idea what the address should be. So another request is made to another DNS server, which is also unlikely to know the answer. However, it can point to a server that might know. So yet another request goes out to the latest DNS server, which may or may not know the answer and may instead refer to *another* server. This goes on until it finally reaches a server that does know the answer. The answer is then passed back to the user's computer and at last she can start the process of connecting to the site.

If this process sounds tedious, it's because it is. However, it's also far better than the original solution, which involved copying a massive text file around. Thanks to caching and the small amount of resources DNS requires, a look-up from a human point of view is actually pretty swift and almost instantaneous. However, if your domain is sitting on an old yellowing PC in the corner of the office and serves results via an extremely busy ADSL line, it might actually take a second or two for that server to be able to respond to a user's request. Even if the web site is on a super-fast server with the world's faster Internet connection, if it takes two seconds to find that server, then your web site will always appear slow.

DNS is often overlooked and it shouldn't be. Not only is it critical to the speed of your web site, it also offers some easy ways of doing load balancing and ramping up the perceived speed of your site. That said, if you're hosting your domain with a half-decent provider, you are unlikely to have any trouble with this aspect.

Connecting to the Server (Finally!)

Now that the user finally has the address, she can start connecting to the remote site. To make a very long story slightly shorter, the web runs over TCP, a protocol that guarantees all data is delivered and (just as importantly) arrives in the order in which it was sent. As developers, we can take this ability for granted. One of the key design goals of TCP is that the developer doesn't need to worry about how TCP performs its magic. However, this magic has its trade-offs. In order to provide these guarantees, it has to do a lot of work under the covers. TCP's companion protocol UDP is far lighter than TCP but it makes none of the guarantees that TCP provides. UDP packets can (and do) get lost in transit, and they can (and do) arrive in any order. Of course, you can write your software with this in mind to give UDP similar properties to TCP, but unless you have a very specific reason for this, you'll probably find you've just recreated TCP.

What can you do about this overhead? Well, you can't replace TCP even if you wanted to. Every web browser and server uses TCP, so if you want to be able to talk to the rest of the world, you need to comply with the same standards as everyone else. However, being aware of how TCP works and the process involved in providing these useful guarantees will allow you to make the most of the resources and thus limit the overhead to just the bare essentials.

On the Server Itself

Okay, now we're at the connection to your site and it's only taken six sections to get that far! You send the request for the page and now you pass over control to the web server. At this stage, pretty much anything can happen. Is the page requested a static page being loaded from the disk? Is it a page that's created on-demand in real time? If it's a dynamic page, does it require access to a database? Does it need to make requests of its own to other web sites? Is any of the data cached?

Web servers are not born equal. For example, the Apache web server out of the box on most Linux distributions isn't particular efficient in either CPU or memory usage. However, it does tend to just work and it offers plenty of support and documentation. If you want a small server that's designed for serving static files at high speed and eats very little resources, you might want to look at nginx. (This isn't to say that one is better than the other, simply that their target audiences are different.)

Note   At this point, some people will be shouting out that Apache can be slimmed down and can compete with nginx. While it is true that you can tweak Apache and remove as many of its modules as you want, why would you bother when there are servers available that were designed for your particular use case? Actually, there are some good reasons, such as only having to learn how one web server works and how to configure it. That said, ask yourself whether stripping down Apache is really any easier to maintain or support than simply installing a server that is already optimized to do what you want out of the box. Like many things in IT, it comes down to personal preference. As long as you have good reasons for your choice, you can use whichever sever you feel is the best fit for your needs.

Next up is the programming language used to develop the site. Different languages and frameworks have difference performance characteristics, but this is really too specialized for a general book on performance; you can find a great deal of information about the various platforms and languages online. Not all of the performance tuning will necessarily work for you; use your discretion and test the solutions to see which help you the most.

Talking to the Database

Once you get past the language, you're now looking at the database. Most dynamic sites have a database of some sort that they use for storing either content or information that the user wants to query, such as statistics or scientific results. Even the simplest of web sites may use a database for storing information on site hits or for providing a member's area. Again, each database has its own pros and cons—as well as a long list of supporters and (more often than not) detractors. If you exclude web sites that need to contact other web sites to generate a page, databases are by far the slowest parts of any web application, even if they are in real terms extremely fast. Caching greatly helps here and is something you will look into in the next chapter.

Quick Look at Caching

Depending on the site itself, there might be some sort of caching involved. Few developers, in our experience, really get their hands dirty with caching; most tend to use whatever the languages or frameworks provide by default. This can range from excellent to non-existent. Usually the server or application looks in the cache before doing expensive calls to the database or content generation, so usually it greatly improves performance rather than impacts it negatively. Again, you'll get hands-on with this in Chapter 3.

If the web site has to make use of other external web resources, you can almost replicate this whole "load a web page" process again for that stage. This is more common than you might think, as many web sites act as middlemen or brokers for other services. For example, resellers often have access to a back-end system via a web API such as SOAP or REST. When a user wants to sign up for, say, ADSL, she puts in her details into a form on the web site and presses the Enter button. The web site collects this data and then sends a request to the actual supplier to run the check for them. SOAP and REST use HTTP, so it's very similar to a standard browser request. If the back end itself needs to contact other services (again, not too unusual; a reseller might contact a broker who contacts the actual supplier) then the chain can get even longer.

If your web site contacts back-end services like this, you need to factor their response times into your system design and see if there is any way you can minimize the impact to the end user. For example, you could show a "Please wait" page so at least the user knows something is still happening in the background.

Back to the Client

All being well, the server now (finally) sends the page back to the user. This is where the browser has to render the page so that the user actually gets to see something. We won't talk much about the browser seeing as we already bored you with that earlier; suffice it to say that if your page contains twenty images and some external JavaScript and CSS, the browser will need to repeat this loading process for each of these resources. In a worst case scenario, on a very busy page this could mean hundreds of requests to the server. In other words, the process we just followed is just for one file; it has to be repeated for as many files as the page requires, which could be substantial.

And so ends this quick look at loading a web page. I've deliberately glossed over things such as server hardware and available bandwidth as we'll talk about these issues in more depth later in this chapter. However, you should now have a greater understanding of the intricacies involved in loading even the simplest of web pages and the myriad factors that can slow down your site. Throughout the book, I will look at many of these and demonstrate how you can either mitigate them entirely or at least manage them as much as possible.

The rest of this chapter takes a more in-depth look at some of the highlights from the previous section. Again, the plan is to give you a general idea as to what's going on in the background so that as you progress through the coming chapters you will have an understanding of how the solutions they provide fit into the grand scheme of things and thus how you can best use them to your advantage.

Taking a Closer Look

After that whirlwind tour you're either regretting picking up this book or you're starting to see that making web sites go faster is not quite as simple as it might appear. It's true that you can get very big gains from even simple optimization, but now you know where these optimizations take effect and why you get the benefits that you do.

To round out the chapter, we're going to look at some of those key areas again, only this time we're going to dip into more of the technical aspects. For example, we'll look at the composition of a web page, the format it's stored in, and how this affects the performance of your web site. As before, this is not intended to be a comprehensive guide to each and every topic. Entire books can (and have) been written on these individual subjects alone. Instead, think of the rest of this chapter as some of the choicer bits. You will no doubt come up with a lot of questions, many of which will be answered in the rest of this book. For those questions that we haven't anticipated, we encourage you to use your favorite search engine to unearth the answer. If you have a question, you're probably not the first; it's often amazing (and humbling) to find entire discussions from years past where your exact question was answered and debated.

The following sections are broken down into various key areas. We start off by looking at the network layer, which includes examining how TCP and DNS work as well as examining the differences between speed, bandwidth, and latency. I then look at the component parts of a web page, specifically HTML and its related text format, and discuss the pros and cons as well as how to get an easy boost using compression. I also look at the concept of hyperlinks and what this means for performance. Next, I take a quick look at how web content is generated and the differences between static and dynamic content. I also briefly look at how this has developed over the years from a performance perspective and how this effects how you should serve the content. I also very lightly touch on the browser itself, and finally, on why databases are the weakest link in terms of performance and why even very simple caching can make incredible differences to performance.

The Network

The two key network-related things as far as web performance is concerned are TCP and DNS. DNS provides the means to find the server you want to talk to and TCP provides the mechanism for moving the data to your browser. I will also take a very quick look at the differences between speed, bandwidth, and latency—and why they aren't the same thing.

TCP

Here's the deal: if you promise not to fall asleep while we very briefly talk about TCP and how it works at a basic operational level, we will promise not to include yet another pretty picture of the OSI network stack or to bore you to death with tedious RTT (round-trip time) calculations. Deal?

TCP is one of the two key protocols used on the Internet today, with the other being UDP. These two protocols are used for very different purposes and have very different characteristics when they're used. The interesting thing, though, is that really there's only one major distinction between the two and all of the differences extend from it. Basically, TCP is reliable and UDP is not.

For that to make much sense, I need to take a step back and look at the Internet Protocol (IP) itself. It's no accident that you usually see TCP/IP written together (although historically it's actually because IP evolved from an unrelated TCP). Previously, it was something of a challenge to make different networks talk to each other. Either there were different network technologies at a hardware level (Ethernet, Token Ring, serial links, and so forth) or they had their own weird and wonderful protocols that wouldn't talk to anything else (NetBEUI and IPX/SPX, for example). The other problem was that networks were fairly static and didn't handle failure very well. If a key distribution point failed, it could cause the whole network to fail. This is far from ideal at the best of times but something you really don't want in your critical infrastructure, such as emergency services or nuclear command and control systems.

IP solved this problem by creating a protocol that didn't require static networks. By putting the address information into each packet and moving responsibility for delivery to the network itself, IP was able to "just work." For example, when you send a packet, it goes to your default gateway. If that is your modem or router at home, it likely knows of just one gateway, the one at your ISP. Your router then passes the packet to the ISP's router. Your ISP knows many more routes but they are usually generic; by this we mean the router might not know the exact location of the destination computer, but it does know which router it knows about is closest to the destination (and thus hopefully also the fastest). The router then forwards the packet on to that router, which repeats the process until the packet finally reaches its destination. This process is done for every packet you send and receive.

Because handling packets like this can be done in a stateless way (the routers don't need to know anything about the packet other than the details provided in the header), they don't need to remember packets they've seen before or keep any complex statistics. Each packet is treated individually and so this system can scale nicely. This is a concept you will see many times in this book.

This system has another benefit. The list of available routers (usually referred to as a list of routes) is dynamic. Each router maintains its own list but only knows about a couple of routes (though some core routers may know many more than this). If a router stops responding, routers will stop sending packets to it and will pick the best alternative route from their list. In fact, it's quite possible that for a given connection that sends ten packets, each one could have been sent via a completely different route.

There is a problem with this system. The simplicity that makes it fast, efficient, and reliable in the sense that a single router failure won't disable the whole network doesn't offer any delivery guarantees. That is, as each router just forwards on a packet-by-packet basis and each packet can take a different route, there is no way to know if any went missing en route. We can't add state to the network itself or we would lose the massive scalability that we've gained—and we'd be back where we started.

This is the problem that TCP solves. It uses IP to deliver and route packets but it guarantees delivery and the order of packets. From a developer's point of view, once a TCP connection is established, what you send down one end is guaranteed to arrive at the other. To do this, TCP uses the concept of sequence numbers based on the amount of data sent. This information is ignored by the routers and only used by the computers at either end of the connection. So we can keep state but we only need to do it at the two end points, not all of the routers in between. By using the sequence numbers, it's possible to determine if any data has gone missing as well as the correct order the packets should be delivered in. Remember, IP packets can take any route so it is quite possible and actually common for packets to arrive out of order. Of course, for this to work, the two computers need to do a bit of negotiation so that they start off on the same page. This is done at the beginning of the connection and is called the *handshake*.

A TCP handshake consists of three stages. They can be summarized (see the note for a more technical version) by the following:

Client: I want to open a connection.
Server: No problem. Do you still want to chat?
Client: Yup! Let's go!

This needs to be done for each connection that is opened. When you download graphics from a web site, ultimately you use TCP to do the downloading. In earlier versions of HTTP, each request and response required a new connection; if you had to download 30 images, you needed 30 connections and hence 30 handshakes. Not surprisingly, if your connection speed is already less than awesome, the last thing you want is an additional 30 "empty" round trips to the server.

Note Okay, the TCP handshake is a bit more formal than that but really it is as simple as it looks (see Figure 2-1)! If you look in a textbook you will find the handshake defined as SYN (for synchronize), SYN-ACK (the server wants to synchronize and is also acknowledging your SYN with an ACK), and ACK (the client acknowledges the server's request). If you think it looks almost like you're negotiating two connections at the same time, you're spot on. Sockets are negotiated in both directions and this allows you to send and receive data at the same time. Cunning, eh?

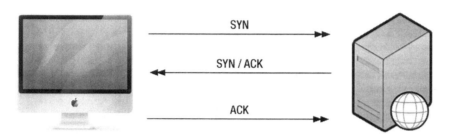

Figure 2-1. TCP Handshake

As promised, this part didn't contain any discussion of the OSI layers and no RTT calculations. However, there are some important points that we're hoping you will take away from this (very) brief tour of TCP. Every time you create a new TCP connection, you need to go through a handshake. There is simply no way around this; the only way to avoid a new handshake is to avoid opening a new connection. The second point is that packets can take any route to get from point A to point B. The idea is that the closest or faster router is chosen, but that isn't guaranteed. It's possible for packets to get stuck in a congested network just as cars get stuck on the motorway. This gives us the second golden rule: to avoid getting stuck in traffic, make sure that points A and B are as close together as possible.

DNS

Okay, now you know how data gets from the server to the client and vice versa but one thing I didn't touch on is that IP has no concept of names. It only understands numbers. An IP address is usually represented as a "dotted quad" number and looks like this: 192.168.1.1. In fact, it's just a 32-bit number that has been made a bit easier to read. While it's nicer to look at, it's still a nightmare to remember. Humans are inherently bad at remembering numbers. There is a reason we have phonebooks and why people write their PIN numbers on the back of their debit cards. Let's be honest; if we can't reliably remember a four-digit PIN number, what are the chances we're going to remember the computer address for every web site we want to visit? And even if we could, what if the site has several computers or the address changes?

I go in to the history of DNS and how we ended up with the current system (and most importantly how you can exploit it to make your sites go faster) in the DNS chapter. For now, all you need to know is that you can change nice human readable names such as www.example.com into the address format that the computer needs.

The reason we're mentioning DNS in this chapter is because although DNS is very efficient for what it does, looking up a name is not free. DNS looks like a big tree with each branch being the next level down. The top of the tree is the dot domain. The next level contains domains like `.com`, `.org`, and `.hk`. Under `.com` is example.com, and under example.com is `www.example.com`. Assuming no one has looked up this name for a while, you must walk the whole tree. It works a bit like sending out a messenger. You go to the top of the tree and ask about `www.example.com`. The top server doesn't know the answer to your request but it can tell you who you need to ask for questions related to `.com`. So you go to that server and repeat your request. You get a similar response this time as well: it won't know the answer to your question but it can point you to the server who knows about example.com. And so on and so forth until we get to the server that actually can answer our request.

This is admittedly a worst-case scenario. Most DNS servers cache requests and each computer keeps its own local copy. In reality, your own computer can often answer the question and your ISP's server (your first port of call usually) handles requests from every customer, so they are likely to have the results for the most common sites already to hand. Sites like `www.google.com` and `www.facebook.com` are almost guaranteed to be permanently cached.

I won't look at the cool things you can do with DNS in this chapter but the key take-away point for this section is that although looking up names is not exactly slow, you take a slight performance hit each time you do it. In other words, the less names you use, the better; then, in a worst case scenario where all the names have to be looked up, there are fewer requests that need to be sent.

Speed, Bandwidth, and Latency

Speed, bandwidth, and latency are the source of much confusion and pain for a lot of people. Everyone intuitively understands *speed* but the other two have definitions that, while quite simple, do sound very alike. *Bandwidth* is the amount of data a given connection can transfer in a particular amount of time. This is generally measured in bits per second. *Latency* is the time it takes for a given request to receive a response. This has a more precise definition but practically everyone measures it with the `ping` command. This command measures the time it takes for a small packet to reach a given server and for that server's response to reach the client.

The confusion stems from the idea that the more bandwidth you have, the faster your Internet connection is. That's not technically true. The more bandwidth you have, the more data you can receive at a given time. So, yes, it takes less time for the data to arrive—but the time taken to actually send each bit of data might actually be slower than a connection that has less bandwidth.

Confused? ISPs have spent the past 15 years telling everyone how if you upgrade to their latest and greatest connection you will get everything so much faster, so you'd be forgiven for thinking that we're talking rubbish. After all, downloading the same file takes 30 seconds on one connection and 60 seconds on the other. Quite clearly one downloads the file quicker than the other, so how can the slow one actually be faster?

Here's an example that actually makes sense. Imagine two cities that are 100 miles apart. Connecting them is a single road with one lane heading from City A to City B. (For some reason, people who go to City B never want to go back to City A.) Let's say that you drive your car from City A to City B at a fixed speed of 50mph (ignoring the fiddly bits of acceleration and laws of thermodynamics so it can cruise perfectly at 50mph from start to finish.) How long does it take your car to get from A to B? Well, if the distance is 100 mph and your car moves at 50 mph, it's going to take you two hours. Okay, that wasn't exactly taxing but what if there are 10 cars that need to get from A to B? Let's say for safety reasons, that there must be a 30 minute gap between each car. This is now getting a bit more complex. Have a look at Table 2-1.

Table 2-1. *Cars Travelling from City A to City B*

Car	Departure Time from A	Arrival Time at B	Trip Time (in hours)	Total time (in hours)
1	0:00	2:00	2.00	2.00
2	0:30	2:30	2.00	2.50
3	1:00	3:00	2.00	3.00
4	1:30	3:30	2.00	3.50
5	2:00	4:00	2.00	4.00
6	2:30	4:30	2.00	4.50
7	3:00	5:00	2.00	5.00
8	3:30	5:30	2.00	5.50
9	4:00	6:00	2.00	6.00
10	4:30	6:30	2.00	6.50

This is getting more interesting. The trip time for each remained the same at 2 hours, but it actually took 6.5 hours for all of the cars to arrive. Now imagine you are a holding an important meeting and you need all 10 people to turn up before you can begin. Your first person turns up at 2:00 p.m. but the last guy doesn't turn up until 6:30 p.m., five and a half hours later. Not ideal.

Now let's look at a slightly different scenario. Let's say that the road contains two lanes. The same rules apply as before: one car can leave every 30 minutes and it travels at a perfect 50mph. Table 2-2 shows the same scenario on the new dual carriageway.

Table 2-2. *Cars Travelling from City A to City B on a Two-Lane Road*

Car	Departure Time from A	Arrival Time at B	Trip Time (in hours)	Total time (in hours)
1	0:00	2:00	2.00	2.00
2	0:00	2:00	2.00	2.00
3	0:30	2:30	2.00	2.50
4	0:30	2:30	2.00	2.50
5	1:00	3:00	2.00	3.00

Car	Departure Time from A	Arrival Time at B	Trip Time (in hours)	Total time (in hours)
6	1:00	3:00	2.00	3.00
7	1:30	3:30	2.00	3.50
8	1:30	3:30	2.00	3.50
9	2:00	4:00	2.00	4.00
10	2:00	4:00	2.00	4.00

Adding an extra lane has cut 2.5 hours off the total waiting time. The meeting can begin at 4:00 instead of 6:30, which is definitely an improvement. But is the road any faster than it was in the previous example? The answer is no. In both cases the cars travelled at the same speed. The latency was the same; it was the bandwidth that changed.

Let's take this example even further by considering 10 lanes of traffic. In this case, all of the cars will arrive after exactly two hours. That's not surprising but what happens if you increase the road to 20 lanes of traffic? You got it; it will still take exactly two hours. There are only ten cars and even if you could split them in half, you wouldn't get any benefit because the bandwidth was already sufficient; the problem is now latency.

Let's go back to networks and data transfer. The IP protocol uses small packets to send data. For most network tests, a packet size of 500 bytes is used as it's close to the average sizes of packets on the Internet. Note that average sizes aren't as meaningful as you might think because different protocols use different sizes. If you think this is cheating, now would be a good time to read the sidebar "Networking and the Facts of Life."

NETWORKING AND THE FACTS OF LIFE

The problem with analyzing networks and the scenarios you've looked at so far is that they represent best-case scenarios. They all assume that none of the cars run out of fuel, that accidents don't happen, that no one gets flat tires, and so forth. They also assume that each car is the same in size and feel. This isn't the case in the real world: glance out the window on any highway and you will see countless different vehicles trundling along at different speeds.

The problem is, if we attempt to take all of that into account (especially when trying to teach the fundamentals), it makes an already confusing scenario much worse. In fact, while the mathematical model for the highway analogy is beautifully simple, if you wanted to make it realistic, you would find very quickly that you can't use simple math—and that what comes next depends on what happened before. Then you start looking at probability and statistics—and quite quickly you wonder why you even bothered asking the question in the first place.

So, to save you from that unpleasantness, let's assume for the time being that the universe is a simpler place and plays by simple rules. The irony is, once you understand how this concept operates under a simple scenario, you will intuitively be able to apply it to the more complex scenarios quite easily without every needing to think about the math behind it.

With this simplified model in hand, you can begin to see the difference between bandwidth and latency. If you need to send an image that is 100KB in size, you need 200 packets (100KB = 100,000 bytes). In two scenarios (one where you receive 10 packets at a time and one where you receive 100 packets), the one that can receive 100 packets will download the image in less time than the other connection. If each packet takes 1 second to get from the server to the client, the total waiting time is 20 seconds for the first connection and only 2 seconds for the second connection. The transit time for the packets is the same (1 second) in both cases, but the extra bandwidth in the second scenario means that more data could be transferred at a given time.

Generally speaking, the faster connection technologies do also boast lower latencies but that is not always the case. For example, some satellite-based Internet connections use the satellite for downloading but a modem for uploading (it's expensive to have a satellite base station in your backyard). Even though the satellite can send data to you much faster than the modem, there is much higher latency because the data needs to be beamed to the satellite and then beamed back to your receiver. This process takes time. Once the transfer has started, it will download quickly. For those sorts of connections, you have very high latency (1,500ms compared to 300ms on dial-up, for example) but much higher bandwidth. This makes the connection fine for downloading large files, but you certainly wouldn't be able to play games like Quake or Counter Strike on it; it would just be too slow. You would be seeing events two seconds after they happened, which means you won't survive very long!

So what's the take-away from this section? Latency and bandwidth are related but they're not the same thing. When optimizing your web site and your content, you need to keep this in mind so that you can play to the latency and bandwidth available to you.

Network Summary

Hopefully that quick tour wasn't enough to put you off. You should now have a pretty good idea how these technologies play a part in the speed of your web site. You learned the basics of TCP/IP—how it gets data from A to B and the overhead involved in accepting guaranteed delivery. You learned how the names of web sites are turned into the network addresses that TCP/IP uses to establish the connection and how that can play a part in web site performance. Finally, you learned the differences between latency and bandwidth, and why bandwidth and speed are not the same thing.

HTML and the Web

This section will be familiar territory for most of you, so we're not going to spend much time on it. Much of this content might seem obvious, but these concepts underpin the majority of what you will read in this book so it bears going over again. If you have a complete grasp of HTML, feel free to skim this section, but do keep an eye out for the subheadings and see if anything catches your eye.

HTML

How many of you have really sat down and thought about what HTML actually is? How many of you simply use HTML (or perhaps even a WYSIWYG designer) as a means to create a pretty web site and leave it at that?

If you fall into the latter category, that's not surprising; HTML was originally designed to be unobtrusive. It was designed to be a very simple way for academics (not programmers) to create documents that were easy to read, compatible on all systems that had the right viewer, and easy to link to other documents.

Today HTML5 has many more tags and a ton of extra functionality. It's certainly more complex than what Tim Berners Lee originally came up with in the CERN lab a couple of decades ago.

They say that the more things change, the more they stay the same. A basic web page written in the originally HTML standard will still render quite happily (if more blandly) on a modern browser. So what else do HTML and HTML5 have in common? They are both text, and they both work by linking to other documents.

Why is Text-Based Important?

Being text-based makes things simple on many levels. For a start, humans can easily read and modify text files in any text editor. No special software is required. Yes, character sets such as Chinese, Russian, and Hebrew are more complicated, but they are still easier for humans to work with than raw binary data. The problem is that text is not the most efficient way to store data; in many cases, a binary representation would be far more compact.

For example, if you are using the ASCII character set (the de facto simple text standard) and you have a line consisting of ten zeros (0000000000), you need 1 byte per zero, so 10 bytes. There are numerous ways to rewrite this to save space. For instance, a simple system such as the character, number of times it appears, and a dot would give you "09.". You can write 9 because you know the character must appear at least once. You've now only used three bytes in this example—less than a third of the original system. A more advanced compression system could potentially save even more, especially over bigger documents.

As usual, it's a tradeoff. You get ease of use, creation, and storage—and a format that requires more space. If you look at an HTML or XML file where a lot of the space is taken up with tags and other overhead, you find that the content-to-overhead ratio is quite low. On the other hand, you can work with your document on any machine without special software. Also, generally speaking, text files make beautiful candidates for compression, which can often reduce their size by 90% or more.

The thing is, you don't want to store the files compressed. True, you can compress them easily but then you have to decompress them before you can work with them. Also, hard disk space is cheap and text files are very small files. The reason you care about how much space the file takes up is not because it's expensive to store; it's because you want to send the page to the browser as quickly as possible—and the smaller the file, the faster it will get there.

To deal with this and make the solution as transparent as possible, all of the major browsers and web servers offer automatic compression. All you have to do is turn it on in the web server and you're good to go. This is actually one of the few performance tweaks you can make that doesn't really have any tradeoff, apart from a little processing power to actually do the compression itself.

So you can have your cake and eat it. You get easy-to-use files and you can send them over the wire in a compressed form. True, you might save an extra few bytes if you did something funky with the text but the benefits would be low and the pain you would cause yourself would likely be high. There are other ways to get even better performance.

Why is Linking Important?

Web sites are made up of documents that link to other documents. Even a simple web site consisting of three pages can actually be pretty complex when you think about it (see Figure 2-2). If you look at the source code for a page on Facebook, you can see that there are links to other pages but also links to resources needed for the current page. For example, all modern web sites require JavaScript libraries and CSS files. Web sites also require images for the layout and background—and the images used in the document itself. Many sites now embed video and music, too.

Think about this for a moment. If you need all these things in order to render the page properly, you can't really show the completed page until all these files have arrived. Often they're not being downloaded from the same site. There are ways around this. For example, when you add an image tag, if you specify the size of the image, the browser can render the page around it because it knows how much space it has to leave. If you don't set that information, the browser can't possibly know how big the image will be until after it has downloaded the image itself. That can take time, and meanwhile the page isn't being rendered properly. In short, your page depends on many other resources, and your page will either not look right or not work properly until all those resources have arrived at their destination.

There are many ways to deal with this issue. In fact, a large part of this book is dedicated to showing you how to work around this problem. We'll show you how to get the content to the user as quickly as possible while providing as much help to the browser so that it can do the right thing. So even if you're waiting for a large image to download, the rest of your page will be readable and look nice.

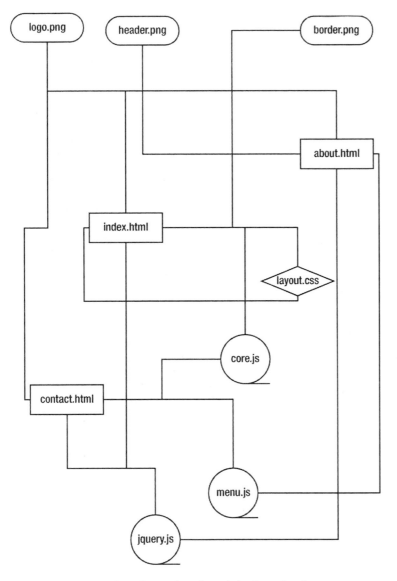

Figure 2-2. *A simple web site that doesn't look so simple*

HTML Summary

HTML is the language for building web sites; as such, it's the key tool in every web developer's toolbox. However, with modern tools, an in-depth understanding of HTML is not required to make nice web sites, so it's easy to overlook the potential issues you might be creating. Sure, a single page doesn't take long to download, but what happens when a hundred people download it? What happens if they don't have ADSL and are downloading over a modem or connecting to your site from another country? Often this side of performance tuning is not considered. Worry not; you'll be looking at these issues and others later in this book.

The Browser

The number of possible browsers, versions, and plug-ins are quite staggering and none of them, as best we can tell, seem to work exactly how they're supposed to. The developer's nightmare used to be limited to trying to make a web site look the same in each browser; these days, that's only one of many problems developers have to face. Trying to ensure that the JavaScript essential to the site's operation works for everyone and that the style sheets apply in the same way (and look decent on mobile devices) are some new issues. Many excellent libraries have been developed to try to resolve these problems but there's always something new to throw a spanner in the works.

Sadly, you can't force a user to use a particular browser on their machine. You also can't tell in advance which browser a user is going to use. The "best" browser seems to alternate on a monthly basis, so it's not even easy to optimize for the most popular browser. Even though you can't control it, the choice of browser certainly plays a part in how fast your site loads and thus the end user experience.

As an example, using a popular JavaScript charting package, a graph with a reasonably large number of points (around 80,000 or so) took 12 seconds to render on Internet Explorer 8 (and a warning about slow scripts) but only 4 seconds to render on Chrome. We're not trying to start a fight over which browser is better, nor are we claiming that our experiment was in any way scientific or conclusive. What we can say is that people who viewed our chart with Internet Explorer complained that the graph crashed their browser or they hit refresh about 20 times before they gave up.

It's not just JavaScript performance that can cause pain, either. Chrome supports WebSockets out of the box and we had no trouble hooking up a nice application to take advantage of it. Unfortunately, the best practice method for using WebSockets on Chrome doesn't seem to work on any other browser, at least not without changing the source. Again, there are libraries (in this case, socket.io) that provide a nice, consistent interface across browsers, but this adds other issues, such as dealing with its dependencies. If you want to use the latest and greatest technologies, you need to make sure they work in all of the browsers you plan to support and that the performance characteristics are similar.

So what can you do about this situation? Apart from being aware of it, there isn't a lot you can do. You need to take each browser's personality into account when you develop your site so that you can provide a consistent service across all of the browsers. Sometimes this means you don't implement certain features. Maybe you limit the special effects you use in a particular browser or use a different charting engine. Maybe you load the data in a different way on the slower browsers so that the user is at least aware that the site hasn't crashed. While you can't control the situation, you can at least attempt to manage it and lower the impact for your users. It's unlikely that you'll get it right each time, and it's unlikely that nothing will ever slip through the cracks. However, if you're aware of the potential for these issues to spring up and bite you, you're already a step ahead of the game.

Web Content

There are really two types of content on the web today. Content is either static or dynamic. In many cases, the distinction has become somewhat blurred as static resources end up being used in a dynamic way. Generally, if you send a resource as-is, such as a file on a disk, the content is static. If you take a resource and alter it or combine it with another resource in some way, the resource becomes dynamic. In short, if you do anything that alters the content before you send it out, the content is dynamic.

One thing to watch out for with Web 2.0 is that rather than generating all the content on the server and then delivering it to the client all at once (the web browser used to be a glorified viewing application), the content can be delivered and updated throughout the time the user has the page open. AJAX, for example, allows a web browser to poll the server for new data. Newer technologies such as WebSockets allow a browser to maintain an open connection that the server can use to send data on demand. The data, and the type of data, generally remain the same even though it is delivered using a different mechanism. Sometimes it's hard to say whether the data being delivered is static or dynamic.

Static Content

Static content is the most basic form of content. It is stored data that is used as-is over and over again. A good example is a company logo .jpg or your site's CSS file. These files sit on the disk until they are requested by a browser. The web server opens the file, sends the content to the browser, closes the file, and that's it. Because these files don't need any special handling, you can make some assumptions that will help you improve performance. For example, you can place them on a server that's optimized for sending out small static files. You can use a content delivery network to put these files closer to the users. With services such as Amazon's Cloud Front and Rack Space's Cloud Files, placing these files in various locations around the world for optimum delivery is both painless and effective.

Remember that you can only get away with this because the content doesn't change and because you don't need to do any special handling or checking. Restricting these files to certain users is more difficult to scale because wherever the file is, the request would need to be checked by your application before it could be released. The take-away: you can get some awesome speed boosts with static files, but they limit your flexibility.

Dynamic Content

All web applications make use of dynamic content. Any web page that responds to search requests or clicking buttons is generated dynamically. That is, a page has to be created in order to respond to request. Some requests are generic and can be cached (more on this later) but if you are showing content based on which users are logged in or you want to display real time statistics, it becomes much harder to cache this content as it is either time sensitive or specific to each individual.

There are techniques for accelerating dynamic content and they all have slightly different approaches. For example, Ruby on Rails offers a simple form of caching: after it creates a dynamic page, it writes the contents out to disk, making it basically just a normal static file. The web server is configured to try to read from disk before it asks Rails to generate the page. This makes for a very simple caching system but one that is very effective. The downside with this technique (and one that is common whenever caching is used) is that the content displayed to the end users may not be the most current. I look at this tradeoff in more detail in Chapter 3 and I touch on it again at the end of this chapter.

Creating Dynamic Content

As you've seen, web pages are simply text documents that are sent over the network. Whether or not that content comes from an actual file or the server generated it specifically for you is irrelevant as far as the browser is concerned. After all, it only cares about the HTML content, not how it was generated.

Originally, the Web was just static pages, making it effectively read-only. There were no forms, drop-down menus, or submit buttons. You could read content and jump to other documents or locations within documents, but that was pretty much it. The biggest benefit was that you could do this on any machine with a browser; apart from the browser, you didn't need to install any special software. This was a big improvement over proprietary formats, and as it was simple to use, people were able to mark up their own content with little effort.

It wasn't long before people started making little programs that could respond with web content. This meant you could view it in a browser but you still couldn't interact with it as such. It was also difficult to program and maintain and a lot of boiler-plating was needed in every application. It was, quite frankly, a bit messy.

The CGI (Computer Gateway Interface) was developed to make everyone's life easier by defining a standard that web servers could use to call programs that would generate dynamic content. This provided a standard way for a script (often written in Perl at the time) to receive variables from the web server about the request and to set variables and provide content for the response. Combined with HTML FORM elements, this provided a very easy way to communicate and generate HTML in real time.

It did have problems. Each CGI request would start a new copy of the program to deal with the user's request. So if 20 people looked at your home page, you'd have to start 20 Perl scripts, including a full interpreter for each one. It was a performance nightmare; even a powerful server couldn't scale very well under CGI. There were two main solutions to this.

- FastCGI implemented the same CGI standard, but rather than executing the script every time a request came in, the FastCGI process would start the script but would leave it open after the request. In this way, it was possible for a FastCGI instance to be re-used for multiple requests and thus save the overhead from starting each request from scratch. FastCGI was fairly successful and most web servers (such as Lighttpd and Apache) still offer it as a mechanism for generating dynamic content.

- The other approach was to embed the interpreter into the web server itself. Rather than open a new process each time a request arrived, the web server would pass the request to the interpreter that it already had in memory. Thus communication between the interpreter and web server was very fast because they were effectively the same process; they didn't need to use any special protocol to communicate. It also meant that the web server could make other optimizations simply because it now had full control over the environment and the way the script was executed.

This was the state of affairs for quite some time; the modular approach was seemingly more popular than FastCGI, which tended to be fiddly to set up and manage. With the modular approach, you simply started your web server and you were done; it's hard to get any easier than that. Interestingly, with the advent of some of the newer web frameworks, we appear to almost take a step backwards.

Ruby on Rails was originally single-threaded; it could only handle one request at any time. The first request needed to finish before the second was processed. On a small and simple site, this might not even be noticeable but if you wanted to scale out to thousands of users, well, even 10 users would probably feel the pain.

The solution was to do something similar to the FCGI approach where a standard web server would sit in front and receive all of the requests from the users and then forward those requests to numerous Rails instances running in the background. For example, you might have two servers each running 10 Rails instances (complete copies of your web site). Then you have your web server sit in front and spread the requests over these 10 instances. This added overhead in the form of network bandwidth and a bit of processing but it provided one huge advantage: you could add as many back-end servers as you needed to meet the load. You weren't restricted to a single machine. The emphasis on being able to scale out rather than scale up is a recurring theme in modern software design and is the de facto standard these days for almost all new systems.

Web Content Summary

Content can be either dynamic or static. You've seen that, for performance reasons, it's often desirable to make dynamic content static (as in the Rails caching system). In a similar vein to the discussions about the user's browser, you're usually limited by what you can make static and what must be dynamic content. It's not always obvious, though, and an appreciation of the basic differences can help you decide the best course of action when planning what to do with your own web resources.

You learned how content is generated and the evolution of that process; you also learned how the Web started off as a simple way for reading documents and gradually evolved into the powerful system that we use today.

Databases: The Weakest Link

Databases are where most web applications spend the majority of their time; in fact, times in excess of 70% are not uncommon in many applications. It's not that the database itself is inherently slow; actually, it's often extremely fast. However, when compared to how fast the server can execute the software itself, the database just can't match it. In many cases, the database has to hunt around on disk for the data—and accessing disk is enough to kill the performance of any application.

I look at databases in greater detail in a later chapter but for now the take-away is that generally speaking, database access is bad and should be avoided whenever possible. This is easier said than done, especially if it's the contents of the database that you want to display to the end user. You can get around this by using caching but that, too, is a tradeoff.

One way to avoid hitting the database is to keep data somewhere else—somewhere very fast and easy to access. There are numerous solutions for this, and MemcacheD is one of the most popular solutions. In effect, when you generate your database content, you stick it in MemcacheD for later use. When you receive a request, you first look in the cache to see if you already have what the user wants. If you do, you simply send that content back and you're done; no calls to the database needed. If not, you make the database calls as normal, but before you send the results to the user, you place it in the cache.

It sounds a bit painful but it's actually really straightforward to implement—just a few lines of code for simple situations. So what's the downside? After all, surely this massive performance boost isn't free. Reading data back from memory rather than querying the database can make a web site much faster and scale from hundreds of users to many thousands. So what's the catch?

The problem is that the data is not necessarily fresh. This may or may not be a problem. If your main database is only updated every five minutes, querying the database in the meantime will always return the same results. In this case, caching is a no brainer because you have nothing to lose. You can even generate the page in a separate script and just update the cache when it's done; this way no one ever sees a slow page.

However, if you want to restrict data or generate different data for different people, you have to do more work to make caching beneficial and support your needs. If it's imperative that users always get the latest data (which updates constantly), you simply can't cache it—but maybe you can cache the data around it. Or if two user requests come within a certain period of time, the same data could be sent to both. There isn't a one-size-fits-all solution, but there's usually something you can do.

Summary

This chapter covered a lot of diverse ground in a relatively small amount of space. You looked at the processes involved in viewing a web page and saw how many individual and unrelated systems need to work in perfect harmony for the World Wide Web to work. As each of these areas has their own performance issues, each area needs to be considered when developing a performance strategy.

You then learned some of the more interesting issues that affect web performance, with a focus on the network, the browser, HTML, how the content is generated, and how you can get the most bang for your buck when it comes to using databases.

The overall focus of this chapter has been to highlight the diverse nature of the ecosystem that powers the Web and how a simple one-size-fits-all performance solution either won't work or won't offer optimal results. Although we didn't mention types of Internet connections, server hardware, infrastructure, and other potentially obvious items, this doesn't mean that they aren't important; I just wanted to focus your thoughts on some of the unsung heroes of the performance world.

In the next chapter, you will take closer look at caching. Even the simplest of changes can make a huge difference to the performance of a web site. Caching is generally easy to set up, easy to use, and offers big gains in terms of performance. It's a great place to start tuning your web site for ultimate performance!

CHAPTER 3

Content Caching: Keeping the Load Light

Caching is one of the key ingredients for an awesomely fast and responsive web site. Yet it's often neglected. It's not that caching is particularly difficult or hard to set up, but it's a very broad topic so it's often hard to know where to start. Caching requires a fair bit of background knowledge because as soon as you start using it, you're inviting all sorts of potential problems that will be a real nightmare to track down if you're not up to speed. Actually, even if you know exactly what you're doing, trying to diagnose issues caused by various different layers of caching and how they may (or may not) interact can drive anyone mad.

Technical books naturally keep pretty close to their core themes. If you buy a book on PHP programming, for example, you would likely be surprised to find a chapter dedicated to Perl or Ruby on Rails. However, when an author wants to introduce caching, they have to compromise: they need to cover enough content to make it useful but it's quite easy to get mired in technical detail that seems important (and under certain circumstances is essential) yet detracts from the main ideas. This is one reason why many books don't touch on the topic at all or gloss over it when they do. Thus many developers end up without a solid understanding of what caching is and when and how to use it.

We have seen this with countless web design consultants. They create beautiful web sites and the web applications work beautifully. They are a joy to use and lovely to behold. Unfortunately, they are vulnerable to Cross Site Scripting attacks and SQL injection, amongst other things. How can these consultants design such great sites yet make these fundamental mistakes? Simple. When they learned PHP or whatever language, the books didn't cover these topics, and they haven't come across them in their travels. It's not that they're stupid, unprofessional, or don't care; it's just that they didn't know these things existed.

And so it is with caching. Caching tends to fall between software development and system deployment—and has nasty habit of disappearing between the two. This chapter, although one of the easiest in the book, is also potentially one of the most important. It explains a technology that will give your web site a big kick in the pants. And it will do all this with very little in the way of work from you.

In the first section we're going to look at what caching actually is, the different technologies, and how they fit together. We won't go into much detail; we'll just lay the groundwork so you can see how all the bits fit together and what their place is in the grand scheme of things. This will pay off in spades in the following sections when we go through a couple of the topics in more detail and start getting into the applications themselves.

Before you get to play with the cool toys, you need to learn some theory. Fortunately, you can get away with just a few key concepts. Then we'll look at why what appears at first to be a simple problem but is actually rather challenging. We will look at how people have tried to solve this problem over the years and the techniques used to make it work. We'll do our best to keep it light but you need to have a rough idea of what's going on in order to appreciate some of the benefits (and challenges) that you'll come across in the rest of the chapter.

For the most part, the in-depth sections can be read independently. Where there is synergy between different layers, we will point you to the relevant section for additional information.

Lastly, due to space constraints, we have had to scale back how much caching goodness we can expose you to. That said, rest assured that the content we cover will get you up and running quickly at least to the point where you can benefit from the technology. Where there are any major gotchas or limitations, we'll make sure to highlight them and provide further information.

What Is a Cache?

A cache is a collection of items that are stored away for future use. Squirrels go to great lengths to find and store nuts (cache comes from the French verb cacher meaning "to hide"). They hide them where they think no one will ever find them. These hidden stores are caches and are very important to the squirrel; when a squirrel discovers his nuts are missing, he gets very upset and storms about looking possessed.

Fortunately, caches aren't necessary for our survival, but they are necessary for super fast web sites. Like a squirrel foraging for nuts, it is much faster to go to a location close by and help yourself from your store than it is to go into the freezing weather and hunt around in the (quite possibly vain) hope of finding some. One is clearly easier and faster than the other, and this is what makes caching so beneficial.

■ **Note** How do you pronounce cache? The problem with words like cache is that although there are two generally accepted pronunciations for the word, the chances are you'll only ever hear one of them. Then one day you have a meeting with someone who pronounces it the other way, and you have absolutely no idea what they're talking about. At least when pronouncing Linux, the two versions are reasonable similar. However, cache can either be pronounced as "cash" or "kay-shh." If you're not expecting it, this can cause you to adopt the expression of a stunned mullet. Fortunately, now that you know about it, your brain won't crash when you hear cache pronounced differently!

Whistle Stop Tour

When people talk about caching, it's usual within a very specific context. They might be talking about a web browser or web proxy. Maybe they've even talking about edge-based caching systems. Or perhaps they're talking about something else altogether. The problem with discussing caching is that so many related technologies all come under the caching banner. Even if we limit ourselves to just the technologies that play a major role in web application performance, we've still got more systems than you can count on one hand. Now "more than five" might not sound all that impressive, but when you consider that you'll have to deal with these potentially all at the same time while simultaneously trying to avoid other possible pitfalls, it's not exactly insignificant, either.

Browser-based Caching

Most people today are in the enviable position of having broadband. Not so long ago, broadband was spoken about in reverent tones. Those lucky souls who had a 2MB ADSL connection suddenly found a fan club of people hoping to share in their good fortune. It was always somewhat depressing to get home and sit through the thrashing warbling noise that our 56K dial-up modems would make while trying to get online.

Sadly, we can distinctly recall visiting Google and watching as the Google logo would download and slowly update the screen. Few people these days believe us when we say just loading Google's front page took four seconds, but honestly it did. Then we would do our search, get the results page, and then wait for the cursed logo to download again. Thanks to the primitive nature of the browsers we were using at the time (which, in fairness, were state of the art at the time) we had to wait another four seconds before we could see our results. If we'd made a spelling mistake in our query, we'd have to resubmit the request—and wait another four seconds for the logo to reach us.

Fortunately, others decided that this situation was intolerable and they set about to fix it. This problem was caused by having to wait for the logo to crawl along the phone line. Although the computer could easily have drawn the logo in an instant, it couldn't draw it before it received it. The obvious solution is to simply remember that we've already seen this particular file before. Sounds easy enough, but how do you know that the file is going to be the same before you've downloaded it? The answer is "with great difficulty" but we'll come back to that in the section on Caching Theory.

Having the browser cache content made a massive difference in performance. By keeping the files on the machine itself and potentially even storing previously rendered pages, the network connection is effectively bypassed. (Ever wondered why when you press the "Back" arrow, the page loads instantly?) When you only need to download a small amount of text rather than bandwidth-hogging logos, the world just seems to be a nicer place!

Web Accelerators

We're going to take a slight detour here to touch on a technology that came to be known as *web acceleration*. There were various applications that you could download (usually for a modest fee) that would promise to make your Internet connection a million times faster. The more legitimate applications did actually make things seem much faster. In fact, when you clicked on the next page, the whole thing would appear instantly. The interesting thing was when you looked at how fast the page appeared and you looked at the maximum theoretical speed of your modem (which no modem ever managed to reach), the numbers just didn't add up.

This performance boost came from sleight of hand—and an ingenious one at that. When it comes to browsing the web, for the most part you have a quick burst of traffic as you load a page and then silence while you read through it. While you're looking around, the connection is sitting idle.

The web accelerator applications would take advantage of this idle time by examining the links on the page and downloading them in the background. Because it was using the connection when it was idle, the user didn't feel any impact. If the user then clicked one of the links the accelerator already downloaded, the files were already at hand so the page loaded instantly. While the user was happily reading the new page, the web accelerator was busy downloading more content in the background. In other words, the best case scenario was an instant page load. The worst case was the speed that it would have taken anyway without the accelerator. In effect, the user couldn't lose.

It also helps to remember that modem connections were generally billed based on how long you remained connected to the server. Rather than being charged for how much you downloaded, you were charged based on how long you were actually online. So there was no cost penalty for downloading pages that were never viewed.

Today, with broadband and mostly dynamic content, these tools aren't particularly useful any more. Many people now pay for the bandwidth they use as their connection is "always on." So when someone talks about a web accelerator today, they are almost certainly referring to a cache that sits in front of a server. If you need to refer to the older solution, you can call it a "preemptive cache" (the name is a good fit because the cache would preemptively fetch pages in the hope that it would download the pages that you were going to visit).

PERCEIVED PERFORMANCE

The reason we say "perceived performance" is because although the site now seems to load almost instantly, in reality the web site and the speed of the connection haven't changed. Many people will scoff at us here and say that there's really no such thing as perceived performance; the web site is either fast or it isn't.

When it comes to the end user, we are quite happy to accept this definition. It is highly unlikely that any of your customers will care how their high-speed experience is created. However, when you're architecting these systems, you need to make the distinction so that when it comes to holding a complex system in your head you don't keep tripping over your own feet.

Abstraction is a normal part of everyday life. We use tools without understanding precisely how they work or how they were developed. Imagine if you had to understand the entire history of the light bulb, electricity, and electrical distribution grids just to use a light switch! So while your users can enjoy the benefits of all your hard work and can simply call it speed or performance, you need to be a little more precise.

Web Proxies

Despite the success of browser-based caches, they had one big limitation. Because they were built into the browsers themselves, it meant that each browser would have its own copy of a given file. For home users, this was rarely a problem, but for businesses it became a real nuisance.

Generally speaking (although it's not as true today) businesses pay more for Internet connections. They often have service-level agreements (SLAs) to guarantee availability or uptime, which in theory provide a superior connection. In exchange, businesses pay more than a home user might pay. As these connections were usually shared across a network, several people could use the connection at the same time. As e-mail and e-commerce took off, businesses spent even more time sending data to and from the Internet.

This created two issues. First, bandwidth was expensive. Either the business paid for what was downloaded or they paid for an unlimited connection at a suitably (much) higher fee. The second issue was performance. If the staff relied on the Web for their daily tasks, and if the Internet then slowed down to a crawl, it affected the company's performance as a whole. Although the business could simply get a faster connection, this would come at a significant cost. What was needed was a way to give better performance while saving money.

Web proxies meet this goal in two ways. First, the proxy sits between the web browsers and the Internet. Rather than having each browser go out on the Web directly, requests are relayed through the proxy. Ultimately only the proxy would ever initiate connections to the Internet itself.

The second part of the solution is an adaption of the cache already found in browsers. When User A visits Google, she makes the request to the proxy. The proxy makes the request on her behalf and downloads all the relevant files, including the logo. The proxy stores these files and keeps track of when and where all the files came from. When User B decides to pay Google a visit, the proxy can serve the logo directly to the browser without having to make a request to Google. As the connection between the user and the proxy is extremely fast, the logo appears to download instantly.

When you have a network with a couple of thousand computers on it and all of them are browsing the Web, a good web proxy can make a massive difference to the amount of bandwidth being used and it can greatly increase performance. While there are many millions of web sites out there, the same ones keep on cropping up time and time again. Google, Facebook, YouTube, Amazon, eBay; these sites are so popular that they are constantly being viewed over and over again. In many cases different people are reading exactly the same content. For this scenario, web proxies are invaluable; they save money and boost performance!

Transparent Web Proxies

It's not just companies and universities that are in on this web proxy business. In fact, almost all ISPs and network providers make extensive use of the technology. If you think about it, it makes a great deal of sense. After all, even a small ISP could have thousands of customers, some of which are big businesses using their own proxies to cut their costs.

So, to avoid being left out, ISPs starting getting their feet wet. Remember, for most entities, sending data on their own network is either free or cheap enough not to be a concern. However, sending data through a network owned by someone else can be very expensive indeed. Just as businesses try to avoid sending too much data to their ISP, ISPs want to avoid sending any more data than necessary to other networks—the same idea writ large.

ISPs used to offer web proxies directly to customers and many also hosted mirrors of popular FTP sites and web sites. This was great for the users because the data they wanted only had to come from the ISP instead of potentially from the other side of the world. The ISPs were rubbing their hands with glee because although they had to provide resources to host these mirrors, it was basically free compared to the cost of thousands of people all dragging down the latest Linux release from outside the network.

The big problem with ISPs offering a web proxy was getting people to actually use it. When the Internet first started getting popular, the first wave of users was fairly technical. They understood the advantages of using local web proxies and they understood that they could benefit by telling their local web proxy to get its content from the ISP's proxy. This built a chain of proxies, each slightly slower than the last, but each having more content. Even though each proxy in the chain would be slower than the last, even the slowest proxy was probably faster than the web site itself.

But time moved on and people stopped caring about web proxies, local or otherwise. With broadband especially, even those who did know about the technology tended not to use it. This was a big backward step for the ISPs because now they had even more users making even greater demands from the network and none of them were playing nice and using the web proxy. An ISP couldn't force the issue (people could always change to a new ISP) and most of the new generation of users had no idea what a proxy even was.

The solution to this problem came in the form of *transparent proxies*. These are a combination of web proxy and some nifty networking tricks that allow a web proxy to intercept a request from a web browser and take it upon itself to fetch the page. The web proxy then returns the cached page to the browser and the browser has no idea that they're not talking directly to the real site.

This solution is very powerful because it's pretty hard to circumvent. If the ISP redirects all traffic on port 80 (the standard web server port) then unless you use a completely different port, you're going to go through their system. As almost every web site in the world runs on port 80, this is a very effective solution.

Now for the downside. You can't see the proxy and have no way to know how many of them are between you and the web site you're visiting. Perhaps there are none, but there could easily be several. Why does this matter? Because sooner or later someone is going to visit your site and it's going to break because some random proxy somewhere decided to cache something it shouldn't. If you don't provide proper caching headers (we cover this in the "Caching Theory" section, but caching headers are simply instructions you'd like the proxy to follow), the proxy will make a "best effort" guess as to what it should cache. It won't always get it right. Most caches are conservative, but in reality a web cache will cache whatever it is told to cache. To make matters worse, the dynamic nature of the Internet means that a given user might not always go through the same cache, a factor that can cause what appear to be random spurious errors. And as your Internet connection probably doesn't go through that particular broken cache at all (hopefully) no matter what you do, you can't recreate the error.

So, if your web application works beautifully from one location but not from another, perhaps it's something between you and the site causing the problem rather than something you've done wrong.

WEB SITE WEIRDNESS

Admittedly, it does sound a bit far-fetched to have an invisible proxy mess things up for your web site. Unfortunately, we've seen it happen. One of our customers had a very simple WordPress web site. WordPress (www.wordpress.org) is an awesome blogging platform that has oodles of plug-ins and features and is super easy to manage. It's used all over the world to quickly and easily create functional yet great-looking web sites.

The newly deployed site was working perfectly in Chrome and then the customer tested it in Internet Explorer. It redirected itself to a missing page and threw an error. Now, while Internet Explorer is not our browser of choice, it is certainly more than capable of displaying a WordPress-based site.

It was obvious that it was doing a redirect, so we looked at the headers. Believe it or not, when Chrome requested the page, it was being given the correct page to redirect to. When Internet Explorer requested the page, it still received a redirect but for a non-existent URL, one that (as far as we could tell) never existed. As this was basically a fresh install and we had done this a hundred times before, this issue was maddening. We even start going through the source to see if there was any Internet Explorer-specific "magic." We couldn't find anything wrong after hours of experimentation. We then migrated the whole site en masse to a completely different machine and it worked perfectly the first time!

It turned out that there was a transparent proxy between us and the server. Whenever it saw Internet Explorer trying to access a WordPress site, it would help out by rewriting the reply from WordPress so that Internet Explorer would get the new direct location. As the proxy was transparent and had all forms of identification turned off, it was only after a lot of trial and error (and finally a desperate phone call) that we discovered the root cause.

So if your application ever starts behaving badly but only when there's a full moon on a Wednesday, don't jump to conclusions. Ask yourself if there might be some third party interference.

Edge-based Caching

Depending on who you talk to, "edge" can mean different things in a network context. Generally speaking, it refers to a server that's as close as possible to the final user but still part of the provider's infrastructure. For example, in Chapter 5 we look at content delivery networks, which often put your data so close to the user it's almost in their living room. (We focus on RackSpace, which uses Akamai, but others include Amazon's Cloud Front and Cache Fly.) Well, okay maybe just their country or city (if it's big enough) but accessing a file from up the road is significantly faster than downloading it from the other side of the world.

However, we're going to look at something a bit different here. This sort of cache usually sits between your application servers and your users. Although for big sites these caching servers sit on dedicated hardware, you can often find the cache and the application server on the same machine. This seems somewhat counterintuitive; if a server was already under performing, how do you improve performance by adding to the machine's workload?

The performance benefit comes from how application servers work. Generally, they are fairly heavy-duty applications sporting lots of features and doing lots of work. They run the actual web application, so they need to be as fast as possible. The problem is, although you could have the web server facing the Internet directly, this means that your web server is handling various different tasks. It's processing orders and updating the stock control system and it's also busy serving graphics, stylesheets, JavaScript and all sorts of other miscellaneous things. This is akin to using a sledge hammer to crack a nut with the additional concern that while dispensing justice to the nut, the sledge hammer is not doing the important (money making) work that it should be doing.

Edge caching fixes this by sitting in front of the application server and handling all the requests from the various users. However, in a similar fashion to a web proxy (these caches are sometimes called *reverse proxies*), the cache tries to answer as many requests as it can without involving the web server. For example, if the front page of a web site is very rich in multimedia, this could put a serious strain on an application server. By placing a cache in front of it, the application server only needs to serve that static content once. From then on, the cache will send it back to the user.

This works extremely well because the cache is designed specifically to deal with requests in this fashion. It is created for the sole purpose of being very, very fast at getting static content back to users. This is all transparent from your application server's point of view. It simply sees fewer requests and so has less work to do over all.

As with other caches, it's really important that the cache doesn't cache things it shouldn't. Remember that the application server won't have any way to tell that something has gone wrong. For this reason, Varnish, one of the best web accelerators (told you this would crop up), only caches content guaranteed to be safe. You can tailor it specifically to your application to eke out every last bit of performance, but in its freshly installed state it won't do anything that might mangle your site. Varnish is one of the applications we cover later in this chapter.

Platform Caching

Platform caching is provided either by the framework you're using to write your application (such as the PHP-based Yii Framework or the ever popular Ruby on Rails) or by a particular library that caches for you (such as the Smarty templating library for PHP). This sort of caching is considered different from application caching (covered later) because it's not usually something you have to implement specifically for your application. In other words, you turn on the feature and it just works, rather than having to make specific calls to methods or functions provided by the framework (which is considered application caching).

Page caching, for example, doesn't much care what the page is, how it was created, or even what language was used. Even with caching individual requests or parts of a page inside an application, often you can leave the heavy lifting to the framework or library. In short, although you might need to think before you make use of your framework's caching support, it is usually the work of a few moments rather than spending hours coming up with a plan.

Because of the huge number of frameworks and libraries out there (each with its own ideas on how best to handle the problem) there simply isn't enough space for us to give even the most popular ones more than a cursory mention. Even if we picked a particular framework to focus on, unless it happened to be your framework of choice, it wouldn't add any value for you.

Instead, if you're keen to give platform caching a go (and you should certainly at least find out what your platform offers), check out your framework's manual or web site. Caching is usually a complicated enough subject that frameworks dedicate a whole section or chapter in their manuals on how to use it properly. This will give you more information on how your framework uses caching plus tailored examples and other platform specific bits and pieces that you should be aware of.

Application Caching

Application caching is similar to platform caching but rather than relying on a framework or plugin to do the caching for you, you do the heavy lifting yourself. There are numerous reasons why you might want to do this. For a start, each web application is different and while most frameworks can give you the basics of template caching and so forth, sometimes you need more.

For example, your site might have a front page that shows the latest news and stories from around the world. The problem is you have so many visitors it's killing your site. You can't keep dynamically creating the page because it is just too resource-intensive, but you don't want to rely on basic static page caching because when you delete the cached page, there will be an upsurge in traffic until the new page is generated. Even then, how long do you cache for? Cache too short and you will still have performance problems. Caching too long and you defeat the whole purpose of having the site in the first place. What you need is some sort of compromise.

And this is where taking responsibility for your own caching can pay dividends. For example, with the above scenario, you could use memcached. Memcached is an extremely fast key/value store. You put data in and you take data out. That's pretty much it. The lack of advanced features is one of its key strengths as it can implement the store in a very efficient way. Memcached is used on some of the world's busiest web sites.

So how would this solve the previous problem? Well, the first thing we do when someone visits our site is see whether that page is in memcached. If the page is in there, we simply retrieve the page and send it back to the user. We don't need to do a database query and we don't need to build a new page. If we don't find the page in the cache, we follow the standard page building procedure as before, but this time once the page is complete we insert it into memcached, which ensures it will be there for the next request.

Memcached allows you to set expiry times for your documents, so if you set a document to expire after 20 seconds, attempting to request the document after that time will fail and the page generation process will start all over again. For many people this works well, but it's still a little bit passive. Specifically, your cache control is based on how much time has passed, regardless of whether any new stories have been added.

One way to deal with this is to create a whole new cached page every minute or so. Even if your site is being hammered by a thousand people, they will all be sent the data in memcached so the server itself is not under much load. Every minute the page in the cache is replaced with a new one, and when people refresh, they simply get the new page. Generating one page a minute is far better than trying to do it thousands of times.

But you can take it further still. Instead of running off a timer, you can simply update memcached when a new story has been added. So if an hour goes by without any new stories, you will only have generated that page the once. When a story finally gets added, you can create the new page and then load it into the cache.

You've gone from the server doing all the work and handling every single connection itself to making the server responsible only for sending out a prebuilt page and generating a new version only when required. In short, caching at this level provides a huge potential for performance enhancement but it requires really knowing your application inside out. Because memcached is deliberately simple, you will need to build your own logic to take advantage of these features. If you're up for the challenge, you certainly won't be disappointed!

Database Caching

Database caching, like databases themselves, is often considered a black art. There is a reason why database experts can charge such large amounts for just a day's work. A good consultant can provide massive improvements for very little effort, just because he or she knows the database inside out and can make it sing and dance.

Out of the box, most databases are pretty fast and they tend to be configured for general performance. In other words, while the performance might not exactly blow your mind, it should be pretty respectable. To turn respectable into warp speed requires a lot of tweaking of the database itself, which disks it uses and how it uses them, the type of tables your database uses, and how you write your queries. There are many other things that can (and do) impact performance, and what works well under one type of load might fail on another. For example, if you have two queries, you might be able to run 1,000 of Query A and 1,000 of Query B before your server runs out of juice. But if you run them both at the same time, you might be surprised to see that you can only run 300 of each. This is because the different queries stress different parts of the system and in different ways.

Yes, trying to optimize and get the most out of a database is really hard. As soon as you change a query or add some new ones, you might find you need to recalculate all those details all over again!

Fortunately, you can leverage application level caching to relieve much of the burden from the database. When it does less work, it can often handle the remainder without any trouble. For this reason, we won't be opening this particular Pandora's Box in this book.

Just the Beginning…

Although this section was only meant as an overview, we actually crammed an awful lot of content into a rather small space. If we were sitting at a cafe talking to you about these technologies, each one could easily last for at least two cappuccinos. With that in mind, don't be too surprised if you've come this far and still have unanswered questions.

Caching Theory: Why Is It so Hard?

The fundamental problem with caching is quite simply that web browsers don't have telepathy. If we send a request right now, the response might be completely different from the response we would have received if we had sent the request 10 minutes ago or if we send it again in 10 minutes time.

Most of the issues with caching flow from this problem. We only want to download a resource if that resource is different from the last time we downloaded it. But we can't tell for sure if the file has changed unless we check with the server. It would be nice if we could rely on the server to inform us of any changes, but because HTTP is a request/response protocol, there is no mechanism for the server to initiate a request. Even if it could inform the browser, that would mean keeping track of many different clients, many of whom no longer care about the status of the file or resource. Because we need to make the initial request, this creates a whole host of other issues such as how often to check for a new version. If we check too often, there's not really much point caching the data in the first place. If we cache for too long, the user will see stale data, which can be just as bad (if not worse) as having to wait ages for the data to arrive.

HTTP 1.0 Caching Support

HTTP/1.0 offered some very basic caching features. Although simple, they worked pretty well for the most part. Basically, a server could use the "Expires" header to tell the browser how long it could safely cache the file before requesting it again. The browser could then simply use the cached file until the expiry time was reached.

The second feature was the IMS (If-Modified-Since) conditional request. When the browser requested a file that it already had in the cache, it could set the IMS header to ask the server if the file itself had changed in the time given. Remember, the time sent should be the time the file was originally downloaded rather than the time the file was due to expire. If the file hadn't changed, the server could reply with the status code 304 - Not Modified. This was relatively small compared to the payload for the file itself and so although a request was made to the server, it could still prevent using bandwidth unnecessarily. If a browser received the 304 status code, it could simply use the cached version of the file. If the file was modified since the time sent, the server replied with the 200 - OK message and sent the file normally just as though the IMS header was not used.

Lastly, it was possible for a client to set "Pragma: no-cache" when sending a request. This indicated to any caches that handled the request that they should fetch the content from the live site and should not satisfy the request by sending data from their cache. The problem with this (and with the other features of HTTP/1.0) is that they were quite basic and didn't provide a way to give specific instructions on how data should be cached or managed. There was an awful lot of guesswork involved; although the caching headers themselves were standardized across browsers, the actual meaning of the headers was somewhat vague. In short, the behavior of a cache was unpredictable and could break applications.

HTTP 1.1 Enhanced Caching Support

HTTP/1.1 was a massive advance on the previous version as far as caching was concerned. The biggest improvement was the creation of an extensible framework with specifications and fixed definitions. Terms that were used casually before were given strict meanings. This meant that the caching system was formalized and thus was relatively easy to implement in a standard and compatible way. It was possible to look at the options and know with a good deal of certainty how that content would be handled. This was simply not possible with the caching features found in HTTP/1.0.

According to the HTTP/1.1 standard, a cached object is "Fresh" until it reaches its expiry time. At this stage the object becomes "Stale" but that doesn't necessarily mean it should be evicted from the cache. When an object becomes Stale it just means that the browser can no longer assume that the object is correct and so should revalidate it before using it. This can be done with the IMS conditional request that was used in HTTP/1.0. HTTP/1.1 expanded on IMS by adding other more specific conditions. For example, it is possible to request an object that hasn't been modified after a certain time (If-Unmodified-Since, or IUS for short).

One problem with the IMS system is that it caches based on time. Time was quite useful when static pages and files were the norm and when the precision of a single second was more than sufficient for determining whether a file had changed or not. However, with modern applications, it's quite possible that an identical URL will return a completely different file and equally possible that a completely different URL will return a file that is already in the cache.

To address this problem, HTTP/1.1 introduced entity tags, which are more commonly referred to as e-tags. These are unique keys for a given file or object. How the server creates the e-tag doesn't matter as long as it ensures that the e-tag is unique for every different file. This is very powerful because it means you can request a resource and provide the exact file that you have and ask the server if the file has changed or not. Thus you don't need to worry about time synchronization issues and can guarantee that you have the file you are supposed to have. You can also specify a list of e-tags that you think might satisfy a request. This means that the server can check multiple files to see if they meet your needs. If one of them has the valid e-tag, the server will generate a 304 - Not Modified response and supply the e-tag of the correct file. Otherwise it will send a normal 200 - OK response.

One of the issues with the HTTP/1.0 cache control offering was that the only way you could issue an IMS type request was by sending a specific time to the server. The problem with this approach is that every machine has its own clock and even when attempts are made to keep that clock in sync with the rest of the world, those clocks tend to drift. It's not uncommon for machines to be out of sync by 10 or even 20 minutes. If you have an application that needs second level caching, you're pretty much out of luck.

In HTTP/1.1, though, you can use the max-age header to specify a relative amount of time rather than referring to a specific point in time. This can be combined with the age header itself, which is used by caches to show how long that data has been sitting in the cache. This provides much more flexibility and transparency to the browser to determine whether or not it needs to send another request.

HTTP/1.1 also sports additional directives such as being able to request that the data is not altered in transit (the no-transform directive), is not cached at all (the private directive), and that the object is not stored (the no-store directive). It is important to note that although these are called directives, in reality they can't be enforced. Good proxies will probably honor them, but there is no way to force that behavior. In short, these directives should be used where appropriate but you should not depend on them. If you are looking for security and to prevent caching of content at intermediary caches, you should almost certainly use SSL.

The Solution

These are the main caching control techniques that you will see in use today. There are more exotic options available but, while they might be able to give you a boost in specific circumstances, it's unlikely that you'll get as much benefit from them as you will from the others. This is partly because not all proxies support all of the options and partly because there can be a lot of work involved in adding support in your application to make it take advantage of the new features. You might also find that once you add support to your application, the stuff you've added to use the new feature may actually add more delay than the new feature will ultimately remove.

In short, go for the lowest hanging fruit first. IMS, for example, is probably the easiest to implement from a programming or development point of view. If you use it, you can cut down on content generation as well as bandwidth used. Once you have it working, maybe look at e-tags if it seems appropriate for the way your application works. There are plenty of things that you can do with the simple stuff before you venture into the darker arts of caching!

CACHING SLOWS THE INTERNET

There has been quite some interest recently in how caching might actually be slowing down the Internet rather than speeding it up. The basic idea is that the Internet is supposed to be a simple network that only concerns itself with moving data from one point to another. It doesn't care what that payload is or where it has come from or where it is supposed to go.

Until recently, the demands for bandwidth and performance were much higher than the technology (not to mention the price of that technology) could supply. This meant that ISPs and related companies had to figure out a way of doing more with less, and caching and various related technologies were a good way to do this.

The problem is that caching introduces latency. It takes a finite amount of time for a cache to receive a request, process that request, and then either send back the cached version or fetch the latest version from the server that actually hosts the site. Although it takes time, historically this delay has been very short indeed compared to the amount of time saved actually sending data. As we don't particularly care where the time is spent as long as that time is reduced overall, this seemed like a good trade-off, and for the most part it has been.

These days, however, we tend to have faster connections with much lower latency and we want to push vast amounts of data around with as little latency as possible (if you need a quick refresher on latency versus bandwidth, flip back to Chapter 2). In this case, caching gets in the way and can slow things down. This debate is still relatively young and the arguments are really just forming at this stage (depending on who you ask, of course). That said, it's likely to become a hot topic for debate as high speed and low latency become more popular and applications start to not only take advantage of them but require them to work.

Caching Isn't as Easy as It Looks

This section discussed the problems faced by the early World Wide Web. We looked at the caching support available in both the HTTP/1.0 and HTTP/1.1 protocols and gave a brief description of how they were used to solve at least some of the problems. We also touched on the issue of caching slowing down the Internet. This is still a relatively young idea but it is certainly gaining some momentum.

The key take-away from this section is that while caching sounds easy on the surface, there are a lot of things that can (and do) go wrong. By getting a feel for the tools available to solve these problems, you will have a greater feel for how caching works and the issues you might come up against.

Web Proxies

You might be surprised to find this in-depth section on web proxies, as these are predominantly used by end users or their ISPs. Even if ISPs are using transparent proxies, there's nothing we can do about it, so why is it being covering here?

Although you won't use a web proxy to directly enhance the performance of your web site, you can use one to test and tweak your site. For example, you can use it to see which files are being cached and can thus ensure it is doing what you expect. Transparent caches generally operate in the same way as a standard web cache (they also usually employ the same software) so you can kill two birds with one stone if you run your site through a proxy.

Whether or not this is worth doing initially is really down to the type of web site you're testing and how much you need to tweak. Most web sites will benefit from caching in some form or another. Generally speaking, unless an application is doing something unusual, a web proxy won't have much effect. That said, if you do happen to hit a brick wall with your application and you're not sure why, firing up a proxy might provide some quick and easy insight into what's going on under the covers.

The Squid Proxy Server

Squid is probably the most popular all-purpose web proxy (or web cache) available today. It was first released in 1996 and has long been the standard web proxy included by most Linux distributions. Just as most people think Apache when they need a web server, most people immediately reach for Squid when they need a web proxy. It certainly helps that Squid is packed full of features including the ability to create complex caching hierarchies (web caches using web caches), in-depth logging, high performance caching, and excellent user authentication support.

Squid also has a strong community with various plug-ins available. Although you might not use them for testing your web site, you might at some point find a use for them. Squid Guard, for example, is a plug-in that provides URL filtering to Squid. This is ideal if you want to block certain undesirable sites, such as advertising or adult material.

■ **Tip** If you really are keen on setting up Squid in order to protect people from some of the darker areas of the Internet, a very good application to investigate is Dan's Guardian. It works in a similar way to a spam filter: it analyzes each page it downloads before sending it back to the browser. We have found that it is extremely effective at filtering content and is very easy to set up. Although it is not a Squid plug-in per se, it does require a proxy to connect through and Squid is often used for this purpose. You can get more information on Dan's Guardian from its web site at `http://dansguardian.org`.

Getting Started

Before you can begin, you need to install Squid. Fortunately, Squid is a common package in almost all Linux distributions and is therefore really easy to install and getting running.

For Ubuntu, the command is

```
sudo apt-get install squid
```

and for CentOS it is

```
yum install squid
```

Well, that was fairly painless! Both distributions include the standard example configuration file. For basic use, you don't need to change much. By default Squid runs on port `3128` but only accepts requests from the machine it's running on (`localhost`). Although you can connect from any other machine on the network (Squid listens on all your network interfaces), you will get an error page if you try to actually visit a web site. This prevents you from accidentally creating an open proxy, which would be a "very bad thing™". The last thing you want is random people on the Internet accessing all manner of sites while making it appear like you're the one doing the browsing!

Still, security aside, a web proxy that won't proxy for you is not particular useful so you're going to need to do some tweaking. You only really have to make one change because the default Squid config file is pretty decent. It is also what the vast majority of Squid caches out there are using, so chances are your Squid server will be very similar to other proxies in the wild.

So without further ado, edit the file with

```
vim /etc/squid/squid.conf
```

You can't just add your rules to the bottom of the file because by default Squid adds a line that denies access from everywhere. If you put your rules after this line, they will have no effect. Instead, you must make sure that they appear above http_access deny all. Fortunately, you can search for "INSERT YOUR OWN RULE" to take you to the right spot. In vim, simply enter /INSERT YOUR OWN RULE and press Enter. Then press O in order to insert a new line. Remember, vim is case sensitive, so you must search for INSERT and not insert. The lines you want to add are

```
acl my_networks src 192.168.1.0/24 192.168.2.0/24
http_access allow my_networks
```

Squid uses access control lists (ACLs) to define who can access the proxy and what they are allowed to do once they do connect. ACLs allow for very flexible configuration using a relatively simple syntax. Even though the building blocks are pretty simple, you can build some very intricate rules with them. The ACL you just created (called "my_networks") will match any request that comes from either of the two networks listed. It doesn't specify what should happen when a match occurs; it just provides a convenient way to refer to these requests.

The next line actually puts this into action. http_access tells Squid that it should allow or deny proxy requests that match the provided ACL. In your case, you have told Squid that you want to allow web proxying from the two networks specified in my_networks. To sum it up, you've now configured Squid to allow anyone on your network to access the Web through the proxy.

Of course the networks listed are just an example and you will need to adapt them to match your own network. You can specify any number of networks in an ACL or you can just specify a single network, which is probably the most common setting for the majority of people.

Now that you're all configured, it's time to fire up Squid. On both Ubuntu and CentOS you can start Squid with

```
service squid start
```

As this is the first time you've run Squid, you will probably see a message about it initializing and setting up its cache directories. On modern machines this should only take a few seconds and it only needs to be done the once. The last thing you need to do is make sure that your browser can connect to Squid. The exact method for doing this depends on the operating system and the browser you are using. Most of them place the proxy options under Networking or Advanced Settings. You want to set it to use the proxy for all protocols and enter the IP address of your server and port 3128. All being well, you should now be able to get online!

▦ **Note** You may get an error saying "Could not determine fully qualified hostname." This just means that Squid can't figure out which name to call itself (used when showing error pages and so forth). If you get this message, go back into the config file (see previous instructions) but this time search for TAG: visible_hostname (/TAG: visible_hostname<Enter>). Press 'O' to insert a new line and then add **visible_hostname myproxy** (or whatever you'd like to call it). Save the file. You should now be able to start Squid.

Troubleshooting

If your browser complains that it can't connect to the proxy server and you're sure you've put in the right IP address and port, it could well be a firewall on your server. To allow access to port 3128 from anywhere on Ubuntu you can use

```
sudo ufw allow 3128/tcp
```

This assumes you're using the ufw firewall management tool, which is simple to use but also pretty powerful. If you want to limit who can connect, you can also do

```
sudo ufw allow proto tcp from 192.168.1.0/24 to any port 3128
```

Again, you'll need to make sure that the network matches your own and that it matches the one you configured in Squid. If you are using CentOS, you're going to need to do some file editing if you want to use the standard iptables script. To do that, open the config file with

```
vim /etc/sysconfig/iptables
```

As before, press Shift+G to get to the bottom of the file and to go into insert mode. You need to make sure that when you add this line it is above the COMMIT line and also above the last rule line which rejects everything. If you add this line after either of those two lines, it won't work. The line you need to add is

```
-A RH-Firewall-1-INPUT -m state --state NEW,ESTABLISHED,RELATED -m tcp -p tcp --dport 3128 -j
ACCEPT
```

Once you've saved the file (press the Escape key and type :wq and press Enter) you will need to restart the firewall with

```
service iptables restart
```

If the proxy connects but you get an error message from Squid itself (you can tell it's from Squid because the error will be in the form of a web page that conveniently has Squid written at the bottom of it), you can usually figure out what went wrong. If the Internet connection is otherwise working fine, it's probably a problem with the two lines you just added. Double-check that they match your network specifics.

Transparent Proxies

We're not going to cover setting up a transparent proxy here because from a performance point of view (at least when it comes to your web application) it won't be very different from what you'd experience with a standard proxy setup. However, if you do want to install a transparent proxy, there are copious amounts of information on how to do it on the Internet.

There are some gotchas that you should be aware of, though. You will need to do some fiddling with the firewall to make it redirect normal web traffic through your proxy. This may involve just cutting and pasting some lines into your firewall config, but if you're not 100% confident with what it is you're changing, you might want to give it a miss. Transparent proxies also don't play nice with SSL. If you attempt to redirect port 443 (https) through a transparent proxy, it will fail due to the way the protocol works. HTTPS can be proxied but only when the browser is aware that it needs to use a proxy. Lastly, a transparent proxy only affects the ports that you specifically redirect through it. If you only redirect port 80 (which is by far the most common) then web sites on any other port will not be proxied or filtered.

In short, if it's a small network and you're looking to build a safe sandbox, simply block all outgoing traffic at the firewall for any address you don't want to have access and then set up Squid as a normal proxy. This will mean that visitors can't get online unless they use your proxy, which in turn means they are subject to your filtering rules and logging mechanisms.

If your plan is to prevent children or teens accessing things they shouldn't, you might need to be more creative in how you lock down the network. Youngsters are extremely resourceful and have a nasty habit of being able to find holes in all but the toughest armor. The sheer ingenuity that we've seen in bypassing what appears to be bulletproof security never fails to surprise (and impress) us. Don't say we didn't warn you!

What's Going On

Although you can often tell a lot simply by using the proxy in the same way that your end user would, it's often helpful to see what's going on under the covers. This is especially important when you have a page that has lots of content and it's not easy to tell which content is being cached and which isn't.

The easiest way is to follow Squid's access log with a tail, like so:

```
tail -f /var/log/squid/access.log
```

This will follow the file (the handy -f flag) so you will see any requests in real time. The output will look something like this:

```
1327843900.435     333 127.0.0.1 TCP_REFRESH_MISS/301 777 GET
http://newsrss.bbc.co.uk/rss/newsonline_world_edition/front_page/rss.xml - DIRECT/63.80.138.26
text/html
1327843901.242     504 127.0.0.1 TCP_REFRESH_MISS/200 8667 GET
http://feeds.bbci.co.uk/news/rss.xml? - DIRECT/63.80.138.26 text/xml
```

The first column is the timestamp of the event. By default Squid stores it as a Unix timestamp, which can be converted at sites such as www.unixtimestamp.com/. This is generally done for ease of parsing of log files because from a developer point of view, it's often easier to work with this simplified format. If you'd rather have a more readable format, you can change this line in the Squid config file

```
access_log /var/log/squid/access.log squid
```

to

```
access_log /var/log/squid/access.log combined
```

You will also need to uncomment the logformat line that defines this formatting style. Search for logformat combined (/logformat combined<Enter>) and uncomment the line (remove the # symbol).

This will give you a much richer format, but it's not ideal for automatic log parsing tools and the like, although many tools do support it. If you're only using this for your own testing and aren't really interested in what sites are being viewed or how often, then there's really no reason not to use the combined format.

Carrying on with the log, the next field is the response time in milliseconds. So in your example, the first request took about a third of a second and the second took slightly over half a second. The next field is the IP address. In this case, the browser is on the same machine as Squid and so is connected via the loopback adapter. The next field is the event that triggered the request, followed by a forward slash and the response code from the server. A TCP_REFRESH_MISS is caused by Squid determining that it should check with the server to see if the file has changed. This could either be because the server has said that the document should only be cached briefly or it could be that Squid's default policies have determined that a check should be sent. There are a huge variety of Squid event messages that can occur and you can find out all about them at `www.linofee.org/~jel/proxy/Squid/accesslog.shtml`. This site also describes the native Squid logging format in considerable detail. If there is anything that you are not sure about based on our explanation, the descriptions on that site might help resolve any confusion.

The first status code was 301, which means "moved permanently." This is quite common in modern sites and is often done in tandem with URL management. The second status code, 200, just means "OK" and that the document has been returned as per the request.

The next field is the size of the resource in bytes—nothing too spectacular there. The next field shows the request method, which will usually be GET or POST. One thing to note is that POST requests are almost never cached because they contain dynamic content (usually form data) and so the response is almost always dynamic in return. It would be rare that you would want to cache such a response, so don't be surprised if many (if not all) POST requests have the TCP_MISS action associated with them.

The next field is the URL that was requested. Although you can't see it in your example, the whole URL (including the GET parameters) is also stored in the logs. You should never transmit sensitive data in a GET request because a system administrator could potentially see it in the logs. Another good reason for not sending data in a GET request is that you might accidentally end up caching a page you didn't want to cache. In short, if you're submitting a form or sending any sensitive data, don't use a GET request; use POST instead. One place where a GET request with parameters is useful is that it makes it easy to create bookmarks to dynamic content and also allows Squid to potentially cache that content.

The hyphen in the next field is used for storing the user's identity. This will always be a hyphen unless you add authentication to your proxy. The next field tells you how the request was made in the cache hierarchy. If you're using the proxy as a standalone service (and you are if you have just followed this section), then you will always see DIRECT here. If you have configured Squid to use a parent cache (for example, if your ISP offers a web proxy service), you will see PARENT here when Squid asks the other proxy for the content rather than fetching it itself. The second part of this field is the IP address or the machine where Squid got the content from. The final field is the content type (or MIME type) of the file. This unsurprisingly describes the type of content the file contains, which is used both by Squid and the browser to determine the best way of handling the content.

Getting a Helping Hand

As you can see, the Squid logs provide a wealth of information but sometimes it can be challenging to see the wood for the trees, especially if you have a lot of data moving through your proxy. If you fall into this category, you might be interested in some of the analysis tools available for Squid such as Webalizer (www.mrunix.net/webalizer/). Webalizer generates graphs and statistics of usage and can give an excellent high-level view of how the cache is performing. Webalizer can be installed in Ubuntu with

```
sudo apt-get install webalizer
```

and CentOS with

```
yum install webalizer
```

Webalizer's documentation is extensive, covers a wide range of use cases, and includes examples. The documentation can be found at ftp://ftp.mrunix.net/pub/webalizer/README or as part of the package your distribution installed.

Squid, the Swiss Army Knife of Proxies

This section offered a really quick tour of the Squid proxy server and why it might be useful for you to install one for yourself. We also touched very briefly on transparent proxies, some of the issues you should be aware of, and alternative ways of creating a walled garden. We covered basic troubleshooting, which (thanks to Squid's ubiquitous nature) is probably something you can avoid. Lastly, we covered Squid's log files, how to tail them, and how to read and understand the somewhat copious information printed on every line. We also recommended Webalizer as a possible graphical tool for log file analysis if you are looking for a more strategically view of the data.

Squid is an excellent tool and is extremely versatile. It will likely do whatever you need out of the box and contains excellent documentation right in the config file. There is also a huge amount of content on the Web covering a myriad interesting (and often mind boggling) configurations. In short, a good grounding in Squid is a very useful thing to have in your toolkit because you never know when it will come in handy.

Edge-based Caching: Introducing Varnish

Varnish Cache has been around since 2006 and, like many of the technologies introduced in this chapter, was designed to solve a real world problem. Admittedly, all applications are written to solve problems but some applications are written to solve a particular pain point that the authors are experiencing. More often than not, those pain points are not suffered by them alone and the software finds a strong following in the community. Varnish certainly qualifies for this distinction!

Why are we introducing Varnish when earlier in the chapter we used Squid, which can also be used as a web accelerator? Those of you who have read ahead will know that in Chapter 8 when we discuss HTTP load balancing, we use nginx even though Varnish can also do this job (as can Squid). Well, there are a few reasons for this. First, we wanted to share a wide range of different solutions so that you can choose the best solution for your particular needs. For example, if you have a requirement to use only official packages from an older Enterprise Linux release, nginx and Varnish might not be available to you. In that case, Squid is a viable alternative. Or perhaps you already have nginx installed and would rather not add an additional application into the mix.

However, unlike the other two, Varnish was designed from scratch to be an awesome web accelerator. It only does HTTP acceleration, unlike Squid, which can cache many different protocols, and nginx, which also happens to be a fully featured (and insanely quick) web server.

One of the interesting features of Varnish is that rather than managing the cache directly (that is deciding what to keep in memory and what to write out to disk), Varnish uses virtual memory. A similar solution is used by the MongoDB database and for much the same reasons. The problem with memory management is that it's very difficult to get right and it almost always depends on how much memory is in the machine and how the individual applications use it. Also, as the application can really only see its own memory usage, it is very difficult to manage the memory and disk access in an optimal way.

The genius of using virtual memory is that it is managed by the operating system itself. Varnish effectively sees a block of memory, which it uses to store the cached data. However, it's up to the operating system to decide which parts of that block are actually in physical memory and which blocks are written to disk. The short version is that Varnish doesn't need to worry about moving data from memory to disk because the operating system will do it automatically behind the scenes. As the operating system does know how memory is being used on the machine (and it should, since one of its roles is to allocate and manage it), it can manage the movement of data in a far more optimal way than any individual application could.

NO SUPPORT FOR SSL

When we tell people about Varnish, one of the things they immediately get excited about is the idea that it can make their SSL connections go faster. Because SSL uses encryption, it requires a lot more resources to use than plain old HTTP. This is not ideal when the machine handling the SSL connection (otherwise known as the endpoint) is also the machine that's handling the application itself. You want to free up as much CPU power as possible to power your application, so if you can get rid of having to deal with SSL, do so.

However, Varnish doesn't deal with SSL at all, and this has caused some confusion or concern that maybe Varnish isn't a mature product yet. In fact, Varnish doesn't handle SSL because there'd be very little benefit in doing so. Many sites that do use SSL use it to encrypt sensitive data, data that is most probably dynamic and is probably not something you want to store in a cache anyway. Moreover, whenever you do SSL, there is always a finite amount of work that must be done no matter how fast you make it. Also, it's not exactly an easy protocol to re-implement. If you build your own version, you then have to worry about all the security issues that you may have created for yourself. It's not exactly easy to test, either. If you use an existing implementation such as OpenSSL, there's very little difference between Varnish using it and another application using it, other than one would slow down Varnish of course!

If you have your heart set on SSL acceleration, there are numerous things you can do, such as adding special acceleration hardware or even configuring another front end server to act as an SSL endpoint. nginx would be an ideal choice and it could still connect through Varnish to ensure that whatever can be cached has been. For more information on load balancing SSL (another great way to boost performance), check out Chapter 10.

Sane Caching by Default

Varnish does *sane caching by default*. This means that it is very conservative in what it decides to cache. For example, any request that involves cookies will not be cached. This is because cookies are most often used to identify people and thus customize the response based on who is requesting the page. What you don't want is for Varnish to take the first page it sees and then send it back to everyone else. At best, you will be sending stale content to your users; at worst, you might send confidential details to everyone by mistake.

Because Varnish only caches what it knows is safe, you can deploy it in front of your web application without worrying that you'll get caught out by any of these problems. Having said that, if your application makes heavy use of cookies, you might find that very little of your application is getting cached. A classic example of a cookie-hungry web site is WordPress. Fortunately, there are plug-ins available for WordPress that make it more cache friendly (available from the usual WordPress plug-ins page in your control panel).

The good news is that Varnish is extremely configurable and allows you to customize pretty much everything about how requests are handled, what items are cached, and even what headers to add or remove. We only cover the basics in this chapter, but the Varnish manual goes into considerable depth on how you can tweak it to match your needs.

Installing Varnish

Installing Varnish is pretty straightforward. Many distributions include it in their own repositories but you're going to use the official Varnish repositories to make sure you have the latest and greatest version. To install on Ubuntu, you first need to install the Varnish key (you'll need to be root for this, so use `sudo -i` before running the following instructions). This can be quickly done with

```
curl http://repo.varnish-cache.org/debian/GPG-key.txt | apt-key add -
```

Adding the Varnish repository to apt just requires adding a single line to the source list:

```
echo "deb http://repo.varnish-cache.org/ubuntu/ lucid varnish-3.0" >> /etc/apt/sources.list
```

Lastly to install, you just to update the package list with

```
apt-get update
```

and run the install command

```
apt-get install varnish
```

Now we're going to cover installing Varnish on CentOS. The EPEL (Extra Packages for Enterprise Linux) also has Varnish packages available. However, one of the main benefits of using an Enterprise Linux operating system such as CentOS is that you can install updates without worrying about things breaking. This can be guaranteed because no packages are allowed to do anything that breaks backwards compatibility, so everything that worked with the last version should work with the new version. In order for EPEL to be useful, it also needs to make that same guarantee, so if at some point Varnish changes something that breaks backwards compatibility, the EPEL will not provide that new version.

To ensure you get the latest version of Varnish, we are going to show you how to install Varnish directly from the Varnish YUM repository. This way you will get all the new versions of Varnish even if they break backwards compatibility. Of course, this is a trade-off. If you do require backwards compatibility, you can always install Varnish directly from the EPEL.

The first thing you need to do is add the repository to your system. Rather than set that up by hand, you can simply install the repository package from the Varnish web site, like so:

```
rpm -i http://repo.varnish-cache.org/redhat/varnish-3.0/el5/noarch/varnish-release-3.0-1.noarch.rpm --nosignature
```

This will add the Varnish repository to your list of sources. The `--nosignature` is needed because at present the Varnish signing key isn't included with Yum. Now all you have to do is install Varnish itself with

```
yum install varnish
```

And you're done! If you want Varnish to start automatically when the machine starts (and you almost certainly do), finish up with the following command:

```
chkconfig --levels 35 varnish on
```

Tip On a fresh CentOS 5.7 install, we got a dependency error when trying to install Varnish. If you get an error concerning "libedit" you can fix that dependency by adding the EPEL repository and rerunning the install. You will be asked whether or not to add the EPEL key, so say yes.

Now let's get Varnish up and running!

Getting Up and Running

Configuring Varnish is a bit trickier than Squid because Varnish needs to know which port to listen on and which servers (called backends) to connect to. By far the most common configuration is to have Varnish running on port 80. This isn't surprising as it is also the standard port that web servers listen on and, in turn, the port to which web browsers will try to connect.

This can become a bit tricky if you're running Varnish on the same machine as your web server, which will also be trying to use port 80. As only one application can bind to a port at any given time, the two can't peacefully coexist. If you are not running Apache on the same machine, you can skip ahead to the next section.

Moving Apache to a different port is relatively straightforward and requires changing two things. First, you need to tell Apache not to listen on port 80 and then, if relevant, you need to update any of your virtual host entries that refer to port 80. On Ubuntu, you can see which ports Apache is using by editing /etc/apache2/ports.conf, which will contain something like this:

NameVirtualHost *:80
Listen 80

Note that CentOS runs SELinux by default and this restricts what ports Apache can bind to. If you get a permission denied error if you use port 81, you can add that port by running

```
semanage port -a -t http_port_t -p tcp 81
```

All you need to do is change the 80 to another port (such as 81) and save the file. The second line is the one that tells Apache what port to listen on and the first line is used for running virtual hosts (being able to host multiple web sites with different names on a single IP address). This line needs to match the definition in each of your virtual host entries. For CentOS, there's no preset location for virtual hosts, and many people just add it to the main Apache configuration file. However, for Ubuntu, those files can be found in /etc/apache2/sites-enabled. Every time you see

<VirtualHost *:80>

you need to replace it with

<VirtualHost *:81>

You will know right away if you've missed one because when you restart Apache, it will warn you if there are any virtual hosts that don't match the one you configured in ports.conf.

Now that you have Apache under control, it's time to tell Varnish to take its place. To configure the port Varnish listens on, you need to edit the main configuration file. On CentOS, this can be found in /etc/sysconfig/varnish and on Ubuntu it can be found in /etc/default/varnish. The config files are similar on both systems but they are structured slightly differently. On Ubuntu, you want to look for DAEMON_OPTS and replace -a :6081 with -a :80. On CentOS, it's a bit clearer: you need to replace the value of VARNISH_LISTEN_PORT with 80.

Once you've set the port Varnish should listen on, it's time to tell it the location of your backend servers. By default it points to port 80 on the local machine. That's not ideal for you because after the quick configuration rejig, this means you'll be serving content from yourself, which will cause problems. For both Ubuntu and CentOS, the default configuration file is /etc/varnish/default.vcl. The bit you're interested in right now is the following chunk (though it might be slightly different from the example):

```
backend default {
    .host = "127.0.0.1";
    .port = "80";
}
```

Although Varnish can handle multiple backends and act as a load balancer, here you're just going to focus on getting things going with as single backend. If you are running Apache on the same machine and moved it to port 81 as per the previous section, all you need to do is update the port number. If your web server is on a separate machine, you need to update the IP address to point to it. If it's not running on the standard port, you should update that as well. When you're done, save the file and exit your editor.

At this point you have Varnish configured. It's listening on port 80 so that it receives all of the web requests destined for the machine. You've told it where to find the web site that you want it to accelerate. All you need to do now is fire it up! This you can do with

```
service varnish start
```

And you're live! You can easily test that things are working as expected by trying to visit the web site. Point your browser at Varnish and all being well you should see your web site.

Of course, this doesn't prove that Varnish is actually caching anything. We've already discussed how Varnish plays it safe when it comes to storing things in its cache. One way to see what is going on is to use the varnishncsa command. This allows you to log in the familiar Apache style and show some Varnish-specific data. Here is the command to see what is being cached:

```
varnishncsa -F '%t %r %s %{Varnish:handling}x'
```

Here the only option you're using is -F, which allows you to manually specify the format. The first element is the time, followed by the type of request, then the status, and finally whether or not it was a hit or miss. An example output looks like this:

```
[05/Feb/2012:17:45:43 +0000] GET http://peter.membrey.hk/varnish.jpg HTTP/1.1 200 miss
[05/Feb/2012:17:45:48 +0000] GET http://peter.membrey.hk/varnish.jpg HTTP/1.1 200 hit
```

You can see that the first request for the image was a miss (not too surprising as you'd never requested that file before). You then requested it almost immediately afterwards, and this time you can see that Varnish had cached it because it was recorded as a hit.

Customizing Varnish

This section provided a quick overview on Varnish and some of its design features. It also showed why it stands above the competition. You got Varnish up and running with a basic configuration (and moved Apache out of the way when necessary) and pointed it to a backend server. At this stage, you have a working web accelerator, but chances are you want to take it further. You can find the excellent manual at `www.varnish-cache.org/docs/3.0/tutorial/index.html`, which covers the various support tools and how to use VCL to really customize Varnish. Although VCL will require a bit of thought and being careful where you put your feet, it will pay off when it comes to boosting performance.

Summary

This chapter is one of the longer chapters in the book but it covers an extensive amount of ground. Each of the different caching layers has its own complexities, and there are subtle issues that seem to interact with each other to create new and interesting (and extremely frustrating) problems to be solved. We could spend entire chapters on each of these topics and even then barely scratch the surface.

The take-away from this chapter is that while caching can be complicated and intricate, there are many simple things that can be done without too much hassle to reap great performance benefits from your application. Some will be more useful than others, depending on what you're trying to do. This chapter exposed you to some of the core concepts of caching and thus provided you with a solid starting point for further investigation. Like many things, once you are able to grasp the thread, pulling it free is very easy!

We started by looking at caching as a whole and why it is a critical technology for good performance in today's Web. We stepped through all the layers of caching that you're likely to come across (as well as some that you probably won't) to give you an overview of what's available to boost your application's performance.

We then dug a bit deeper into the basics of caching theory and looked at the tools that browsers provide in order to make caching a reality. We covered some of the problems and looked at how they might be solved. We also touched on a relatively new idea that caching might be slowing the Internet down instead of making it faster.

Next we introduced Squid, discussed the pros and cons of setting up your own proxy, and showed how you could use it to look at the caching characteristics of your application. We highlighted some issues with transparent proxies and talked about some tools to make your proxy more secure and child-proof. Then we introduced Varnish and covered how to get it installed and powering your site. We mentioned some of the issues with using a web accelerator and how to customize Varnish to your exact needs.

That wraps up our whirlwind tour of caching! We would have loved to spend more time on this subject and cover the applications in more depth, but we lacked the space. Hopefully we've been able to give you an idea of what's out there; after all, it's hard to find something when you don't even know that you want to find it!

The next chapter covers DNS and how you can quickly leverage it to your benefit for some simple but effective load balancing!

CHAPTER 4

DNS Load Balancing

DNS load balancing is the simplest form of load balancing. That said, it's also very powerful. It can be used to solve many performance problems very quickly as it allows you to direct incoming traffic to any one of a set of servers. But as with all quick and easy solutions, there are many things that DNS load balancing can't do. If it was a panacea, after all, we would not have had to write this book.

DNS Details

First, let's talk a little about DNS: specifically what it is and what it does. Without DNS, the Internet as we know it today could not function. DNS is really that important. However, it's also something that even experienced developers often know little about. So let's get stuck in.

The IP Address

Let's start at the beginning: the basics that underlie DNS. The key thing that DNS, and consequently the whole Internet, is built on is called the Internet Protocol (IP for short). Each machine has at least one unique address (imaginatively called an IP address) that allows other machines to communicate with it. For example, your home has an address that people can use when sending letters by mail. This address is unique to your home and no other residence in the world has the same address. If two places had the same address, how would the postman know which should get a certain letter? It would be most inconvenient!

Once you have your unique address, you then require the name of the recipient. This really means "At this physical location, there is a person called Peter." Again, this sounds simple enough. Families share a home, they each have unique names, and so it is obvious to whom it is directed. Even when people share the same name, they often have a suffix such as "Senior" or "Junior" to tell them apart. However, if two people have the same initials, such as John and Jane Doe, and a letter arrives for "J Doe," it's impossible to know to whom it is directed.

So what does any of this have to do with the Internet, IP addresses, DNS, and load balancing? IP works in a very similar way. First, each computer (or, more accurately, each network interface on a computer) has a unique IP address. This makes sense; otherwise the network wouldn't know to which computer it should be delivering the data. As for the addresses' names in the mail example, that ties in nicely with port numbers. Each program that listens to the network uses a unique port to identify traffic directed to it. Port 80 is the standard port for HTTP traffic. Port 443 is the standard port for HTTPS or secure web traffic. (You don't need to worry about port numbers at this stage). As you can see, an IP network really has a lot in common with the postal service.

There are two IP protocols in use today. The most common is IPv4, which has been the foundation of the Internet since its inception (well, since 1981 anyway). The other is IPv6, which was created to overcome the limited number of IP addresses in IPv4 (no one expected the Internet to explode the way it did). In theory, IPv4 has run out of addresses, so everyone is migrating to IPv6 as fast as they can. The reality is that IPv4 isn't going anywhere and most ISPs don't provide IPv6 addresses to their end customers anyway. For a much more in-depth look at IPv4 and IPv6, Chapter 14 covers both protocols, their limitations, and how they impact load balancing.

An IPv4 address looks like this:

127.0.0.1

It is also known as a dotted quad number (a number made up of four decimal numbers ranging from 0-255 and separated by periods). Each machine attached to a network (such as the Internet) has one of more of these addresses assigned to it.

The Problem

The problem is that people are generally very bad at remembering numbers. It's one thing to remember `www.google.com` but quite another to remember `74.125.237.81`. And that's just one web site. So, humans can't remember numbers and computers can't readily use textual addresses. What's to be done?

The solution turned out to be very simple. You create a file called `hosts` and in this file you write each IP address and its equivalent hostname. That way whenever the computer sees `www.google.com`, it looks in the hosts file, finds the IP address, and tries to connect. Seriously, this is how it used to work: each machine had a huge list of names and addresses. In fact, this file still exists. Under Unix (Linux and Mac), you will find it in `/etc/hosts`. It can also be found under Windows in `C:\windows\system32\drivers\etc\hosts.`

The problem with this solution is that you need to know all the names in advance, which is something of a fatal flaw. However, back when this solution was devised, the number of hosts on the Internet was in the hundreds, not the hundreds of millions we have now. In short, it was a simple solution that worked. Even back then, though, it was noticed that there were some fairly obvious issues of scale.

First, you need to make sure that everyone has the same contents in that file. If you've ever tried working on a Word document with other people, you know that it gets messy very quickly. When you take into account that each machine needs this file and ideally they should be the same, trying to keep them all in sync is a challenge of Herculean proportions.

The original `hosts` file was maintained by a single group of people. The file was then put on a server where everyone could download it. This solved the problem of people overwriting each others' changes but it meant that all the work involved in maintaining the file fell onto just a handful of people. This quickly proved to scale badly as more and more people were requesting changes. Also, the bandwidth used by thousands of people downloading the updated version every few hours was problematic.

The Solution

What was needed was a system that would spread out the workload—for both humans (updating files) and computers (bandwidth mostly). To do this, the system needed strong caching support and it needed to be distributed. In other words, it needed to be built in such a way that the people responsible for a particular domain were the ones who had to maintain and update it. This system became DNS, and it is still in use today. It has scaled extremely well, especially considering when it was first designed and how much the Internet has grown since then.

Taking a Step Back

So, DNS maps names to IP addresses and vice versa. Although it's good practice to properly map an IP address to the correct hostname, don't be surprised if you come across IP addresses that map to some weird, wonderful, and completely unexpected names. Reverse DNS is more difficult to set up because the people in charge of the IP address block have to handle the changes. For an ISP, this can be something of an administrative nightmare, and as very few applications actually care about reverse DNS (mail servers being one), it's rarely a problem. It won't affect your load balancing so let's ignore it.

For a given hostname, then, you can have one more or more addresses. This is affectionately known as "poor man's load balancing." The IP addresses are handed out in a round robin fashion. For example if you had

```
www.example.com    192.168.1.1
www.example.com    192.168.1.2
```

the DNS server would alternate between these addresses whenever anyone asked for www.example.com. In effect, this means you can send requests to as many different servers as you wish. The reason it isn't considered an ideal technique is because there are inherent problems. For example, if one of the servers were to fail, the DNS server wouldn't be aware of it and would still send out the IP address of that server to the client.

DNS in Depth

Now let's discuss how DNS actually works! The basic principle is something akin to a distributed version of the hosts file. The distribution of these hosts files is central to an understanding of DNS. This distribution is called a tree hierarchy (so called because its structure looks like an upside down tree). In Figure 4-1, you can see how from the single top (called a root) node, it expands down, and each of these branches forks further.

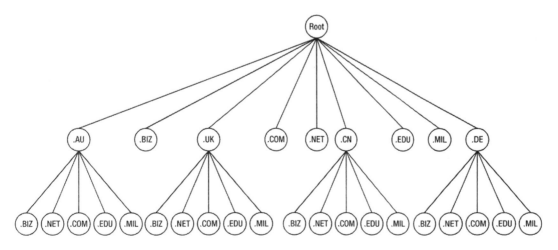

Figure 4-1. DNS hierarchy

Although there is a single root zone, for scalability and redundancy purposes it is replicated across several servers. Currently there are 13 geographically distant servers dedicated to this task. These servers (also known colloquially as root servers) don't hold any host information themselves but instead point to another tier of servers that look after top level domains such as .com and .net. If you're thinking that this looks suspiciously like a URL, you're right; each dot in a URL points to the next level down in the tree (which may or may not be on a different server). The structure of the URLs we all know and love is simply a manifestation of the way DNS manages the tree.

So, if tier one consists of 13 core servers, what exactly is tier two? Well, they are broken down like parts of a URL. So think about the following URL: `www.google.com.hk`. There are four parts `www`, `google`, `com`, and `hk`. Each part represents a different portion of its makeup by DNS.

- hk: Short for Hong Kong, this portion represents the location. Every country has one (except the USA because it is the "base" of the Internet).

- com: Short for commercial, this means that the domain is owned by a business.

- google: The name of the entity you are searching for; this is Google's domain.

- www: The World Wide Web subdomain of the google domain, this tells it to go the World Wide Web server that is attached to the `google.com.hk` domain.

Now that you know how a URL is put together, you might guess how a DNS query (the process of looking up the name itself) works. A basic DNS query goes to one of the 13 core nodes. From there it queries the top level domain for the first portion of the URL, the region. Once it has queried the region, it goes to the regional DNS server and queries it for the commercial domain server.

From that server it makes a request for the google domain and then finally it reaches the name server for the google domain itself, Google's DNS Server. From here you can retrieve the IP address of `www.google.com.hk`, but you could potentially retrieve the `google.com.hk` domain's IP or the `mail.google.com.hk` domain as all of these domains could have entries within the `google.com.hk` DNS Server.

Querying Yourself

Now that you understand how DNS works, try it for yourself! There are a large number of tools to query DNS servers. The first and by far the most common is dig. Dig is short for Domain Information Groper and is one of the most widely used tools for performing queries on a domain. Syntactically, dig is very simple to use. The invocation is just

```
dig <domainname>
```

As a trial, we executed a lookup for `www.google.com.hk`.

```
root@archie:~$ dig www.google.com.hk

; <<>> DiG 9.7.3 <<>> www.google.com.hk
;; global options: +cmd
;; Got answer:
;; ->>HEADER<<- opcode: QUERY, status: NOERROR, id: 57130
;; flags: qr rd ra; QUERY: 1, ANSWER: 2, AUTHORITY: 0, ADDITIONAL: 0
```

```
;; QUESTION SECTION:
;www.google.com.hk.                   IN        A

;; ANSWER SECTION:
www.google.com.hk.       19994    IN        CNAME     www-hk.l.google.com.
www-hk.l.google.com.     172      IN        A         74.125.237.88

;; Query time: 21 msec
;; SERVER: 10.0.0.1#53(10.0.0.1)
;; WHEN: Mon Jan 23 22:31:56 2012
;; MSG SIZE  rcvd: 84
```

As you can see, it has returned two answers from our one query: www.google.com.hk, which in actuality is the server www-hk.l.google.com, and this server has the IP address 74.125.237.88. If you wish to check this, you can perform a simple ping to www.google.com.hk and you will see the ping routed to the IP address of the domain name.

```
root@archie:~$ ping www.google.com.hk
PING www-hk.l.google.com (74.125.237.88) 56(84) bytes of data.
64 bytes from syd01s06-in-f24.1e100.net (74.125.237.88): icmp_req=1 ttl=56 time=17.9 ms
```

Voila!

Advanced DNS Queries

A more advanced query is called a DNS traversal or a DNS walk. This means that it will attempt to query all the name servers that lead to the goal. To perform this, we again invoke dig. This time, however, we gave dig the +trace option, which tells dig to provide the full trace of all the servers it queries when looking up the DNS entry for the domain in question. Again, we queried www.google.com.hk for the information.

```
root@archie:~$ dig  www.google.com.hk +trace

; <<>> DiG 9.7.3 <<>> www.google.com.hk +trace
;; global options: +cmd
.                       105602   IN        NS        g.root-servers.net.
.                       105602   IN        NS        e.root-servers.net.
.                       105602   IN        NS        i.root-servers.net.
.                       105602   IN        NS        k.root-servers.net.
.                       105602   IN        NS        j.root-servers.net.
.                       105602   IN        NS        d.root-servers.net.
.                       105602   IN        NS        b.root-servers.net.
.                       105602   IN        NS        l.root-servers.net.
.                       105602   IN        NS        a.root-servers.net.
.                       105602   IN        NS        m.root-servers.net.
.                       105602   IN        NS        f.root-servers.net.
.                       105602   IN        NS        c.root-servers.net.
.                       105602   IN        NS        h.root-servers.net.
;; Received 512 bytes from 10.0.0.1#53(10.0.0.1) in 22 ms
```

```
hk.                          172800   IN     NS         b.dns.tw.
hk.                          172800   IN     NS         z.hkirc.net.hk.
hk.                          172800   IN     NS         ns1.hkirc.net.hk.
hk.                          172800   IN     NS         ns2.cuhk.edu.hk.
hk.                          172800   IN     NS         ns2.hkirc.net.hk.
hk.                          172800   IN     NS         sec3.apnic.net.
hk.                          172800   IN     NS         adns1.berkeley.edu.
hk.                          172800   IN     NS         hk-ns.pch.net.
;; Received 500 bytes from 128.63.2.53#53(h.root-servers.net) in 245 ms

google.com.hk.               28800    IN     NS         NS2.GOOGLE.COM.
google.com.hk.               28800    IN     NS         NS3.GOOGLE.COM.
google.com.hk.               28800    IN     NS         NS1.GOOGLE.COM.
google.com.hk.               28800    IN     NS         NS4.GOOGLE.COM.
;; Received 117 bytes from 137.189.6.21#53(ns2.cuhk.edu.hk) in 244 ms

www.google.com.hk.           86400    IN     CNAME      www-hk.l.google.com.
www-hk.l.google.com.         300      IN     A          74.125.237.24
;; Received 84 bytes from 216.239.38.10#53(NS4.GOOGLE.COM) in 191 ms
```

The output for the dig with trace is much more complex. The first thing to notice is that there are 13 servers in the top section. These are the actual root servers of the Internet and we queried them directly! Then it goes into the query of the hk domain; you can see all of the Hong Kong name servers that were resolved. From the Hong Kong name servers, it resolves directly to google.com.hk's, resolving domains NS1 to NS4 of the google.com domain. These NS servers are called nameservers and they provide DNS functions for the domain name google.com. This shows that there are actually four DNS servers working in concert to provide DNS name resolution for google.com.hk!

DNS Caching

By now, you must have realized that this is nowhere near efficient enough. To query the root nodes every time you want to browse www.google.com.hk would be extremely taxing on the root DNS servers. You have seen the output of dig; there can be quite a bit of information for one web site alone. Now multiply that by the number of web sites on the Internet and then again by the number of people who browse the net. Take that number and multiply again for every Smartphone, nettop (Internet desktop), and Internet-enabled device out there. Needless to say, it's quite a lot.

Although all of the core DNS servers are actually clusters of servers that respond to queries as a group (which gives them a lot of power and bandwidth), it's still nowhere near enough to power every single DNS query for the whole planet! The solution is called caching. *Caching* means that your system will keep its own list of known servers and DNS servers to allow it to look them up from its own storage. This cuts down on the amount of time it would take to do a full walk of the DNS tree for a server you have visited before. It also reduces the number of queries sent to the primary nodes. For example, our server that has been doing the dig lookups of www.google.com.hk will already have in its memory the nameserver for the hk domain that it has looked up and the DNS entry for Google.

Querying your DNS Cache

If you are a regular Windows user (and who isn't, willingly or otherwise), you can perform a simple query to inspect your current DNS cache. To show your current DNS cache, open a Windows command prompt and then execute `ipconfig /displaydns`.

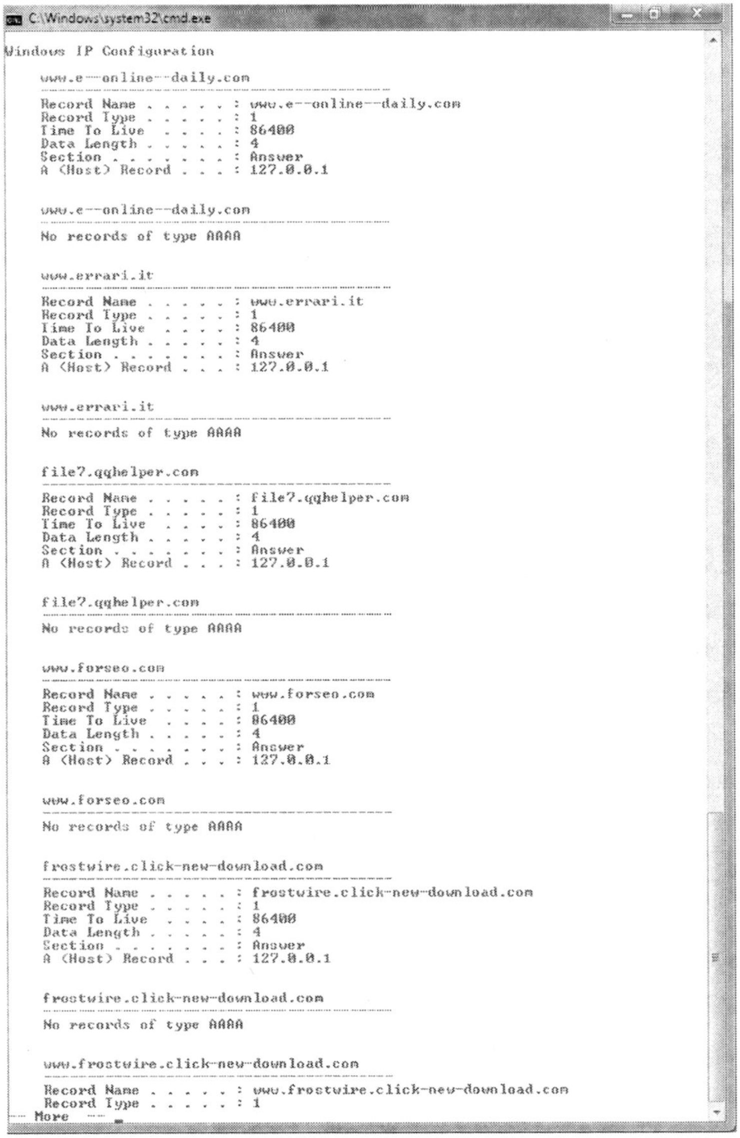

```
C:\Windows\system32\cmd.exe

Windows IP Configuration

    www.e--online--daily.com
    ----------------------------------------
    Record Name . . . . . : www.e--online--daily.com
    Record Type . . . . . : 1
    Time To Live . . . . : 86400
    Data Length . . . . . : 4
    Section . . . . . . . : Answer
    A (Host) Record . . . : 127.0.0.1


    www.e--online--daily.com
    ----------------------------------------
    No records of type AAAA

    www.errari.it
    ----------------------------------------
    Record Name . . . . . : www.errari.it
    Record Type . . . . . : 1
    Time To Live . . . . : 86400
    Data Length . . . . . : 4
    Section . . . . . . . : Answer
    A (Host) Record . . . : 127.0.0.1


    www.errari.it
    ----------------------------------------
    No records of type AAAA

    file7.qqhelper.com
    ----------------------------------------
    Record Name . . . . . : file7.qqhelper.com
    Record Type . . . . . : 1
    Time To Live . . . . : 86400
    Data Length . . . . . : 4
    Section . . . . . . . : Answer
    A (Host) Record . . . : 127.0.0.1


    file7.qqhelper.com
    ----------------------------------------
    No records of type AAAA

    www.forseo.com
    ----------------------------------------
    Record Name . . . . . : www.forseo.com
    Record Type . . . . . : 1
    Time To Live . . . . : 86400
    Data Length . . . . . : 4
    Section . . . . . . . : Answer
    A (Host) Record . . . : 127.0.0.1


    www.forseo.com
    ----------------------------------------
    No records of type AAAA

    frostwire.click-new-download.com
    ----------------------------------------
    Record Name . . . . . : frostwire.click-new-download.com
    Record Type . . . . . : 1
    Time To Live . . . . : 86400
    Data Length . . . . . : 4
    Section . . . . . . . : Answer
    A (Host) Record . . . : 127.0.0.1


    frostwire.click-new-download.com
    ----------------------------------------
    No records of type AAAA

    www.frostwire.click-new-download.com
    ----------------------------------------
    Record Name . . . . . : www.frostwire.click-new-download.com
    Record Type . . . . . : 1
-- More --
```

Figure 4-2. Windows DNS cache

Figure 4-2 shows a snippet from our DNS cache. As you can see, there are a large number of entries pointing to 127.0.0.1. This address is a special reserved IP address called a Loopback or Localhost address. Computers use the Loopback address as a quick way of referring to themselves. Having these web sites appear in our DNS cache with 127.0.0.1 means that they are resolved automatically to our local machine. As we obviously don't run those sites and there isn't a web server running on this machine, we will never be able to open a connection to the remote server. This can be an especially effective way to prevent your computer from connecting to unwanted servers such as those serving adverts on web pages.

If you wish to empty your DNS cache, you can execute `ipconfig/flushdns`. While this is never an ideal solution, it can be useful when web sites are not resolving because they have changed their IP address or moved.

DNS Cache in Linux

By default, many server distributions of Linux don't come with DNS caching enabled. There are a number of applications that can perform this function; one of the easiest to install is nscd, the Name Service Cache Daemon. While we will cover nscd here, we don't recommend running nscd on a DNS server because having cached addresses requires additional maintenance and adds nothing to the function of your DNS server.

To install nscd, execute the following code.

Ubuntu:

```
sudo apt-get install nscd
```

CentOS:

```
yum install nscd
```

You will also need to enable nscd caching for DNS by editing

`/etc/nscd.conf` and ensuring that the line

```
        enable-cache            hosts           yes
```

is set within your configuration. To start, simply execute

`/etc/init.d/nscd restart`

Now that you have nscd running, you can perform the following commands to play with your DNS cache: `nscd -g` shows statistical information about usage rates of your cache and `nscd -i hosts` flushes and clears your DNS cache by invalidating all of the entries currently stored within it.

The Real Stuff

You may be wondering why we spent so much time covering DNS. Well, it's really important. Without a fundamental understanding of what DNS is and how it is used on the Internet, you won't be able to take full advantage of DNS load balancing. So, without further ado, let's start configuring your DNS server.

The first thing you need to set up your DNS server is a Domain name, a static (unchanging) Internet-facing IP address, and another name server to provide lookups for your DNS Server. When you purchase a domain name, the registrar will often ask for an IP address to point to for your name server. This should be the static Internet-facing IP address of the server you are building now!

With this basic information in hand, you can begin. Probably the world's most abundantly used DNS server is BIND, the Berkley Internet Naming Daemon.

BIND9

Start by installing BIND on your server!

Ubuntu:

```
apt-get install bind9
```

CentOS:

```
yum install bind
```

Now that you have installed BIND, you need to configure it. BIND is notorious for being hard to configure; while it can be complex, it's not beyond the skills of mortal man to configure. To start, go to /etc/bind and check the file list. You can see there are a few files, but for your purposes you only really need to worry about a few.

- *bind.keys*
- *db.0*
- *db.127*
- *db.255*
- *db.empty*
- *db.local*
- *db.root*
- *named.conf*
- *named.conf.default-zones*
- *named.conf.local*
- *named.conf.options*
- *rndc.key*
- *zones.rfc1918*

CentOS doesn't store its files in the same place as Ubuntu and instead stores them in /var/named. It also does not install the example configuration files directly for you; instead they can be found in /usr/share/doc/bind-9.x.x/sample/. You can copy the files over with

```
cp /usr/share/doc/bind-9.x.x/sample/named.conf /etc/
cp -rf /usr/share/doc/bind-9.x.x/sample/var/ /var/named
```

The list of files shows the standard config files plus some db files. These db files are the key to BIND; they are databases of key DNS entries. When you configure a DNS server, you create your own DNS database. A DNS database has two discrete sections, the first of which is the header and looks like the following:

```
$TTL    604800
@       IN    SOA     ns1.example.com. info.example.com. (
                          2011102401          ; Serial
                                7200          ; Refresh
                                 900          ; Retry
                             2419200          ; Expire
                              604800)         ; Min
;
```

The first portion of a BIND database is the TTL, or Time To Live, flag. This is a throwback configuration and isn't used by DNS for tracking. Its purpose is in fact duplicated by the expiry configuration. The 604800 represents 7 days (60 seconds *60 minutes *24 hours* 7 days) and it means that a server will keep this information in its own cache of nameserver information for 7 days.

After this comes @   IN   SOA   ns1.example.com. info.example.com. This line represents the domain you are managing. This line says that the domain @ (wildcard meaning the one hosted locally) is provided here; you are the Start of Authority server for the listed domain and are issuing as ns1.example.com; and the administrator can be contacted at info@example.com. (That's not a typo. The e-mail @ symbol is denoted by a period in a BIND configuration file, as the @ symbol is used to donate a self reference.) Next is an open bracket, which MUST be on the same line as the SOA.

■ **Note** In this example, there are periods at the end of the domain names. This is because you are providing fully qualified domain names. The period at the end is a required part of this syntax.

DNS DB Header

The next section is about the information that will come from your nameserver. The first part is everyone's favorite, the serial. The serial is a unique identifier placed in your DNS database that is the equivalent of a version tracking number. It provides a single field entry that allows other servers to determine if things have been updated and if they should perform a full refresh of their entries for your server. Every time you change your DNS db you must change the serial; this can't be stressed enough. The format used in the previous example is the year, the month, the day, and then a two-digit revision number. This means on a given day you can theoretically go through 100 entries without issue—and that is normally plenty. When doing your initial testing, you can simply use incremental numbers from 1 onwards until you have a final version, which also removes any chance of needing to re-use a serial.

■ **Note** Everyone forgets to change the serial (even when they are reminded mere seconds before saving their changes).

Refresh

Refresh represents the amount of time a server should wait before querying this server again to perform another lookup. It is recommended that this number be between 1200 and 43200. This represents 30 minutes to 12 hours. Your example uses 2 hours as the refresh time, a value that represents a decent length for a user session.

Retry

Next is retry, which is the value that says how often this server should be retried if the server is unavailable when performing a refresh. Standard values range between 120 and 900, representing 2 to 15 minutes (although higher is possible).

Expire

After retry comes Expire. This is how long the entry should remain valid in another server before it should be re-queried. The expire value means that if a request to refresh the DNS data is made and the nameserver for this domain is down, then the current DNS information will still be available from the time of the last refresh until the time of the expire. The standard length of an expiry is from 1209600 to 2419200 (2-4 weeks); this means that DNS entries will last for plenty of time and continue working despite an extended outage of a domain's nameserver.

Min

The final value is Min, which is the negative caching length value. So, if given a negative answer to a DNS query on a server, this is how long the negative answer should remain valid. This is a new addition in BIND9 and it won't take a value over 10800 (3 hours).

In your example, you can see that, following the Min value, there needs to be a closing bracket ')' on that line to close the header for the file. The semicolons represent comments, so anything after the semicolon is ignored. Now, onto the actual meat portion of a DNS database!

DNS Database Entries

Now that you know how the DNS data is to be managed by other servers, you can make a database of entries. A DNS database entry contains a few things.

1. The name of the address you are providing the entry for.

2. The keyword IN

3. The type of record

4. The value for that entry

Next you'll see a large number of examples of a basic DNS configuration.

```
@                      IN    NS    ns1.example.com.
@                      IN    NS    ns2.example.com.

example.com.           IN    MX    10      mail.example.com.

example.com.           IN    A     123.123.123.123
mail                   IN    A     123.123.123.123
```

63

```
ns1                     IN      A       234.234.234.234
ns2                     IN      A       234.234.234.234

www                     IN      CNAME   example.com.
ftp                     IN      CNAME   example.com.
```

Here are four example styles of DNS entries: an NS entry that denotes a nameserver entry; an MX entry (which is a mail exchanger and is normally the mailserver for a domain); an A record that links an IP address to a name; and a CNAME entry, which is a Canonical Name entry or an alias.

Note   There are additional DNS types, but the ones covered here are all you should need for a basic to medium setup.

Nameserver (NS)

The first thing you will notice is the two nameservers have "@" symbols. These are self reference elements and both state that this server is both ns1.example.com and ns2.example.com. These entries allow you to serve the names of the nameservers to the public. Additionally, the address of this server has also been lodged with an upstream provider as the Authority on this domain. "Authority" in this case means that the server has the ability to speak as the authority as to where members of that domain may be contacted.

Mail Exchange (MX)

Note the number value in the MX entry. This is an additional field in MX entries called the pref, which is a simple performance and load balancing metric for name servers! This value (normally set to 10) says how much preference should be showed to a particular mail server. In this example, it represents the primary mail server for the domain. Sub mail servers would use values such as 20, 30, and so on.

A Records

Next are A records. These are the bread and butter of a DNS setup. They represent all the domain names that run under a domain's header. In this example, there are entries for the fully qualified domain, the mail server, and ns1 and ns2. Any of the domain names that end in a period are considered to be fully qualified domain names, as discussed earlier; those without are sub domains of the fully qualified domain set in the header. This means that the entries for mail, ns1, and ns2 are actually entries for mail.example.com., ns1.example.com. and ns2.example.com..

Note   The IPv6 implications to DNS are covered in Chapter 14.

Canonical Name (CNAME)

The final entry that you are concerned with in this chapter is the CNAME entry. A CNAME entry takes a name just like an A entry, but instead of providing an IP address, it provides another name. This is the equivalent of saying that something is also the same IP address something else. So in the example, `www.example.com.` is the same as `example.com.`, which is also the same as `ftp.example.com.`

Loading your DB

Once you have your DB file written correctly, you need to tell BIND that it should load it. The configuration file is `/etc/bind/named.conf.default-zones` (or `/etc/named.conf` if you're on CentOS). This file is called a *zone file*. This file contains a list of entries that allow you to add multiple DNS databases, so you could in fact host multiple domains off the one DNS server. The format can be seen in the following example (remember for CentOS the files will point to `/var/named/data/`):f

```
zone "." {
        type hint;
        file "/etc/bind/db.root";
};

zone "localhost" {
        type master;
        file "/etc/bind/db.local";
};

zone "example.com " {
        type master;
        file "/etc/bind/db.example.com";
};
```

The zone file contains a list of entries for each zone that is owned by the server. The first two zones in this example are two internal references that contain entries for the root servers (`db.root`) and for your local machine's internal DNS (`db.local`). The third entry is that of the `example.com` domain. The entry starts with zone `"example.com"`, which says that the entry below is for the zone `example.com`.

Following the zone header is a curly brace and then a type entry. For your purposes you will make a master entry, which says that the zone you are serving is the master authority for that domain. Finally, you need to link your own DB file that you have created. This is done the same way as when you linked the db you created earlier to the zone entry.

Checking the Config

Once you have written your config, you can check it with `named-checkzone`. The syntax is `named-checkzone <Domain> <DB File>`. An example of a working config is

```
root@archie:/var/log$ named-checkzone example.com /etc/bind/db.example.com
zone example.com/IN: loaded serial 2012013001
OK
```

Or for CentOS:

```
root@archie:/var/log$ named-checkzone example.com /var/named/data/db.example.com
zone example.com/IN: loaded serial 2012013001
OK
```

Once you have checked over your config and linked it in the zone file (and double and triple checked that darn serial value), you can start or restart BIND.

Common Issues

To diagnose issues with your BIND installation, we suggest first reading over your system logfile (normally found in **/var/log**). Look for entries relating to Named and something akin to

"Jan 30 20:11:56 archie named[10120]: zone example.com.in-addr.arpa/IN: loaded serial 2012013001".

This shows that the server started correctly, loaded the serial, and is serving that domain. However, read further and look for entries like "/etc/bind/db.example.com:12: ignoring out-of-zone data (example.com)", which denotes that a portion of your DNS table has not loaded correctly. If so, perform the following checks:

- You are using semicolons for comments.
- The open bracket is on the first line.
- The close bracket is on the last line with the Min value.
- Your MX entries have MX values.
- All fully qualified domain names have periods on the end.
- Your zone name is the name of the domain you are trying to provide for, so if your db contains entries for example.com., your zone should be example.com.

Again, once you have made any changes, check again with named-checkzone.

Testing your DNS

Now that your DNS is running, you can test it by using the nslookup command. NS, as you'll probably remember, is shorthand for name server, so you are doing a nameserver lookup. nslookup is a significantly cut-down version of dig. You could use dig in this situation, but we find that nslookup is just as effective (not to mention far easier) for these kind of simple queries. The usage of nslookup is nslookup <server to look for> <dns server to use>.

In this example, you are going to look up the example.com domain using the 127.0.0.1 special loopback address. (Yes, you're going to talk to yourself!)

```
root@debian:/etc/bind# nslookup example.com 127.0.0.1
Server:         127.0.0.1
Address:        127.0.0.1#53

Name:   example.com
Address: 123.123.123.123
```

And that's it! If you were unable to resolve the IP address for the domain you set up, check that BIND is running and that you have no errors. Go over the config checks, validate your BIND config (see "Common Issues" section for a refresher), and ensure you have updated (and triple and quadruple checked) your serial value.

DNS Load Balancing

As for the actual load balancing, it is fairly dumb in how it works. It uses a simple method called round robin to distribute connections over the group of servers it knows for a specific domain. It does this sequentially (by going first, second, third, etc.). To add DNS load balancing to your server, you simply need to add multiple A records for a domain. Yes, it really is that easy! BIND takes care of the rest!

For example, consider the following setup, which provides four servers that will resolve to the name example.com. As ever, when you configure your server, remember to check your config with named-checkzone and to increment your serial!

```
example.com.        IN      A       123.123.123.123
example.com.        IN      A       123.123.123.124
example.com.        IN      A       123.123.123.125
example.com.        IN      A       123.123.123.126
```

Or you can provide a number of IP addresses to one entry, like so:

```
example.com.        IN      A       123.123.123.123
                    IN      A       123.123.123.124
                    IN      A       123.123.123.125
                    IN      A       123.123.123.126
```

To check that your DNS load balancing has taken effect, you simply need to nslookup the address in question. Just as you did earlier, you can test with nslookup; your results should look something like the following:

```
root@archie:~# nslookup example.com 127.0.0.1
Server:         127.0.0.1
Address:        127.0.0.1#53

Name:    example.com
Address: 123.123.123.123
Name:    example.com
Address: 123.123.123.126
Name:    example.com
Address: 123.123.123.124
Name:    example.com
Address: 123.123.123.125
```

Advantages of DNS Load Balancing

DNS load balancing provides several important advantages.

- *Simplicity.* As mentioned earlier, there may be situations where you can simply increase your load by adding an additional duplicate system to allow you to process more traffic. Or you may have multiple low bandwidth Internet addresses that you route to one server to provide a larger amount of total bandwidth to the server.

- *Easy to configure.* As you have seen, configuring DNS load balancing is a breeze. You simply add the additional addresses into your DNS database and off you go! It can't get much easier!

- *Simple to debug.* There are a plethora of tools that you can use to debug and work with DNS including dig, ping and nslookup. Additionally, BIND includes tools to validate your config, and all the testing can be done using the local loopback adapter.

- *Builds into additional infrastructure.* Because you have a web-based system, you will need to have a DNS server to have a domain name. This means that without a doubt you will have a DNS server at some point down the line. Adding DNS-based load balancing allows you to quickly extend using your existing platform!

Issues with DNS Load Balancing

DNS load balancing also has its fair share of limitations. As with everything we share with you in this book, you should consider a blended solution to maximize effectiveness, and you should use the information we provide to come up with a full plan on how to achieve maximum performance within your system.

- *Stickiness.* This is a problem suffered by dynamic applications and rarely affects static sites. As discussed in Chapter 2, HTTP (and thus the Web) is a stateless protocol. It has chronic amnesia and can't remember from one request to the next. To get around this, you send a unique identifier to accompany each request. This identifier is the cookie, although there are other sneaky ways to achieve something similar. This unique identifier allows the web browser to keep a collection of information relating to your current interaction with the web site, all tied to that one key. The issue here is that this data isn't available between servers, so if a new DNS request is made to determine the IP, there is no guarantee that you will return to the server that has all the previously established information.

- *Processing load.* As mentioned, you can wind up in a situation where one out of every two requests is a high intensity request, and one out of every two is easy. If the absolute worst possible situation occurs, all the high intensity requests could wind up going to only one of the servers and all the low intensity to the other. This is not a very balanced situation and something you should avoid lest you ruin the web site for half of the visitors.

- *Fault tolerance.* The DNS load balancer can't tell if one web server goes down so it will still send traffic to the empty space left by the downed server. This means that half of all requests would die, and the end user could sit there refreshing to get to a working server ad infinitum.

So given all the issues, why use DNS load balancing at all? Well, it's a very simple system and that really counts for something. You don't need to debug a complicated infrastructure to figure out what went wrong; it should be pretty easy to spot. Simplicity is highly underrated, and this simple form of load balancing might be more than sufficient or can be used as one part of a much larger load balancing effort.

Summary

This chapter covered the configuration and usage of the Berkeley Internet Naming Daemon (BIND to its friends) to provide DNS for your domain. You now know the strengths and simplicity of configuring DNS load balancing and how you can do simple diagnostics to confirm that both your DNS and DNS load balancing are working.

CHAPTER 5

Content Delivery Networks

This chapter covers a topic that you probably won't be able to recreate by yourself. Or at least you wouldn't (or shouldn't) want to. Content delivery networks (CDNs) have become quite prominent in recent years. The way they work is very simple and this hides some of their intrinsic power.

For example, Peter lives in Hong Kong and is blessed with a 100Mbps Internet connection. When he downloads updates from Microsoft or Apple, he can download at around 10Mbps. The reason is because Hong Kong has awesome connectivity. It is quite realistic for an individual to have a 1Gbps fiber optic network connection here. However, while this provides ping times for Quake 3 in the low single digits, all of this stops at Hong Kong's border. At this point everything gets shuttled back and forth via relatively slow links, and your lightning-fast connection gives you no advantage.

So, how can he download the updates so fast? The answer is really rather straightforward: the files he needs are physically in Hong Kong. But what happens for people outside of Hong Kong? Surely they'll have the same issue in reverse: if it's fast for Peter, it's going to be deathly slow for them. As it happens, this isn't a problem because the files are in most other countries, too.

Okay, so that doesn't sound particular awe-inspiring, does it? Big deal, you have the file in more than one place. Not rocket science. True, but what is really cool is that you access all those files—regardless of where they are—with the same address. In other words, if you use the URL in Hong Kong, you download from the Hong Kong mirror, but if you're in the United States or the United Kingdom, you would get to the local mirrors. In short, you would always connect to the server that's closest to you and thus get the highest possible speed available.

So, same URL, same file, different locations. Isn't that cool?

When the World Wide Web took off and it became critical for a web site in the United States to be equally fast and responsive when browsed from Tokyo, it hit a problem. The easiest solution (and one you still see occasionally) is for a company to have servers in more than one place. You go to their main site and then you'll get redirected to a local mirror. You can usually spot these by the different hostname, such as the following:

```
http://www.example.com/
http://hk.example.com/
http://uk.example.com/
```

These addresses point to individual machines, usually in the region they are supposed to serve.

Note   Funky hostnames don't necessarily mean that the server is different. For example, applications like Basecamp from 37Signals use different hostnames to differentiate individual customers. It's a great example of using the environment to make the application simpler and easier to maintain.

The problem with this system is you have to maintain a server for each region or country. You need to apply updates to all of them individually and make sure the content is always up to date. That said, if you are specifically targeting only two countries, you might want to look into this solution. The rest of us need a solution that's just going to work, be fast, and make the boss and customers happy. We need a content delivery network.

Building complicated networks that span the world is not a cheap thing to do. In fact, it's hideously expensive. The interesting thing is that although you need to set up the servers and have good coverage, once the network is in place, it will spend most of its time sitting on its hands waiting for something to do. That's not a very efficient use of your huge investment.

Content delivery networks get around this little problem. One company builds the network and then shares it with others—for a fee, of course! This has many benefits for people like us, as we merely need to use a small portion of the network's bandwidth and don't fancy the high costs of its implementation. We just pay for what we intend to use, nothing more.

Choosing a CDN Provider

So now what you know the details of what a content delivery network really is and what it can do for you, you can start by choosing one for your purposes. There are many commercial content delivery network providers available: Amazon Web Services offers the Amazon CloudFront, which is optimized to work with other Amazon Web Services they offer, such as their Elastic Compute Cloud, or EC^2. Another frontrunner in the field of CDN is Limelight Networks, which was founded in 2001 and has an extensive portfolio with well-known customers and a good reputation. Finally, Akamai is another key player; delivering between 15 to 30% of all web traffic and running over 95,000 servers worldwide, it is definitely a market leader.

The CDN provider you'll be looking at in this chapter is Rackspace. Rackspace offers many services, including their Rackspace Cloud Files service. The Cloud Files service is currently hosted using Akamai's content delivery network at a very decent price, paid per GB of storage per month. Naturally, it's eventually up to you to choose which content delivery provider to use, but we've been very satisfied with their services and how their API integrates.

Getting Started with Rackspace

Before you can start uploading any data, you first need to register an account using their web site. The process should be pretty straightforward and involves selecting the services to use (in this case, the Rackspace Cloud Files service) and providing them with some basic information, such as your contact details, payment information, and so on. Once done, you will receive an e-mail from them that includes your login details with a link to their web site that you can use to get started. For now, let's assume that your username is loadbalancer, and your password is LoadBalance01.

Use your browser to navigate to their web site, which will prompt you for your login credentials, as shown in Figure 5-1.

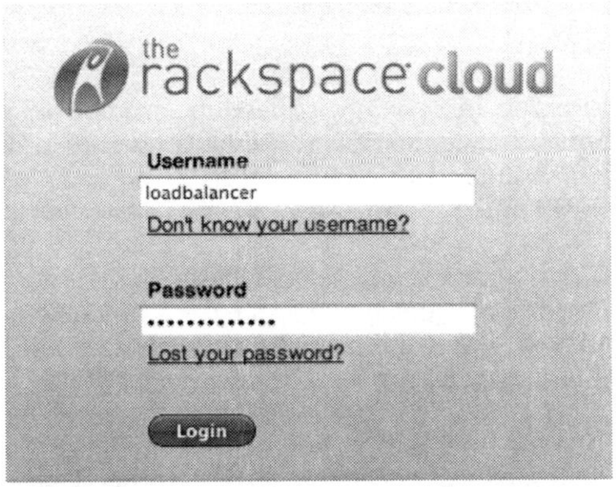

Figure 5-1. Rackspace Cloud login prompt

The first time you log into the account, you'll be asked to read and accept the terms of conditions and set up password recovery information in case you forget your password. Then you will get to the Rackspace interface. The management interface is quite self-explanatory and offers a number of options to modify your account, request support, view some tutorials, and of course, manage your hosted files. More importantly, you will be shown an overview of your account's activity per rented service; this includes the total amount of bandwidth used and disk space rented throughout the past month.

Specifically, Bandwidth In tells you the total amount of data transferred into your Rackspace Cloud Files account. Bandwidth Out tells you the total amount of gigabytes transferred to external users via the Web, so this will tell you how active your web site or application has been the last few weeks. Bandwidth CDN informs you about the total amount of data delivered to others using the Akamai content delivery network, which Rackspace employs. Next, Disk Space informs you about the total amount of gigabytes used by all objects on your account. Finally, Operations summarizes the number of actions you've performed recently on your account, such as initiating uploads, downloads, creating new storage containers, and so forth. An overview of the default layout can be seen in Figure 5-2.

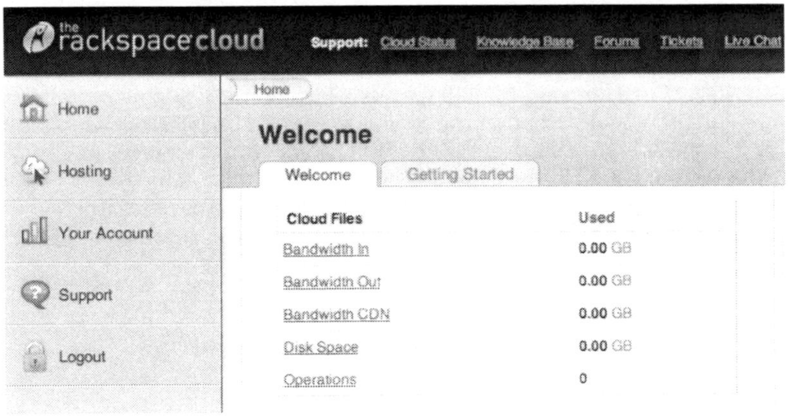

Figure 5-2. Getting started on your fresh Rackspace account

Adding Content to Your CDN Account

Before you can get started on adding your data to the Cloud Files account, you first need to generate an API access key. The API access key will be required for authenticating against the RESTful API before being able to perform any calls (or actions). The RESTful API is discussed later in this chapter, so you don't need to concern yourselves with the details on how the API and authentication scheme works yet, but you do need to generate this key before you can get started.

To generate the access key, you need to navigate to the Hosting menu and select Cloud Files. Here, you'll be prompted to generate the API Access Key by clicking Activate Now. Once done, the blank fields will be populated with your API Key and your account's username. You will require this information later on when you start working with language-specific APIs. For now, you can proceed by clicking on Start Cloud Files.

Initially, no containers will be listed the first time you open the interface, as you can see in Figure 5-3. Containers are used to store the content you wish to serve and are best compared to directories. That said, it is mandatory to create at least one before you can upload any data to the CDM. To do so, select Add Container from the menu, which allows you to specify the name of your container (for example, website or AwesomeApp, depending on what you prefer). Fill in a name for the container and click OK to generate it.

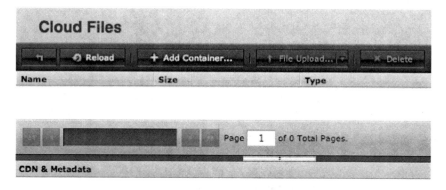

Figure 5-3. *The initial view showing no containers or data*

Once generated, the container will be listed, and additional options will become available in the CDN & Metadata frame below. Here you can specify whether the container should be publicly available using the Publish to CDN option or if it should remain private. By default, every container is set to private, meaning its contents will only be published to the CDN and made publicly available when configured so using the container's properties. Additionally, Enable CDN Logs can be enabled to generate log files, keeping track of your visitors. The size of these log files do count to your disk usage, however.

For now, enable the Publish to CDN option as shown in Figure 5-4 and leave it at that. Now you're ready to upload some content!

Figure 5-4. Publishing your container to the CDN

Before going any further, note that Rackspace Cloud Files does not currently support nesting containers or creating subdirectories within a container. Instead, it allows you to use pseudo-directories by adding directory marker objects and ensuring the file names are set to match these.

Say you've previously created a container named Images. If you want to create a pseudo-directory in it named HongKong, you first need to create a (zero-bytes) file lacking any extension and name it HongKong (this can be done using the create_paths function, shown later on). Now, if you wish to ensure a file is reachable using Images/HongKong/IMG_1234.JPG, you need to rename the file to HongKong/IMG_1234.JPG, where the / would act as a path element separator. Note that the forward slash is a regular character and will be accepted in any filename.

This way, you can also create additional nested directories. Keep in mind that for each nested pseudo-directory a directory marker object needs to be created.

Moving on! You can now proceed to upload data to your container by selecting it and selecting File Upload from the menu. This allows you to browse your local files or the network and select them for uploading. You can upload several files at once (all of which will be listed in a separate window from where they can also be removed if necessary). Now, assume you have built a killer app that's going to make you very rich and so you wish to publish it to the CDN (in this example, your killer app is called AmazingApp and the file is AmazingApp-1.0.0.tar.gz). So you simply add it to the list of uploads, and select Upload, as shown in Figure 5-5. It's that simple! The file(s) is now well on its way to a number of servers from where it can be downloaded using the high-speed network that Akamai provides.

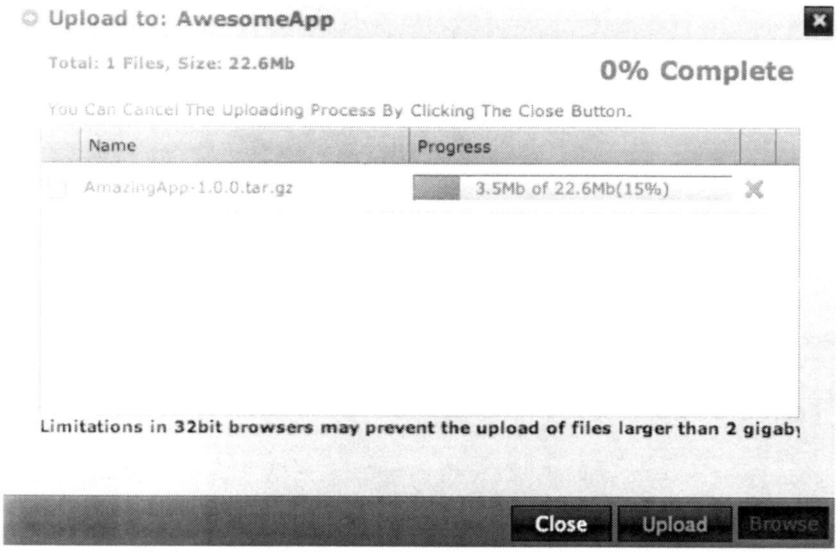

Figure 5-5. Publishing your data to the CDN

Once the upload has finished, the data will be listed under the container previously created, as shown in Figure 5-6. Its size and file type will also be displayed. When highlighting the file, the CDN URL will be presented, which can be used to directly download the file over the high-speed network. This is exactly what's so cool about a CDN: one URL, different servers, but a guaranteed high-speed connection available from wherever the file will be requested.

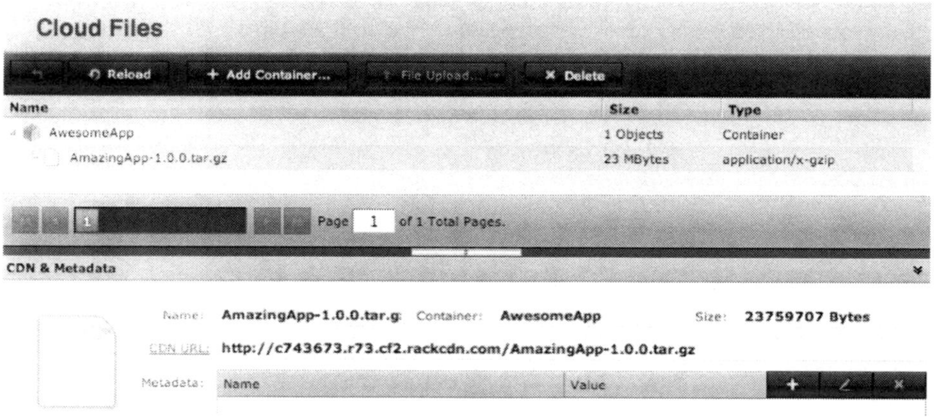

Figure 5-6. An overview of the published file and its details

The Rackspace Cloud Files API

Other than the web interface, Rackspace also offers a number of language-specific application programming interfaces, or APIs. These can be integrated into your own application, allowing you to interact with your CDN containers without requiring the web interface. Using the API, containers can be created, modified, and deleted; files can be listed, uploaded, and removed; and much more. Essentially, it allows you to do exactly the same actions that can be done via the web interface. In fact, the same API, called RESTful, is utilized, and the language-specific APIs simply provide another layer of abstraction on top of the RESTful API, preventing you from work directly with HTTP requests and responses to manage your data.

That said, any requests made and responses received to and from the API are being done using standard HTTP calls. These calls are performed using HTTPS (port 443).

In the remainder of this chapter, you'll look at the RESTful API for PHP. PHP is a popular programming language on the web, and there's a fair chance you'll be using it for developing your own web applications. The current version of the RESTful API requires PHP version 5.x with the following modules enabled:

- cURL
- FileInfo
- mbstring

Throughout the remainder of this section, we will assume you have a solid understanding of the basics of PHP.

■ **Note** All the language specific APIs are hosted at and can be obtained from GitHub at
`http://github.com/rackspace`.

Integrating the API into PHP

Before you can start using the API, you first need to integrate it into your PHP page. By doing so, you load all the API classes available, allowing you to call functions otherwise unknown to the native PHP language. To do so, you first need to download the PHP API from the GitHub repository and extract its contents to the web server, ensuring the source code files are in your PHP include path.

Once extracted, open your PHP file and include or require the cloudfiles.php file in your script, like so:

```php
<?php
  require('cloudfiles.php');
?>
```

And that's it! Simple, isn't it? Now you're all set to start using the API. Remember that the examples shown here will solely focus on your API, not on any additional code.

Authenticating with Your API Key

When you first started using your Rackspace account, you were asked to generate an API access key before you could proceed to upload any files to the CDN. That key is the same one you will use to identify yourselves with the RESTful API, allowing you to interact with your data.

To authenticate, you need to call the authenticate() function. However, in order to do this, you are first required to create an authentication instance by invoking the CF_Authentication class.

```php
<?php
  require('cloudfiles.php');

  # First, create the authentication instance providing our username and API Key
  $auth = new CF_Authentication("loadbalancer", "12345");

  # Perform the authentication request by calling the authenticate() function
  # on our instance previously created
  $auth->authenticate();
?>
```

Once authenticate() has been called, it will verify the username and API key provided against the RESTful API and will return 1 if successfully authenticated. If the API returns an AuthenticationException, it means the provided credentials (such as the username/API key) are incorrect and must be rechecked.

Optionally, to confirm authentication has succeeded, or if you are still authenticated, the authenticated() function can be called, which will return 1 if successful. The authenticated() function requires no parameters to be specified and also exists within the CF_Authentication class.

```php
<?php
  require('cloudfiles.php');

  # First, create the authentication instance providing our username and API Key
  $auth = new CF_Authentication("loadbalancer", "12345");

  # Perform the authentication request by calling the authenticate() function
  # on our instance previously created
  $auth->authenticate();

  # Confirm we've successfully authenticated
  $status = $auth->authenticated();
  print $status;
?>
```

The CF_Authentication provides several other functions that allow you to toggle debugging (setDebug), export, and load authentication information from cache (export_credentials, load_cached_credentials) and ssl_use_cabundle, which can be used to leverage the Certificate Authority bundle included in the API. The functions described, however, are the ones most commonly used.

Connecting and Disconnecting

Once authenticated using the CF_Authentication class, you can pass on the validated authentication details, stored in $auth, to a connection instance in order to connect to the storage system. To do this, the CF_Connection class can be used, with $auth as its parameter.

```php
<?php
  require('cloudfiles.php');

  # First, create the authentication instance providing our username and API Key
  $auth = new CF_Authentication("loadbalancer", "12345");

  # Perform the authentication request by calling the authenticate() function
  # on our instance previously created
  $auth->authenticate();

  # Establish the connection instance
  $conn = new CF_Connection($auth);
?>
```

In order to close a connection using the API, you can call the close() function also provided by the CF_Authentication class.

```php
<?php
  require('cloudfiles.php');

  # First, create the authentication instance providing our username and API Key
  $auth = new CF_Authentication("loadbalancer", "12345");

  # Perform the authentication request by calling the authenticate() function
  # on our instance previously created
  $auth->authenticate();

  # Establish the connection instance
  $conn = new CF_Connection($auth);

  # Disconnect from the storage system
  $conn->close();
?>
```

Working with Containers

As well as establishing connections, the CF_Connection class can also be used to work with containers. For example, you can use the class to create new containers, list the ones you have, delete and modify containers, and retrieve an overview of the files available and their total size, among other things. This section will look at how to perform the actions most commonly used. First, let's have a look at how you can retrieve a list of containers currently available to your storage system.

Listing the Containers

There are three different methods available for listing your containers. First, there's the list_containers function. This function can be used to return an array of strings that contains the names of all containers available on your account. The list_containers function takes two parameters: limit, which can be used to restrict the total number of results returned, accepting an integer, and marker, which can be used to return results greater than whatever string has been specified. Let's look at an example used to list all available containers, using the list_containers and print_r functions, like so:

```php
<?php
  require('cloudfiles.php');

  $auth = new CF_Authentication("loadbalancer", "12345");
  $auth->authenticate();
  $conn = new CF_Connection($auth);

  # Create an array containing the names of our containers found
  $containers = $conn->list_containers();

  # Print the array using print_r
  print_r($containers);

  $conn->close();
?>
```

The results will look as follows:

```
Array
(
    [0] => "AwesomeApp"
)
```

The second function available to request a list of containers is the list_containers_info function. Like the list_containers function, this one also generates and outputs an array containing the names of all available containers. However, other than the names, it will also print out the total number of objects available within the container and its total size in bytes. As with list_containers, list_containers_info also accepts the two parameters: limit and marker.

```php
<?php
  require('cloudfiles.php');

  $auth = new CF_Authentication("loadbalancer", "12345");
  $auth->authenticate();
  $conn = new CF_Connection($auth);

  # Create an array containing the names of our containers
  # found, including its details (size, total number of items)
  $containers_info = $conn->list_containers_info();

  # Print the array using print_r
  print_r($containers_info);

  $conn->close();
?>
```

As expected, its results will contain a nested array for each container available.

```
Array
(
    ["AwesomeApp"] =>
        Array
        (
            ["bytes"] => 23759707,
            ["count"] => 1
        )
)
```

The third function available for listing your containers is the list_public_containers function. This function can be used to return a list of names of all containers ever published on the CDN. That said, it will also include any containers that were previously CDN-enabled, regardless of their current existence. list_public_containers takes one Boolean parameter. If set to true, list_public_containers will only return the currently enabled CDN containers rather than any that ever existed. By default, this option is set to false.

```php
<?php
  require('cloudfiles.php');

  $auth = new CF_Authentication("loadbalancer", "12345");
  $auth->authenticate();
  $conn = new CF_Connection($auth);

  # Create an array containing the names of our containers
  # that are now, or were previously, made publicly available
  $public_containers = $conn->list_public_containers();

  # Print the array using print_r
  print_r($public_containers);

  $conn->close();
?>
```

The resulting array would look like the following:

```
Array
(
    [0] => "AwesomeApp"
)
```

Creating and Deleting Containers

Two other methods that the CF_Connection class provides are create_container and delete_container. As their names imply, create_container is used to create a new container on the storage system, whereas delete_container is used to delete an existing, but empty, container.

The create_container function is extremely straightforward to use as it only accepts a single string as its parameter: the container's name. If the supplied name already exists, a SyntaxException will be reported back, and you would require specifying another name. Let's look at an example.

```php
<?php
  require('cloudfiles.php');

  $auth = new CF_Authentication("loadbalancer", "12345");
  $auth->authenticate();
  $conn = new CF_Connection($auth);

  # Create a new container named "Images"
  $conn->create_container("Images");

  $conn->close();
?>
```

Likewise, delete_container also takes a single string representing the container's name as its parameter.

■ **Note** Containers should be emptied before they are removed. This can be done using the delete_object function provided by the CF_Container class.

```php
<?php
  require('cloudfiles.php');

  $auth = new CF_Authentication("loadbalancer", "12345");
  $auth->authenticate();
  $conn = new CF_Connection($auth);

  # Delete the (empty) container named "Images"
  $result = $conn->delete_container("AwesomeApp");
  print $result;

  $conn->close();
?>
```

If the delete_container command returns the NonEmptyContainerException, it, quite obviously, implies that the container is not yet empty, and thus can't be removed. Additionally, if the container's title wasn't typed properly, a NoSuchContainerException response can be expected. If all goes well, however, a True will be returned to indicate the container was removed as expected.

Using a Container

Before you can start making modifications to your containers, you first need to know how to use them. Sure, you've seen how to list, create, and delete containers, but you haven't looked at modifying them yet. In order for you to do this, you must first require assigning an instance to the container or containers by using the get_container or get_containers functions respectively, as provided by the CF_Connection class.

The first function you'll be interested in is the get_container function. As with many functions, this one also takes a single string as a parameter, used to identify the name of the container for which you're creating the instance.

```php
<?php
  require('cloudfiles.php');

  $auth = new CF_Authentication("loadbalancer", "12345");
  $auth->authenticate();
  $conn = new CF_Connection($auth);

  # Create an instance for our Images container, named $container
  $container = $conn->get_container("Images");

  $conn->close();
?>
```

Once the instance ($container) has been specified, you can make modifications to it, such as changing its public visibility, removing it, and so forth. You will learn how to do this later.

You can also create an array of container instances using get_containers. When using this function, an array will be returned that also includes some specifics about the containers it includes, such as the number of objects and the number of bytes stored within each container. The get_containers function accepts two parameters: $limit, and $marker. $limit can be used to restrict the total number of results returned, accepting an integer, and $marker can be used to return results greater than whatever string has been specified. Let's look at a practical example and its results.

```php
<?php
  require('cloudfiles.php');

  $auth = new CF_Authentication("loadbalancer", "12345");
  $auth->authenticate();
  $conn = new CF_Connection($auth);

  # Create an array of container instances, named $containers, limit to 2 results
  $containers = $conn->get_containers(2);
  # Print the array's details in a decent way
  foreach ($containers as $contdetails) {
    echo "Container name:" . $contdetails->name . "\n";
    echo "Objects:" . $contdetails->count . "\n";
    echo "Bytes stored:" . $contdetails->bytes . "\n";
  }

  $conn->close();
?>
```

The resulting output will look similar to this, depending on the number of containers and the contents found, of course:

```
Container name: AwesomeApp
Objects: 1
Bytes stored: 23759707
Container name: Images
Objects: 0
Bytes stored: 0
```

Modifying Container Settings

Now that you've seen how to make, break, and use containers, let's have a look at how to modify the permission settings on them. Using the CF_Container class, you can leverage two functions to modify the containers' privacy settings. The first function, make_private, takes a single string as a parameter used to specify the container's name and can be used to disable sharing a container on the content delivery network. The function will work for both new and old containers, but be aware that any data already cached in the CDN will remain publicly available from the CDN's cache until the TTL expires.

Let's look at a practical example on how to privatize an already existing container using make_private.

```php
<?php
  require('cloudfiles.php');

  $auth = new CF_Authentication("loadbalancer", "12345");
  $auth->authenticate();
  $conn = new CF_Connection($auth);

  # Create an instance for the Images container, named $container
  $container = $conn->get_container("Images");

  # Privatize this container
  $container->make_private();

  $conn->close();
?>
```

In a similar fashion, you can also make the container publicly available using the make_public function. When doing so, you will need to specify two parameters: the container's name and the default TTL specified in seconds. As expected, a CDN-enabled URL will be returned to your browser, which you can print out using the print or echo function PHP provides.

```php
<?php
  require('cloudfiles.php');

  $auth = new CF_Authentication("loadbalancer", "12345");
  $auth->authenticate();
  $conn = new CF_Connection($auth);

  # Create an instance for the Images container, named $container
  $container = $conn->get_container("Images");
```

```
    # Publish this container on the CDN, with a TTL of 30 days (1 day * 30)
    $url = $container->make_public(86400 * 30);

    # Print the public URL
    print $url;

    $conn->close();
?>
```

Working with Files

Okay! By now you should have a solid understanding of how the API operates, the overall structure of the functions it provides, and how the output is returned. You know how to make adjustments to your container collection and how to retrieve useful information about them. However, you haven't looked at storing anything in them yet. What good is creating and managing containers via the API if you still require the web interface to stuff it? This section will cover how to list, upload, remove, and download files using the PHP API.

Listing Your Files

The first function you should know about is the list_objects function. Using this function, you can retrieve an array of strings that contains all the items in the selected container. The function takes four optional parameters: $limit, $marker, $prefix and $path. $limit can be used to restrict the total number of results returned, accepting an integer; $marker can be used to define an offset (number of items to skip); $prefix takes a string and is used to list only those filenames starting with what has been specified and which path can be used; $path can be used to only return the items listed under the given pseudo-directory.

Let's look at some examples to clarify this.

```php
<?php
    require('cloudfiles.php');

    $auth = new CF_Authentication("loadbalancer", "12345");
    $auth->authenticate();
    $conn = new CF_Connection($auth);
    $container = $conn->get_container("Images");

    # List all the files within the Images container
    $files = $container->list_objects();

    # List only the first 5 files within the Images container
    $files = $container->list_objects(5);

    # List only 10 files within the Images container, but skip the first 10 files found
    $files = $container->list_objects(10,10);

    # List all the files found within the container that start with "IMG_"
    $files = $container->list_objects(0,NULL,"IMG_");
```

```
# List the first 10 files found within the Images container
# HongKong/Day1 pseudo directory
$files = $container->list_objects(10,NULL,NULL,"HongKong/Day1");

# Output the array
print_r($files);

$conn->close();
?>
```

Using Your Files

As is the case with containers, you must first create an instance for a file before you can start working with it. To do this, use the get_object function, which takes a single parameter: the file name you wish to modify or act upon. Keep in mind that you first need to create a container instance. The following is an example:

```
<?php
require('cloudfiles.php');

$auth = new CF_Authentication("loadbalancer", "12345");
$auth->authenticate();
$conn = new CF_Connection($auth);
$container = $conn->get_container("Images");

# Create an object instance for one of the files in the Images container:
$file = $container->get_object("IMG_1234.JPG");

$conn->close();
?>
```

Another such command you can use to "select" your files is get_objects. This function allows you to create an instance of a whole number of files, rather than one. The get_objects function takes four optional parameters: $limit, $marker, $prefix and $path. $limit can be used to restrict the total number of results returned, accepting an integer; $marker can be used to define an offset (number of items to skip); $prefix takes a string and is used to list only those filenames starting with what has been specified and the path to be used; and $path can be used to only return the items listed under the given pseudo-directory. Here's an example:

```
<?php
require('cloudfiles.php');

$auth = new CF_Authentication("loadbalancer", "12345");
$auth->authenticate();
$conn = new CF_Connection($auth);
$container = $conn->get_container("Images");

# Create an object instance for all files in the Images container:
$files = $container->get_objects();
```

```
# Create an object instance for only the first 10 files found in the Images container:
$files = $container->get_objects(10);

# Create an object instance for only the first 5 files found, skipping the first 10 items:
$files = $container->get_objects(5,10);

# Create an object instance of all files starting with "IMG_"
$files = $container->get_objects(0,NULL,"IMG_");

# Create an object instance of the first 8 files found after skipping 16,
# located in the Images container's HongKong/Day1 pseudo directory
$files = $container->get_objects(8,16,NULL,"HongKong/Day1");

  $conn->close();
?>
```

Once the instance has been created, you can start requesting information of your files and make modifications to them!

Getting the Public URI

One of the first functions you should know for working with your files is the public_uri function. As the name implies, it allows you to retrieve the public URI of the instance you are currently working with. When executed, the function will return either the public URI if successful or NULL if no public URI is available. Let's look at a short, but practical, code example.

```
<?php
  require('cloudfiles.php');

  $auth = new CF_Authentication("loadbalancer", "12345");
  $auth->authenticate();
  $conn = new CF_Connection($auth);
  $container = $conn->get_container("Images");
  $file = $container->get_object("IMG_1234.JPG");

  # Retrieve the URI from the file, and display the file in the browser
  $uri = $file->public_uri();
  print "<img src='$uri' />";

  $conn->close();
?>
```

Uploading and Removing Files

Now let's look at something more interesting: uploading files. A very simple and effective tool for uploading data to your Rackspace account is the HTML form. They are simple to create, easy to modify, and easy to integrate to pretty much any web-based application. That said, for the following piece of PHP code it is assumed you've set up an HTML form containing at least one input field, named name. Not exactly original, we admit, but at least it's self-explanatory! Now let's get some work done.

Assuming you've created your HTML form that includes type=file input field named name, you can start looking at your PHP script. To upload a file to your Rackspace account, you need to look at two functions not covered yet: create_object and load_from_filename. The create_object function is (not surprisingly) used to create a new object in your current container and works like a placeholder for the file to be uploaded. It takes a single parameter used to identify the file itself. This is where the form's name field will be inserted, as this represents the name of the file you've uploaded.

The second function is load_from_filename. This function is used to upload a file to an instance that is returned by create_object, previously executed. load_from_filename accepts two parameters: filename and verify. Naturally, the first parameter is most relevant to you, as it allows you to specify the location of the file that you wish to upload. This file is, in fact, placed in a temporary location on your web server, and it inserts its location in the $_FILES array. In the example code, this location is represented directly by the $tmp_name variable, which is thus the first parameter you will use. The second parameter, labeled verify, can be used to check if the uploaded file's MD5 checksum matches that of the original file on the web server. This parameter is Boolean and thus requires a True or False.

Now, let's have a look at the actual code itself.

```php
<?php
  require('cloudfiles.php');

  $auth = new CF_Authentication("loadbalancer", "12345");
  $auth->authenticate();
  $conn = new CF_Connection($auth);

  # Store information based on the uploaded data using the form
  $filename = $_FILES['fileupload']['name'];
  $localfile = $_FILES['fileupload']['tmp_name'];

  # Create an instance for the container where we wish to upload the file to
  $container = $conn->get_container("Images");

  # Create a new object with $filename as its name. Return an instance for it ($upload)
  $upload = $container->create_object($filename);

  # Upload the file to the container
  $upload->load_from_filename($localfile)
  $conn->close();
?>
```

Other than uploading files, there will also be times when you want to remove a file from your Rackspace collection. To do so, you can use the delete_object function provided by the CF_Container class. The function takes either a filename or an instance as its parameter, which will represent the file to be removed. Let's look at a simple example for both of them. First, let's look at how to remove a single file by specifying the file name directly.

```php
<?php
  require('cloudfiles.php');

  $auth = new CF_Authentication("loadbalancer", "12345");
  $auth->authenticate();
  $conn = new CF_Connection($auth);
  $container = $conn->get_container("Images");
```

```php
  # Delete an object from the Images container
  $container->delete_object("IMG_1234.JPG");

  $conn->close();
?>
```

Downloading Files

Another useful thing the API lets you do is download files from the cloud. Now, you may think: aren't we given URLs for that? Well, yes, this is generally true, but not if the container is set to be private, for example. When this is the case, you can choose to download the file and store it locally using save_to_filename, feed its contents to the browser using read, or stream it using stream. So, there are lots of options available. Let's have a closer look at each one to see when each is best used and what the code would look like.

Before you can download a file, however, you need to create an instance for the file you wish to download. As you might remember from earlier, this is done using the get_object or get_objects function. Here's a simple example that creates an instance named $file for one of the JPG files found in the Images container:

```php
<?php
  require('cloudfiles.php');

  $auth = new CF_Authentication("loadbalancer", "12345");
  $auth->authenticate();
  $conn = new CF_Connection($auth);
  $container = $conn->get_container("Images");

  # Create an object instance for one of the files in the Images container:
  $file = $container->get_object("IMG_1234.JPG");

  $conn->close();
?>
```

If you wish to save this object locally on your web server, you can use the save_to_filename function. save_to_filename is all but complicated: it takes a single parameter used to specify the location where the file is to be stored locally. Here's an example:

```php
<?php
  require('cloudfiles.php');

  $auth = new CF_Authentication("loadbalancer", "12345");
  $auth->authenticate();
  $conn = new CF_Connection($auth);
  $container = $conn->get_container("Images");

  # Create an object instance for one of the files in the Images container:
  $file = $container->get_object("IMG_1234.JPG");
```

```
# Save this file locally on the hard drive
$file->save_to_filename("/var/www/IMG_1234.JPG");

  $conn->close();
?>
```

If you directly wish to feed the contents of the file to your browser, however, you need to look either read or stream. It is suggested to use read for relatively small files, such as text files, image files, and so forth. read takes a single parameter that can be used to define specific custom HTTP headers to the file, such as Last-Modified, If-Match, and so on. Additionally, you want to use the header function provided by PHP to set the page's content type to whatever the file's content type really is, which you can find out using content_type. Let's look at an example.

```
<?php
  require('cloudfiles.php');

  $auth = new CF_Authentication("loadbalancer", "12345");
  $auth->authenticate();
  $conn = new CF_Connection($auth);
  $container = $conn->get_container("Images");

  # Create an object instance for one of the files in the Images container:
  $file = $container->get_object("IMG_1234.JPG");

  # Figure out the content-type using content_type, and use it to set the header of this page
  header("Content-Type: " . $file->content_type);

  # Read the file, and feed its contents to the browser. After that, print it:
  $data = $file->read();
  print $data;

  $conn->close();
?>
```

When you are dealing with larger files such as video files or a large number of images, you need to look at the stream function instead. stream relies on fopen (provided by PHP) to bind a file to a stream. As with the read function, stream also requires you to set the content type of the page using header to ensure the contents are properly displayed in your browser. Here's an example:

```
<?php
  require('cloudfiles.php');

  $auth = new CF_Authentication("loadbalancer", "12345");
  $auth->authenticate();
  $conn = new CF_Connection($auth);
  $container = $conn->get_container("Images");

  # Create an object instance for one of the files in the Images container:
  $file = $container->get_object("IMG_1234.JPG");
```

```php
# Figure out the content-type using content_type, and use it to set the header of this page
header("Content-Type: " . $file->content_type);

# Star streaming the output to the browser
$output = fopen("php://output", "w");
$file->stream($output);
fclose($output);

  $conn->close();
?>
```

Other Useful Functions

There are two more helpful functions that the API provides and they can really make your life easier. The first one is create_paths, which is timesaving when working with pseudo-directories.

As you've seen earlier on in the chapter, Rackspace Cloud Files doesn't allow the creation of subdirectories or subcontainers. Rather, it lets you use pseudo-directories by creating directory marker objects. This way, you can still simulate a hierarchical structure in your containers. Note, however, that you are required to manually create these directory marker objects for each (nested) pseudo-directory you want to have, consisting of a zero- or one-byte file of the content-type application/directory.

Luckily, the API lets you do this automatically using the create_paths function. You can do this by creating an object instance of a file containing the path separator symbol (a forward slash, `/`) in its name, and passing this instance on to create_paths. Here's a simple example that will clarify:

```php
<?php
  require('cloudfiles.php');

  $auth = new CF_Authentication("loadbalancer", "12345");
  $auth->authenticate();
  $conn = new CF_Connection($auth);
  $container = $conn->get_container("Images");

  # Create a variable for one of the files in the Images container:
  $file = "Holidays/2011/HongKong/Day1/Resized/Small/IMG_1234.JPG";

  # Use the create_paths function to create pseudo-directories
  $container->create_paths($file);

  $conn->close();
?>
```

This script will create a total of six directory marker objects:

```
Holidays
Holidays/2011
Holidays/2011/HongKong
Holidays/2011/HongKong/Day1
Holidays/2011/HongKong/Day1/Resized
Holidays/2011/HongKong/Day1/Resized/Small
```

If you now wish to upload a specific photo, video, text file, or any other type of file in to any of these directories, you simply need to rename the file so that it is prefixed with the pseudo-directory's name. For example, to place a video in the Day1 folder, you need to ensure the file name is renamed accordingly, like so:

`Holidays/2011/HongKong/Day1/video.mp4`

To wrap up this chapter, we would like to mention the get_info function. The get_info function provides you with some relevant information about your Rackspace Cloud Files account. It creates an array that reports the total number of containers available and the number of bytes used in your Rackspace account. This not only gives you a quick overview of your account, but it can also be used to calculate your monthly costs, for example. Here's a code snippet of how it looks. Note that it doesn't require any parameters to be specified.

```php
<?php
  include cloudfiles.php;

  $auth = new CF_Authentication("loadbalancer", "12345");
  $auth->authenticate();
  $conn = new CF_Connection($auth);

  # Create an array storing your account's information
  list($containers, $size) = $conn->get_info();

  # Output the results in a pretty way
  print "Containers: " . $containers . "\n";
  print "Total bytes: " . $size . "\n";

  $conn->close();
?>
```

Summary

This chapter introduced the concept of content delivery networks. Content delivery networks allows you to distribute your data across the planet while consistently providing top-notch download rates. Without them, your data would be tucked away on a single server, which although very capable locally, would quickly reach its limit when requests came from across the border. Content delivery networks get around this little problem by using a hideously expensive and complicated network that spans many countries to store all the data at each location. Today, you can use this very same service for a small fee without maintaining the servers and paying the fat bills for it.

We've also covered the basics on how Rackspace works and how their web interface can be used to create and modify containers, upload files, and retrieve the URL for the uploaded data.

To finish, we've covered the majority of functions the Rackspace Cloud PHP API provides. The API is available for several programming languages, and each allows you to perform an extensive amount of actions on your collections and files. Leveraging the API and the CDN's services, you can provide a solid, simple, and high-speed web application that is guaranteed to run smoothly.

CHAPTER 6

Planning for Performance and Reliability

This topic has always been a bit of a groaner. Everyone knows the importance of planning (who hasn't heard the adage "failing to plan is planning to fail"?) but no one really wants to do it. Let's face it, planning is simply not as fun as writing code. It's very easy to come up with reasons why the planning can wait.

The problem with this approach is that by the time you start thinking that planning might have actually been quite a good idea, you're already miles out to sea and heading off into even deeper water. So deep, in fact, that a sign proclaiming, "Here be monsters!" would not only not go amiss but might even be considered mandatory. Now you're thinking that starting off with a plan might have been a swell idea. But if you're not entirely sure where it all went wrong, it probably won't be all that obvious what you can do to fix it.

Fear not! Help is at hand! As the famous Chinese saying goes, "if you want to know what lies ahead, ask someone coming back." In short, the best way to avoid ending up waist-deep in a swamp is to speak to more experienced developers and ask them for help and guidance.

This chapter aims to provide a map that you can use to help steer yourself past the worst bits. Some of the things covered here will seem obvious, others hopefully less so. There's no magic sauce here; all of this stuff is fairly straightforward. (But everything is straightforward once you know about it!)

We'll start off with a very basic look at project management and how to plan your way through any project. It's a lightweight process with a focus on giving you some structure to follow. You are most welcome to take what works for you and ignore anything that doesn't. Feel free to enhance it in any way that suits your needs. What we provide here is really just a starting point; you should change whatever you need to change to make it as useful as possible to you.

The last section is admittedly a bit of a stretch for a chapter on planning in a book on performance. However, the number of sites we've seen taken down or severally damaged due to poor backups is really quite disturbing. So we'll cover some of the basics of making good backups, the different types, and how to go about it.

yoU MAke DInner In TiME

As promised, we're going to start off with good old planning and management. You might be strongly considering skipping this section. We strongly suggest that you at least skim through this section! Even if you only pick up one new idea that rings true, it will pay dividends from now on!

Because project management can be boring and because few people really want to read huge tomes on the subject (certainly not us, anyway), we're going to introduce a very powerful yet refreshingly simple system. As luck would have it, the system has an easy to remember mnemonic of

yoU MAke DInner In TiME

which breaks down to

1. Understanding

2. Making Decisions

3. Design and Implementation

4. Installation

5. Testing

6. Maintenance

7. Evaluation

We cover each of these points in the following sections. Although it looks pretty full on, it's really easy to use; quite honestly we've never found anything better! Although these ideas are mostly applied to development projects, they can also be easily applied to developing your system for performance. In fact, you can apply these techniques to pretty much any project successfully. The idea is that with this roadmap you'll stray from the path less than if you just winged it (which is what most of us tend to do). So even a passing familiarity with this stuff will likely be quite helpful in the long run.

yoU

Geeks (or computer professionals, if we want to be politically correct—but we don't) are often a little trigger-happy when it comes to problem solving. There is nothing like a good problem to stretch those mental muscles, especially as we spend most of the day explaining where the Start menu is and why when you left-click you really do need to click the left mouse button and not the one on the right. Perhaps this is why we tend to jump into a problem with both feet—to recover from the mental starvation we have been suffering. Whatever the reason, this approach has a nasty habit of either backfiring immediately or helping us to paint ourselves into a corner.

Now, before anyone else says it, we know that sometimes those really simple problems really are that simple. Sometimes when we say "It will just take a minute," it actually does. More often that not, though, what was described as a really easy problem turns out to be a rat's nest of tangled requirements, dependencies, and confusion. And let's not forget deadlines, which are usually as realistic as founding a unicorn ranch staffed by fairies. The problem is that most of the time we find out about the hidden hell under the carpet once there's no possibility of turning back.

Fortunately, there is a solution. Before jumping into the pool of project happiness, have a look around first. Speak to people and try to understand more about the situation. If you find out during your conversation about the piranha-infested swimming pool, you will be very grateful you didn't decide to test the waters using yourself as bait.

Joking aside, it's important to get a thorough understanding of the problem before you get started. This invariably starts with discovering whether the problem you've been given is actually the problem you want to solve.

For example, we were working on a project where the user wanted us to put together a solution using OCR (optical character recognition; see the note for more info) to scan in the student number on the 5,000 forms she received on a regular basis. She currently had to type those in by hand. This is the bit where we had to resist the urge to Google for the latest OCR libraries. Instead, we asked her questions to try to get to the root of the problem. Why did she want to scan the student numbers? Well, she wanted to save time inputting all the forms. What were the forms? Why was she inputting data? The forms were student confirmation forms that the college sent out to every student at the beginning of term. The data she was inputting was whether or not the form had been returned.

Note Optical character recognition is something the computing industry has teased us with for many years. It goes right along with voice recognition software in that it offers a lot but often falls short of your hopes and expectations. OCR software has greatly improved (as has voice recognition software, to be fair) but it is far from perfect. In effect, the computer has to look at a picture and work out whether it contains letters or words. This is exceptionally easy for a human but very challenging for a machine. When you consider all the different forms the letter "e" might take, and how each person's handwriting is unique (and there are thousands of computer fonts), it's easy to understand why there could be some mistakes. Plus recognizing a character at any angle is easy for a human but requires vastly more effort from a computer, so the potential for mistakes is quite large. When you need to reliably enter information (in this case a student ID number), OCR is not an ideal solution; in fact, it's something you'd want to avoid.

This gave us some useful information right away. First of all, the forms were generated in house. Second, all she was doing was typing in a student number and pressing Enter. So we spoke to the people who created the form. They had a little application that queried the student database to produce a PDF form ready for printing. We asked if they'd be adverse to us adding anything to the form, and they were quite happy to oblige as long as we didn't alter the data on it.

The solution: a bar code on each of the printed forms. Then our user scanned the barcode to confirm that the student had returned the form.

Had we simply taken the user's problem *as stated* and run with it, we'd have built a complex OCR system and still the user would have had to at least double-check what had been scanned. Even if the application worked perfectly (ever seen OCR work perfectly all the time?), it would still be far inferior to the bar code scanning solution. By taking the time to look deeper, we were able to uncover other options and, in this case, a better solution. You won't always uncover a better solution but at least you can be more confident that the solution you are proposing is the best one.

The same issues arise when you have great ideas of your own. It is very easy to have a fantastic idea and sit down to build it without truly understanding what it is you're building or why. What makes this idea so awesome? What problem are you trying to solve with this idea? Is there a better solution already available? Don't waste time trying to reinvent the wheel.

This doesn't mean you can't be creative. In fact, just being technical is not enough; you need that spark and curiosity to be a great developer. But you also need to be smart. You need to stack the odds in your favor so that the chances of making your latest project a success are as high as possible. Sure, you can beat the odds just by being awesome, but why not take all the help you can get?

So, where do you start? You start by asking questions. You ask as many people as many questions as you can come up with. Dig deeper into the problem. People have a tendency to see the solution in terms of the problem rather than thinking about the best solution overall. In our earlier example, by digging deeper and finding the underlying issue (how to quickly record a student's return), we were able to come up with a much better solution.

In other words, once you know the problem, take a step back and decide whether this is the underlying problem or whether it's just a surface issue. If you're not convinced it's the underlying issue, keep on digging until you're sure!

Tip Emanuel Lasker, world chess champion for an unmatched 27 years, once said "When you see a good move, look for a better one." If you've come up with a fantastic solution, keep looking for an even better one. The more great solutions you come up with, the more likely you are to find the very best solution of all.

Once you're done asking all your questions, you need to do some research. This doesn't have to be heavy-handed or involve hours staring at a screen. The idea is to take a look around and see how others have solved the problem you're now facing. If it's landed on your desk, chances are it has landed on someone else's desk at some point in time. If you're really lucky, they will have written up a nice blog post telling you what to avoid and how to fix the problem. Even finding a post to an e-mail list with the exact problem but little in the way of answer tells you something about what you're trying to do (most likely that it's not going to be an easy ride). The Internet is a wealth of information; in a very short time you should be able to dig up some useful information on solutions, libraries, or tools that might help you.

By this stage, you should be confident you've identified the real problem and you should have some ideas on how it has been solved (or not) elsewhere and what tools might help you build a solution. Armed with this information, you're ready to go on to the next stage!

Wait! Before you go running off to work on your design, take a minute to think about how you see this project ending.

- Have you covered everything you need to cover?

- Can you see in your mind's eye how you want this to play out?

- Based on what you've found so far, is your master plan a good fit?

- How hard will it be to backup and maintain this solution in the long term?

- Are you painting yourself into a corner without even realizing it?

Before you move on, take a moment to think about what you've decided and check that everything is still on track.

MAke

This stage is where you need to make some decisions. You know what needs to be done and you have a few ways that you might go about doing it.

Although this section is about making decisions, you first need to think about the constraints your project is facing. The most common constraints are time and cost but can also include things such as available hardware, operating systems, or a particular programming language. In the example from the last section, one of the criteria was that we use the .NET platform, which was the college's standard. This meant that the library we wanted to use (which was only available for Python at the time) was not an option. There were also cost restrictions, which affected our ability to buy a commercial library. From these restrictions alone it became clear that we'd need to find a .NET-based open source library or, failing that, we'd have to write our own.

No matter what solution you come up with, it has to have an overall positive effect. If it costs a lot of money to run, that might be acceptable if it quadruples the number of users. If it takes six months to build, that might be okay if over a period of years it will generate vast amounts of income. These criteria are like shifting sands; they are different for every project and can actually change during the project's lifetime.

This is why it's important to understand the goals and constraints of a particular project so you can decide the best course of action. As the reigning professional, it is up to you to look at the pros and cons and then start making decisions. This can either be very easy or it can pose a serious challenge with trade-offs. You must also consider the possibility that there might be no feasible solution for a given problem and set of constraints. Many of the failed projects we've seen didn't fail because of poor design or programming; they failed because they tried to do the impossible.

We don't want to talk too much about decision making because you've probably already done most of this (at least in your head) during the understanding stage and thus this task is really just a formality. Still, it does help to get things down on paper and to make sure that you've covered all your bases. Once you've got this section down pat, it's time to move on to design.

Or not! It's that time again! Take a break and think about the issues we raised at the end of the last section. Once again, think through your decisions and think about how you see this project ending.

- Are you still on course?

- Has anything changed that you need to be worried about?

When you're happy all is well, you can move on to design.

DInner

At last, it's time to start designing and building the solution! This part is pretty much down to individual taste, and the methods involved are as unique as the problem itself. However, it can still be broken down into at least three separate parts.

First, you need to have some sort of design in mind. Although writing code is a form of design in its own right, if you start coding right off the bat, you might very well code yourself into a corner.

Once you have a solid design, it's time to finally build it. There are various ways to approach this, and everyone has their personal favorite. We're assuming your technique isn't horrific, so we won't focus too much on the prototyping stage.

Next, it's time to configure the application and make it production-ready. When we say production-ready, we're not suggesting that you should have something immediately deployable (after all, you haven't fully tested it yet). However, when you finish this part of the process, your application should be in the same form that you see it being deployed in.

So how do you go about designing the solution? A lot of books at this stage would tell you the best way to go about the design process. We're not going to go that deep into it because the best technique depends on your own experience and skill set. From your research, you should have a strategical view of what you want to build. Now you need to start filling in some of the blanks and fleshing out the design itself. Because you already have a good idea of what it will look like, and the tools and constraints that you have to work with, the design process can be pretty straightforward. In most cases, it's just a matter of connecting the dots you created during the research stages.

But what if your overview doesn't work quite the way you planned now that you've take into account some of the finer details? If you need to change your strategy, it's not a problem. At this stage you haven't started building anything yet so you're free to make whatever changes you see fit. This gives you a great deal of freedom to experiment and try a wide range of possibilities with little cost, risk, or waste of time. Once you write your first line of code, you are already creating a mental line in the sand that makes it much harder to go back and try new ideas. Even if you do decide quite quickly that you're heading in the wrong direction, there is always that urge to keep on going. As soon as you realize you're travelling on the wrong path, turn around and head back!

When you do push an issue back to the research stage, you should also fix it there. Whatever your new overview looks like, it should be supported by evidence from the research phase rather than a gut reaction. Keep your foundation solid so that you can always confidently justify your decisions.

Once you have a workable design, it's time to build it. At last, you get to have some fun! As promised, we won't talk about actually writing code in this section but if you find you're building something that is pushing the limits of your design, you should stop and review the design. If you find that your design needs changing or doesn't quite fit your overall strategy, it's time for a quick trip back the research phase. Each trip doesn't require a complete overhaul; you just need to confirm or refute any new issues.

So now you have your solution, one that solves the problem within the original constraints, is based on solid research, and is well planned and designed. Now you just need to configure it and set it up in the way you see it actually being used in production. Again, that doesn't mean you take the solution live, but you want it to the point where it looks the same as if you were going to deploy it.

Wait! It's time for yet another pause and a good think on what you just did.

- Are you still on track?

- Is all progressing as planned?

- Have you made sure that your design takes into account your end goals and hasn't been distracted by any cool technologies or great ideas for new features?

Stay focused on the goal. You can always tweak later, but solve the problem you set out to solve first.

In

Implementation can be either exciting or terrifying, depending on how the other stages went. Either way, it's time to get your application hooked up and ready to save the world. Of course, it's not as easy as just switching your application on. You need to make sure that people know how to use your application and that they actually want to use it. Your project will be significantly more successful if the users are waving the flag for you. You also need to make sure that the migration and cutover from the old system happens as smoothly as possible.

Installation should be fairly straightforward because the production environment should be all but identical to the system you set up in the last section. Even when you're building things for your own interest, you still need to make sure that when you install your solution, you do it right. This sounds obvious, but we've seen it happen more than once where someone has deployed their latest and greatest creation but forgotten about a key dependency or didn't remember to change the database settings.

Then the whole thing implodes when they go to fire it up—and we all know that first impressions are the most important!

So take your time with this stage. Make sure you know your solution needs. Double-check all of the dependencies and configuration details. If your application needs to send e-mail, finding out from the administrator that direct e-mail is blocked and that you must go through a relay is information you want well in advance when you can easily do something about it. It is also helpful to have some form of test script that exercises all of the key points in your application. This might not be possible depending on the solution, but if you can use such a script, you should do so! Every little bit helps!

But even when your application is installed, you are far from finished. You should have a plan for switching out the old system with your new and improved solution.

- Do you need to import any data?

- Can you simply work with the existing database or do you need to set up something new?

- Will people start using your application immediately or will you gradually phase it in over a period of time?

These issues aren't unique to development; any solutions where you are making changes to critical systems (such as installing caches or load balancers) should be rolled out on a small part of the system rather than doing an en masse migration. Sometimes the softly, softly approach is your best bet. Sometimes, though, you really have to do it in one big jump, in which case you need to have a plan to follow if it goes wrong.

These sorts of plans don't have to be intricate. You don't have to answer every single question that might come up. However, you should know what to do when a particular issue arrives. In the world of financial trading, the markets are in a constant state of flux. When you take a position, you need to already know the conditions for getting out of that position. Then, when something goes wrong, you can react immediately before it gets any worse. If you haven't considered the issue, then you freeze while you think about what to do next. Freezing can cost a trader an awful lot of money, just as not having a plan to deal with any issues in your system might damage your reputation. So, like the professional trader, have a good idea of what could blow up in your face and a rough idea of what to do about it.

The next thing to look at is training staff and getting their buy-in. Many people greatly overlook the importance of getting a buy-in from the people who are actually going to be using a project. It's important to realize that an inconsequential change from a developer's point of view can ruin a particular user's workflow. Taking away their most relied-upon feature is not going to make them your friend. However, you can head this off before it even happens by talking to the users and showing them what you're doing and why. Most importantly, when you get feedback, make sure you act on it. Even if you don't agree with it, you can demonstrate why that idea won't work or would cause problems. Show that you didn't simply just dismiss it out of hand. You might also get some excellent ideas that you never considered because you're not working at the sharp end. If users are already lining up to use your solution before you've even released it, then even if there are teething problems you'll find that your users are willing to give you an awful lot of goodwill and support.

This leads nicely into user training. The ideal piece of software requires little in the way of user training. Wherever possible, find someone to test your app—someone who has no idea what it is supposed to do or how to go about doing it. Ideally, even they should find the software easy to use, though whether or not they can actually make use of it is an entirely different matter. This sort of test can unearth glaring issues that the intended user of the software might simply work around or not consider worth mentioning.

Many solutions (such as deploying a web cluster) don't involve training users. However, there will be administrators that need to know what you've done. Even if it's just you running your own cluster, it doesn't hurt to spend some time writing up documentation. It's all clear as day to you now. But at 4 am six months from now when something catches fire, it won't be nearly so fresh in your mind. You might need to really dig around to solve a problem that could have been solved with a single command, had you just remembered which one to use.

So training isn't just for the users; it's for anyone who might come into contact with your solution—and that includes you. (We won't go on about the different ways of providing training as there are thousands of books on that already.)

Wait! It's time for another sanity check. If you sanity check yourself each step of the way, you're never going to get truly caught out; any issues that turn up are still relatively easy to fix. So take a look at the original plan, the original problem, and your solution.

- Is it still focused?

- Have you solved all the problems you intended to solve when you started out?

- Have you drifted from the one true course?

If you've drifted a bit, no problem. Just bring it back on course. If you're still on the right heading, it's time to jump to the next section.

TiME

TiME breaks down into testing, maintenance, and evaluation. The type of testing mentioned here isn't the same as the testing you did during the design and implementation phase. This testing is done throughout the life of the solution simply by using it. When looking at how it is used over a period of time, the stresses and problem points begin to make themselves evident. For example, maybe the solution isn't fast enough or perhaps one of the components needs some tweaking. The issues that you pick up probably won't make or break the solution, but they do highlight that it is not running optimally.

Once you've found a particular issue and you've determined that it needs to be fixed, you can do this as part of the maintenance cycle. The maintenance cycle is really used for two things: for fixing the issues that you've highlighted and for clearing out any cruft that has built up during daily use. For example, you might clean out any temporary files or tidy up the database—anything that works towards making the application run smoother.

Evaluation involves taking a step back and determining whether your initial solution solves the problem. Ideally you'd want to have solved it on the first try and then each maintenance cycle can improve or enhance the system in some way. Often that's not possible and it requires a few tries to actually hit the mark.

The TiME cycle continues for as long as the solution is in use. For simple or mature systems, this cycle can be almost glacial; changes might happen perhaps every six months to a year. For newer systems, it might happen on an almost daily basis. When deploying a system into production, that's rarely the last time you'll ever touch it. Something almost always crops up that requires anything from a minor tweak to an almost complete rebuild (see the box on the Y2K bug if you're not convinced). So while you shouldn't sit around worrying about it, you should be comfortable with the idea that anything you build and deploy is quite likely going to need to change at some point.

Again, stop and think about what happened in this step and your ultimate goal. If your solution is designed to be easy to support and easy to maintain, and you've focused on this goal throughout the process (as you will have done if it was in your original plan and you've been sticking to it), then by the time you get to this stage, you will have a solution that's easy to maintain and support. You reap what you sow, but a lot of effort goes into making sure you're actually sowing the seeds you intended to sow (in the right place, at the right time, and hopefully in a field that you own). Ultimately, you will end up with a much better solution that's much easier to work with if you take a break every now and again to check the compass to make sure you're still heading in the right direction.

THE Y2K BUG

The Y2K bug (named after the year 2000) was probably one of the most hyped issues leading up to the new millennium. There were fears that nuclear missile silos would get confused and fire their rockets and that planes would fall out of the sky. Or that people receiving pensions would suddenly have a negative age and so stop receiving any payments.

All of this hysteria was caused by a very simple problem—a problem that at the time it was created was not a problem at all. In fact, it was a great way to cut costs, speed up processing, and make more efficient use of very expensive computers. It all came down to storing the year as a two-digit number instead of a four-digit number. For example, rather than storing 1983, the system would only store 83. Being able to halve the amount of storage required at a time when 10MB of memory was only found on million dollar computers was a good idea! It didn't occur to anyone that this might pose a problem in the year 2000. After all, that was some 30 years away. Surely no one would still be using these systems by then!

Guess what? We were and many companies didn't really catch on to the problem until relatively late in the game. If you happened to know COBOL in 1997, you could (and many did) set yourself up for life updating the systems in a panicky haze.

For example, many systems would calculate the age of a person by taking the current year and then deducting the year of birth. To use the previous example, 2012 - 1983 = 29. However, if you just use the last two digits, all of a sudden that person becomes -71 years old. How much do you charge a -71 year old for a year of car insurance?

The solution was relatively easy, even though it was fiendishly tedious: simply lengthen all the data fields to support four-digit years and then go through all of the software and make sure that anything that touches dates has been updated to use the new system.

So was there really cause for panic? As it turns out, 2000 came and went without much in the way of problems. However, the issue was known decades before and many years passed when this fix could have been made part of general maintenance, a fix that would have saved an awful lot of worry not only for companies but for their customers as well.

The Importance of Planning

And so ends our quick detour into project management. We tried to keep it as light as possible and avoid any of the current buzzwords. The most important thing we'd like you to take away is that having a plan or a structure to follow can really make a huge difference in any project.

For those still wondering why we've just taken half a chapter to talk about project management in a book on performance, it's because many of the performance issues we see in the wild were caused by people not truly understanding the problem or not really thinking their designs through. This led them to create suboptimal solutions that couldn't scale. By the time we were brought in, these systems were in production and were too expensive and critical to the business to replace, so we had to do the equivalent of a quadruple bypass to get the thing working at an acceptable level.

Had the developers for those projects sat down and truly understood what it was they were building and why, they would have been able to come up with a much better design, one that probably wouldn't have caused the performance bottleneck in the first place. As the old saying goes, an ounce of prevention is worth a pound of cure.

You can make the argument that many applications are properly designed and it's simply that they have far more users than the current infrastructure can support. But any well designed piece of software should be relatively easy to scale. Applying this project management technique to your new load balancing and caching cluster design will ensure that you deliver the best possible solution for the application, regardless of how well it was designed.

So this part of the chapter has been all about helping you to think of the big picture while keeping track of the details that tend to trip people up. Even the professionals often forget to do this; it's much more common even among IT professionals than we care to admit. At the very least, the ideas laid out here should help to give some structure to your ideas, even if you only take one or two of them to heart.

Although we've covered a good project management framework, we haven't really looked at the issues with developing software itself. There are many interesting problems that really only apply to software engineering that other forms of engineering seem to have been able to avoid. For example, unlike building a skyscraper or a bridge, software is almost fluid in nature and has a tendency to sprawl in all sorts of unanticipated directions. When building a bridge, the distance between the two end points never changes. The distance between the ground and the deck of the bridge never changes. In software, core concepts can change all the time and frequently do. Imagine trying to build a bridge where the end points keep moving and the height is never the same two days in a row; it's not hard to see why writing software can be so stressful.

■ **Note**   It has been pointed out to us that the distance between two points can indeed change and that it is quite possible for the distance between the ground and the deck of the bridge to change as well. In fact, there are specific engineering solutions available to resolve both these issues. However, we feel our point still stands: at least when you build a bridge, you don't suddenly find out you need to build an airport, which three weeks later becomes a skyscraper before finally (usually a day before the deadline) reverting to its previous bridge-like configuration.

When writing software, we make many design decisions. We decide where to put code and whether or not to use stored procedures in a database. Each of these decisions has an effect on the future. If we decide to use stored procedures now, what happens when our growth determines we need a new database, one that does not support our stored procedures? What happens when we need to add an API to our application and realize that the core business logic is spread throughout the whole system so adding an API will require almost a total rewrite? These things aren't theoretical; they've happened to us, and we've seen many companies get caught in the same trap.

Hindsight is a wonderful thing. There are many things that we would have done differently had we known at the time how they were going to turn out. Until the geniuses in Cupertino release the iCrystalBall (we would also settle for CrystalBall+ from Mountainview or CrystalBallXP from Redmond) the future will remain mysterious and off limits. Because we can't tell what will happen, many people unfortunately use this as an excuse not to worry about it. If something goes wrong, they reason, they will fix it then. The problem is that by the time it goes wrong, it is likely to be extremely difficult and expensive to fix (assuming it can be fixed at all).

So this section will give you a mini super power: you will know what problems might crop up! Now that you know about them, you can take them into account so that if they do occur, it's a minor inconvenience rather than a full-on panic attack.

Backups

Unfortunately, making proper backups is one of those things that no one takes seriously until they lose six months worth of work. At which point, they curse themselves for not having proper backups and vow to do something about it—at some point.

If you're one of the relatively few people who have awesome backups, feel free to skip the rest of this section. If you have tactical and strategic backups, you are already covered. If you're wondering what a tactical back is, read on!

■ **Note** Awesome backups are defined as backups that you are absolutely certain can be restored and are located in multiple places that you are absolutely certain you can get to in a form that you are absolutely certain will not be affected when you lose your production system. If this sounds like overkill, remember, they're called awesome for a reason!

Why Backups Are so Important

Backups are important because some things are not replaceable. For example, if you have a web site with many large high quality images, chances are you will have many thumbnail images to allow for easy browsing. These thumbnails should be backed up as a matter of course, but if you were to lose them, it's not a massive problem because you can recreate them from the original images. However, source code and other items are irreplaceable. If you lose the source code for an important class, there is no way to magically get it back. You have to reconstruct it from scratch, which is especially difficult because a single class is enhanced and improved over a period of time to add features and abilities that might not be obvious on the first attempt.

Imagine if you ran a very popular web site akin to Facebook and you lost all your source code. You want to make a simple change? Sorry, you can't do that until you've replaced everything that has been lost. All those hours of research, testing, and planning? They need to be redone. If keeping the source code safe was your responsibility, you're probably going to lose your job. You could be in a world of legal pain as well; losing a company asset potentially valued at millions of dollars is not a good thing.

You should make good backups for no other reason than you don't want to retype and do all that hard work for a second time. Backups can save you typing and testing—and nobody wants to do any more of that than they have to!

There May Be Trouble Ahead

Computers have the very nasty habit of blowing up at the least opportune time—usually without bothering to tell anyone and leaving enough intact that a cursory glance won't notice anything amiss. This usually happens just before a presentation or when you're about to launch that awesome new feature you've been planning for months.

That much is a given, but even knowing this in advance (and every computer user has their fair share of horror stories filed under When Technology Goes Bad) few people take this seriously. Even people who have had their servers catch fire get caught out again by the same problem because for some reason they believed that lightning never strikes twice!

But it does, and it has a tendency to know which people will be affected the most. It doesn't matter if you have the best hardware or your computer is brand new or you're going to make a copy tomorrow night when you get home. You need to accept the idea that your system can fail at any time for any number of reasons. Once you accept this, you will begin to appreciate the enormity of the problem. Hopefully you'll decide right here and now to sort things out so that you know you'll be covered.

Backups are an insurance policy. Like an insurance policy, no one likes to fork out the premium, but everyone is very glad they did when it comes to making a claim. And everyone who didn't pay the premium wishes they had!

IT REALLY CAN HAPPEN

We were working on a project to build a custom thin client server solution to be deployed across an entire city. It had a secure connection to a central server for filtering, user authentication, and sharing files, and each server had a fairly complex desktop set up with the latest and greatest software. Add to this a huge array of fine-tuning and weeks worth of experimentation and you have the prototype server ready for deployment.

After testing the new server thoroughly we were finally convinced that it was ready for prime time. We decided to have a cup of coffee before taking an image of the disk. It was 7 pm and we had to pick up another colleague from the airport 250 miles away at 6 am the following morning to help with the deployment. So far, so good; we could image the disk, get five hours of sleep, and all would be well.

It was while we were adding the sugar to our coffees that we heard a nasty crash. On returning to our office, the server was on the floor. This was somewhat odd as it had been firmly seated on the desk. As we went to pick it up, we could hear a somewhat pitiful "whirr-clunk" sound. For those not in the know, this indicated a shattered and totally useless hard disk. The fully tested and completed build was gone.

We didn't get any sleep that night and amazingly we did have a working prototype to install the next day—but it was six hours of solid panic. Had we taken the image before we went to make coffee, perhaps we would have had a good night's sleep.

We still don't know how the server ended up on the floor, but it certainly demonstrates that bad things can happen without any warning. Had we made a backup, it would have been a minor annoyance. But we didn't, so we nearly had a collective heart attack instead. Learn from our mistake! Make regular and complete backups!

Automation is a Must

If your backup system requires that you must actually do something, then we promise you that your system will fail you at the worst possible time. The reason is that humans are inherently lazy. We tend to put things off. Why stop to make a backup now when there's just a few more lines of code to go? I'll just watch the rest of this episode and then I'll definitely make the backup! Then your machine crashes and you realize that the last workable backup you have is actually from three weeks ago, long before you made the critical changes you were polishing up today.

For a backup to be safe, it needs to be automatic. This can be run from a cron job on Linux or an application that runs all the time on your Mac. Whatever the solution, you really want it to take care of the whole process for you. That way, regardless of what you're doing or thinking, your work will be saved.

Tactical Backups

A *tactical backup* is a backup that runs constantly while you're working on things. It allows you to jump back in time and recover recent work that you've either lost or edited to the point where it is hopelessly broken. On our Mac we use Arq2 (many people use Apple's own Time Machine). It takes a snapshot every 20 minutes and then encrypts and sends the backup to Amazon S3 for safe storage. This means a checkpoint is set every 20 minutes that we can jump back to if necessary.

This is ideal for things like editing text (in fact we're using it right now in case the laptop dies, as we really don't fancy writing this chapter again from scratch!) but when you're working on source code you might (read almost definitely) need finer control. Source control systems such as Git, Mercurial, or Subversion track and store the history of every file in your project. However, they only commit changes when you actually make a commit, and especially with distributed systems such as Git and Mercurial, the data is only transferred to a remote server when you specifically do a push.

This means that even if you're religiously using source code management (and you should be), it is not the same as a timed backup. They do different things. Source control is there to track changes in your application and to allow you to easily move between current and previous revisions. It is not designed to protect you from disk failure. Backups, on the other hand, are not interested in tracking the minutia of each file and instead simply find the changes and copy them off the machine for safekeeping. While you can argue there is some overlap here between the two, the goals are quite clearly different.

So a tactical backup is a solution that allows you to get your hands quickly on data that you might lose or might have replaced, thinking you didn't need it any more. Whatever solution you use, it should allow you to quickly recover data and should be easy to use. You should feel at ease pulling data back from the past and it should be second nature to you.

Strategic Backups

Strategic backups are a bit different from tactical backups in that they do not necessarily have to be instantly accessible. They are usually created based on specific times or events.

For example, every time you deploy a new version of your site, you might make a complete backup. This would be a strategical backup because you're not planning to actually use it any time soon; it's just there in case you need it. Source code management systems allow you to do something similar using tags so that you can easily mark a particular revision as a specific version. However, these solutions are not a replacement for backups. After all, you should be making a full backup of your code repository after a big release just in case something goes wrong.

Alternatively, you might create *time-based strategic backups*. This is when backups are made based on the amount of time that has passed. For example, you might schedule a full backup of your code repository once per month. Maybe you then encrypt and upload it to Amazon or burn it to a CD or DVD.

Generally, you want to do a combination of the two (i.e. make backups at each key event and on a regular basis). Again, the backups should be automated wherever possible so that you don't need to think about them.

Incremental vs. Full

To quickly recap, a full backup is a complete and self-contained resource that can be used to reconstruct all the data. It is the only file you need to get all your data back. However, each time you take a full backup, you are going to duplicate data, which means you'll eat up huge amounts of disk space.

The solution to this is to make *incremental backups*. This is when, having taken a full backup, you only store the changes from your current system. Because you're not storing duplicate data, you save a huge amount of space. The downside is that you need all the files leading up to your current backup in order to do a restore. If you lose any of the files, you won't be able to restore the backup.

So which is better? As always, it's a trade-off between space and safety. Personally, we avoid incremental backups for critical things because we don't want to be hunting around to locate the various parts of the backup that we need. That said, Arq uses incremental backups, and as it stores them all in the same place on Amazon S3, the risk of losing a critical file or it being damaged is very small. So far, this has worked really well for us.

Ultimately, you need to weigh the pros and cons and make a decision that best fits your needs and requirements.

Please, Please Perform Test Restores!

If you are going through all the hassle of making regular backups and making sure all the important files are covered, you should be given a pat on the back because you're already ahead of the game. However, it never fails to amaze us that so many people who put in all that effort making good backups never actually test that the backups are working. Usually they find out that all is not well in the land of backups when they actually try to restore a critical file and find out that they can't.

This happens a lot, even in big companies. A huge amount of effort is spent on making sure backups are running, but relatively little (if any) time is ever spent verifying that those backups are recoverable. For example, one of the backup tools we were using quite recently was backing up data quite happily, only we didn't know (and apparently nor did the application in question) was that the index itself was corrupt. Data was being stored nicely on the remote server; it just wasn't possible to actually recover any of it. Fortunately, we found out by a routine test. Every week we attempt to do a full restore to another machine, and that restore failed. This freaked us out, but the problem was easy enough to resolve: we just dropped the backup and created a new one.

There's no telling how long this problem might have gone undetected if we hadn't attempted the test restore. We could have potentially lost months or even years worth of data.

So please, if you're making backups, test them on a regular basis. Depending on the system you're using, you can also automate a test restore. However, there's no substitute for hands-on experience. Proving to yourself that your backups are solid is a great way to help you sleep at night!

Summary

This chapter has admittedly taken us off the beaten path as far as performance goes, but we hope you agree that it was worth it. We started off by looking at a nice lightweight framework for project management and how you can apply it to practically any project you work on. We highlighted that many of the performance-related issues we see in the real world could have been prevented with a little forethought and that applications tend to be much easier to scale if they have been well designed in the first place.

Then we took another slight detour to touch on backups and what sort of things you should be looking for from your backup solution. This section covered the differences between tactical and strategic backups, the pros and cons of incremental and full backups, and the importance of testing the restore process.

We hope this chapter has sparked a few ideas or at least given you pause to think about the way you manage your own projects and its related assets. This chapter is certainly not meant to be an all-or-nothing affair; help yourself to the bits that meet your needs and feel free to ignore the ones that don't. If you're completely happy with your existing methodologies and strategies, that's great, too; at least you can be more confident that nothing has slipped through the cracks!

The next chapter introduces the core concepts of load balancing, building the foundation you need for the rest of the book. It discusses the various things that can be load balanced and the importance of really knowing your system so that you can get the most out of it.

CHAPTER 7

Load Balancing Basics

Load balancing means the ability to spread the load of processing for an application over a number of separate systems for an overall performance increase in processing incoming requests. This seems very simple; just splitting up the load helps it all gets done quicker. But although the concept is simple enough, there are a number of factors that can add heavy levels of complexity. Anyone who has ever managed a large group of people can attest to this.

This chapter explains the complexities in a load balanced environment. The information here should give you an introduction to the core concept of what load balancing is about. Armed with this knowledge, you should be able to progress into the later chapters that cover some very in-depth examples on how to perform several different types of load balancing. This chapter covers the following:

- What is load balancing?
- What resources are in play?
- How is it accomplished?
- The guiding principles of load balancing
- Understanding your system
- Planning for load balancing
- Monitoring load balancing

What Is Load Balancing?

Load balancing represents the ability to transfer any portion of the processing for a system request to another independent system that will handle it concurrently. It splits the load that comes into one server among a number of other devices. This has the advantage of reducing the amount of processing done by the primary receiving server—allowing it to handle more requests and increasing performance—as there is less competition for resources and there are more devices processing the whole of the load.

Often your systems will already be partially load balanced, as having a separate database server from your web server is indeed load balancing. This is a great example of traditional load balancing: adding additional servers to share the processing load of complex requests. It is right here that you can see the previous examples shine through.

Once your initial single web/database server reaches the point when each additional request placed upon it slows down the processing of other requests, you need to expand. This gives a significant performance increase to both the database and the web server, since they are no longer competing for CPU time to process their respective requests. While splitting up different applications that are used to process a request among separate servers is normally the first step, there are a number of additional ways to increase your ability to split up and process loads—and all for greater efficiency and performance.

What Computing Resources Are Available?

As mentioned, much of load balancing is about the distribution and allocation of resources to complete a task. In order to better understand how to allocate resources, you should understand these resources. As it stands, there are four major resources that make up a server. They are

- Processor (CPU)
- Memory (RAM)
- Network
- Storage (Disk)

Each of these resources is important in its own right and can adversely affect your system performance, so it is therefore important for you to understand them all!

Processor (CPU)

Everything that is done by a computer is processed in some form or another. From driving your display to dealing with every move of your mouse and every tap of your keyboard, the CPU of your system needs to process these inputs and use this processing to determine what needs to happen in response to these actions.

On top of creating actions and responses, your processor also powers your operating system. At all times your operating system is processing in the background—even an action as simple as keeping time. This means that the processor is one of the key performance measures on any system as it represents the ability to take a basic input and turn it into the correct output. Without enough processing power you can't keep up with the demand on your system. The example of separating a web site and database to different servers helps illustrate this. With the database on a new server, the web server now has all of the processing capabilities that were being used by the database, which includes the following:

1. Keeping the database server alive and watching for requests.
2. Taking requests for data from the database.
3. Calling up the database and looking through it for each specific piece of information to match your query (this is a big one!).
4. Making changes to the existing database tables (if applicable) for the query that it has received.
5. Altering the data collected for the query into one cohesive response in the format you requested, even if it is the default format.

6. Packaging and transferring the collated response to the portion of the system that requested it.

7. Tracking that this request has been made, by whom, how it went, and what happened.

From these tasks, you can see that a simple database can use a large amount of processing; the larger and more complex a database, the more processing power it takes to maintain and use. While databases are heavily optimized to allow this to be done very efficiently, this is still a heavy consumption of resources. So giving your database its own server is very advantageous because it removes the competition between your web server and database, allowing them to process on their own with no interference. Splitting up different applications or different portions of applications to increase the processing power available to each is, in our view, the very core concept of load balancing.

Memory (RAM)

Memory is information that is stored by your OS in high-speed, short-term storage. This is where most of the common components of your operating system live; they live here because they can be accessed by the processor significantly quicker. RAM overutilization is not as big a problem as CPU overconsumption but it can still cause significant performance impact. One of the functions of most modern operating systems is called virtual memory, which is the ability for the operating system to begin writing portions of the data held in memory to long term disk storage. This, of course, means that the memory is slower to access, as disk storage is much slower than RAM.

Disk storage plays into the previously mentioned web server/database example. Most database systems consume a large portion of memory because they want to keep as much information as possible in memory so it can be accessed quicker. In cases when you have a large volume of processing requests on your web server, you can wind up writing portions of your database or web requests to disk, slowing you down. As with the processor, separating the two functions into two different servers means that you can increase the performance of both your database and web server.

Checking Performance of CPU and RAM with top

The Linux command *top* (Linux is case-sensitive) is used on most Linux systems to allow you to see the current processing, memory, and CPU use of your system. It is a great tool for diagnosing how each individual process on your server is performing. top allows you to see how much processing power and memory each individual application is using. To look into this in more depth, see Figure 7-1.

```
top - 11:38:23 up 5 days, 12:22,  1 user,  load average: 0.02, 0.03, 0.05
Tasks: 118 total,   1 running, 117 sleeping,   0 stopped,   0 zombie
Cpu(s):  1.7%us,  0.2%sy,  0.0%ni, 98.2%id,  0.0%wa,  0.0%hi,  0.0%si,  0.0%st
Mem:   4047504k total,  4013908k used,    33596k free,    68552k buffers
Swap:  4182012k total,    54476k used,  4127536k free,   100808k cached
```

PID	USER	PR	NI	VIRT	RES	SHR	S	%CPU	%MEM	TIME+	COMMAND
839	minecraf	20	0	3717m	3.0g	2472	S	9	78.6	2437:28	java
660	mysql	20	0	169m	13m	3276	S	0	0.3	3:22.23	mysqld
680	root	20	0	15780	504	420	S	0	0.0	2:05.09	irqbalance
1	root	20	0	23988	1356	756	S	0	0.0	0:01.54	init
2	root	20	0	0	0	0	S	0	0.0	0:00.00	kthreadd
3	root	20	0	0	0	0	S	0	0.0	0:02.15	ksoftirqd/0
4	root	20	0	0	0	0	S	0	0.0	0:21.29	kworker/0:0
6	root	RT	0	0	0	0	S	0	0.0	0:00.00	migration/0
7	root	RT	0	0	0	0	S	0	0.0	0:00.00	migration/1
8	root	20	0	0	0	0	S	0	0.0	0:08.99	kworker/1:0
9	root	20	0	0	0	0	S	0	0.0	0:03.90	ksoftirqd/1
11	root	RT	0	0	0	0	S	0	0.0	0:00.00	migration/2
12	root	20	0	0	0	0	S	0	0.0	0:01.92	kworker/2:0
13	root	20	0	0	0	0	S	0	0.0	0:03.56	ksoftirqd/2
14	root	RT	0	0	0	0	S	0	0.0	0:00.00	migration/3
16	root	20	0	0	0	0	S	0	0.0	0:03.53	ksoftirqd/3
17	root	0	-20	0	0	0	S	0	0.0	0:00.00	cpuset
18	root	0	-20	0	0	0	S	0	0.0	0:00.00	khelper
19	root	0	-20	0	0	0	S	0	0.0	0:00.00	netns
20	root	20	0	0	0	0	S	0	0.0	0:00.00	kworker/u:1
21	root	20	0	0	0	0	S	0	0.0	0:01.29	sync_supers
22	root	20	0	0	0	0	S	0	0.0	0:00.03	bdi-default
23	root	0	-20	0	0	0	S	0	0.0	0:00.00	kintegrityd
24	root	0	-20	0	0	0	S	0	0.0	0:00.00	kblockd
25	root	0	-20	0	0	0	S	0	0.0	0:00.00	kacpid
26	root	0	-20	0	0	0	S	0	0.0	0:00.00	kacpi_notify
27	root	0	-20	0	0	0	S	0	0.0	0:00.00	kacpi_hotplug
28	root	0	-20	0	0	0	S	0	0.0	0:00.00	ata_sff
29	root	20	0	0	0	0	S	0	0.0	0:00.00	khubd
30	root	0	-20	0	0	0	S	0	0.0	0:00.00	md
31	root	20	0	0	0	0	S	0	0.0	0:00.23	khungtaskd

Figure 7-1. An example of top

From Figure 7-1 you can see that the top section contains information dealing with the number of tasks on our system, followed by the current total processor usage (1.1%) for the whole system. Following this is the memory usage, which shows that 99% of our memory is currently in use. Finally, you can see the breakdown of which applications are using which resources at any given moment. This data shows that our most resource-consuming application is a Java application with process ID (PID) 839, which is consuming 78.6% of our memory and 9% of one of our CPUs; in other words, this application is consuming the most resources on this server—and of those resources it is consuming a significant amount of RAM but not really any CPU.

This kind of information is incredibly useful in diagnostics. In this instance, we were able to determine that we have one application that is consuming most of the memory; from there we can determine which process. From knowing which process, we can examine deeper to find out why this application is using resources and whether we should restart or terminate the application.

Network

Network represents the current throughput of a network device and the proportion currently being used for data transfer. In addition to the throughput, this also represents the time taken to transfer data between two points. Both of these can be crucial—if not enough capacity is available, no data can be transferred from point to point. As with all other metrics, excessive usage of these can have a severe impact on your system's performance. In this case, if your bandwidth is saturated, messages can be delayed or lost, so the determent here is evident. Even having a slow transmission speed can be severely detrimental; the packets may expire before they reach their destination, causing them to be lost.

```
bwm-ng v0.6 (probing every 0.500s), press 'h' for help
input: libstatnet type: rate
|       iface              Rx                    Tx                 Total
==========================================================================
           lo:       170.56 KB/s          170.56 KB/s          341.12 KB/s
         eth0:        21.70 KB/s           40.24 KB/s           61.93 KB/s
--------------------------------------------------------------------------
        total:       192.26 KB/s          210.80 KB/s          403.05 KB/s
```

Figure 7- 2. bwm-ng example

To monitor your bandwidth (amount of data in/out) you can use a tool called bwm-ng (bandwidth monitor). The output looks like Figure 7-2 and gives an "at-the-moment" snapshot of how much bandwidth you are using. This can be useful for knowing how much usage you are consuming moment to moment. In addition to bwm-ng, there are two other tools that can be used for network testing: ping and traceroute. These two tools are the bread and butter of network testing. Note that ping shows the availability of a connection to a particular host and the time it takes to return from it, and traceroute shows the same information plus the times taken on every single network "intersection" it crosses on the way to its destination. Ping is usually employed first to establish if connectivity is available and working in an acceptable manner.

▪ **Note** Invocation of ping is `ping <IP address or URL>` and invocation of traceroute is `traceroute <IP or URL>`.

Keep in mind that traceroute differs from ping as it as a more sophisticated tool for diagnosing specific problems such as finding a bottleneck (point with delay) or finding where a connection drops off. This point can then become your basis for diagnosis, as you have now isolated where any connection issues stem from and can examine what may be causing these issue there—or you can point the finger at someone else.

Storage (Disk)

Storage refers to the amount of physical storage available to your server at any moment. Like network, this can be measured in two parts: the disk I/O (amount of disk input/output per second) and total volume consumed. For your purposes, disk I/O is fairly irrelevant as most of your applications will not be writing to disk regularly. Of course, there are advantages in monitoring and watching disk I/O, but these will be as beneficial as in other areas. We have said disk IO is not supremely important, but disk space usage is! When your server runs out of storage space, all kinds of errors can occur, any virtual memory that was in use can be over-written, and your system can grind to a halt.

```
dhows@archie:~$ df -h
Filesystem          Size  Used Avail Use% Mounted on
/dev/sda1           455G  1.7G  430G   1% /
none                2.0G  192K  2.0G   1% /dev
none                2.0G     0  2.0G   0% /dev/shm
none                2.0G   64K  2.0G   1% /var/run
none                2.0G     0  2.0G   0% /var/lock
dhows@archie:~$ sudo du -sh /
du: cannot access '/proc/12312/task/12312/fd/3': No such file or directory
du: cannot access '/proc/12312/task/12312/fdinfo/3': No such file or directory
du: cannot access '/proc/12312/fd/3': No such file or directory
du: cannot access '/proc/12312/fdinfo/3': No such file or directory
1.5G    /
```

Figure 7- 3. *du and df example*

As you can see from Figure 7-3, it's easy to monitor your disk usage with two simple commands *du* and *df. du;* they show the usage of every item and all subitems within its usage (in the example, you can even see errors that would prevent seeing the portions of the disk that the user doesn't have access to). This can be useful but consumes a lot of screen space, so it's normally used in the form du -sh (*s* standing for summary and *h* standing for human readable), which gives a nice neat output of the current usage of the disk. The second command *df* gives a brilliant output showing the current state of all the logical partitions attached to your server. This can be used to give you quick notification if one of your disks is full.

Load Balancing in Practice

Now that you have an understanding of the resources that one normally has to worry about, you can begin looking at how these resources can be effectively allocated. This allocation of resources to increase the effectiveness of applications is the core of load balancing and therefore our focus. The primary ways that load balancing is accomplished are as follows:

1. Split applications over a number of servers, balancing the load over a number of servers (such as separate web and database servers).

2. Add specialist components to applications in order to balance the amount of processing needed for each application function, such as caching of common web site data, saving time on the collection of this data from disk, or the creation of this data from database entries, etc.

3. Create additional servers that can collectively share the load, which can greatly increase the amount of processing power available to complete the tasks required by a server.

Over the course of the next few chapters we will introduce several concepts for dealing with the second and third methods of load balancing, which includes things like SSL acceleration, SSL offloading, creating a load balancer to allow multiple servers to share load, and creating a highly-available (HA) cluster for processing requests.

Guiding Principles

With load balancing, as with just about any form of system modification, there are a number of guiding principles that inform most of what you are attempting to accomplish. Understanding them is key to successfully load balancing your system and will make the job of maintaining and further improving your load balancing and system performance easier.

Understand Your System

Principle one is understanding your system. This may seem easy at first, but is actually quite an in-depth undertaking. Understanding your system, in simple terms, is having knowledge of how your system goes about performing its day-to-day business tasks.

For example, in a web server you need to be aware of how connections come into your system and where they go. Once they get to their destination, what happens to the requests, what kind of response comes out, where does the information in that response come from, and how does this data get back to the initial requester? In addition, you should also look at understanding the normal traffic flow to your web site and the traffic pattern.

The traffic flow means how a user interacts with your web site, so you will learn how they log in, request common data, etc. This kind of information allows you to make tweaks to the areas of your system that you know will be trafficked significantly more, by having unchanging data (like a company logo) stored in cache or by having a cut-down view in your database that allows quicker request time for username and passwords (allowing quicker user logins).

Traffic patterns can be much more cryptic to understand but provide much more insight once deciphered. Each request that a user makes will have an impact on your system; however, under normal circumstances the actions of one user are insignificant. The actions of your entire user base are much different. Consider a football scores web site: it will be most active during the football season, on game day, during the hours that football games are being played. This kind of pattern allows you to preempt traffic problems by adding additional resources to cope during these peak periods.

The combination of these three items can be dynamite. Continuing with the football example, think of it this way: on game day you will see an increase in requests for the scoreboard pages and these requests place a heavy load on your database. In response, you can add a quick cached database view that shows only the current scores as relevant; in addition, you can cache certain versions of this page for "relevant" periods (say a minute or two). This means that anyone who requests access to your football scores would get the cached version of the page, which is updated every minute. The scores are still displayed and updated in near real time (on the timescale of a football fan), the load on the database is mightily reduced, and the pages can load quicker since they are cached and ready to display at a moment's notice.

Planning

Principal two is planning. Planning builds upon what was briefly mentioned in principle one and acts much as a yang to its yin. This is to say that planning is much less useful without information, and the information itself is not acted upon without good planning. Planning is about setting a goal, establishing the parameters of what you wish to accomplish, and finding out ways to accomplish what you have established.

Most IT texts talk about a number of things in this area but the key is simple: be proactive (act to prevent or pre-empt) rather than reactive (act in response to). If you are proactive in understanding your system, you will understand when your system is at its worst and you will take steps to lessen any issues before they occur.

Monitoring and Testing

Principal three works with both the two previous principals. Principal three is that you should monitor your system and that any change that you make should be monitored while it is tested. One of the key human foibles is that we are often wrong about things; this most certainly includes performance tweaks made to IT systems. As part of understanding your system, you need to monitor and be aware of how long a connection takes, or how much load you are expecting. Then extending this knowledge to your testing to make sure that any changes you make actually have a positive outcome.

This brings us to one of the biggest caveats that you will encounter during the course of this book. Not all performance tuning is suitable to all situations. We have tried to be as general in our focus here as we can and we have tried wherever possible to ensure that these changes are universally of benefit. This, however, isn't always the case, so with this in mind, always test the changes that you make to ensure that you are getting benefits from your changes.

Summary

Using these three principals means that you will take a very active focus on your system performance and load balancing. This active focus is what this chapter is about—having an understanding of what you are working with and a clear goal of where you want to go. Using the concepts covered in this chapter should give you a good grounding of what you can do to ensure that the rest of the advice and configurations in the latter chapters of this book provide as much advantage as possible.

CHAPTER 8

Load Balancing Your Web Site

When hearing the word "Apache," most people will think of three things: a group of Native American tribes, a US military battle helicopter, or the open-source HTTP web server project. Now, assuming you didn't pick up this book to learn about American battle helicopters or the Apachean people, you are probably thinking of the web server.

While it's certainly true that the brand name Apache is mostly known for the web server project, the name Apache on its own has little meaning. Rather, it is the Apache Software Foundation that has developed and released the Apache HTTP Server as one of their projects, among many others. It is this Apache HTTP Server software we'll be discussing in this chapter. You'll learn how to fine-tune it for better performance and how to apply load balancing to it.

You'll also have a look at optimizing and load-balancing nginx (`engine x'), which is another open-source cross-platform package capable of hosting web sites as well as acting as a reverse proxy and an IMAP/POP3 proxy server that can be used for e-mail. Where Apache HTTP is process-based and highly extensible using modules, nginx is well known for being a high-performance, event-driven, and lightweight solution instead; it also has a very small memory footprint, which is exactly what you need to speed up your web site!

Don't worry! While both Apache HTTP Server and nginx have their strengths and weaknesses, there is no need to start deciding which one to pick. Would it be Apache HTTP because you're so comfortable with it, or should you go with the new kid in town, nginx, that quickly earned its stripes due to its efficiency? Why not use them both? Remember, this isn't about choosing teams. Instead, your purpose is to make your web site load faster, so why not reap the benefits of both if you can: nginx running on the foreground for serving static content (HTML files, images, and so forth) as well as the load balancer using its proxy module (which is very simple to set up) and several Apache servers running in the background for the dynamic content (such as PHP pages).

Measuring Web Server Performance

Before you can get started on speeding up your web server, you first need to know its currently capability. How else are you going to tell if the steps you took to speed it up actually worked? There are several tools and packages available to benchmark your web server: some are expensive, others are free. One that has proved to be helpful is the tool called httperf. Optionally, you can use ab, which comes with Apache.

httperf is a very powerful command-line Linux tool that can be used to establish a (high) number of connections to a web server to give you an impression of your server's performance. Not only is it flexible enough to send along specific headers (such as the Accept-Encoding header), there's also a perl wrapper available called autobench, which allows you to increase the number of requested connections per second on each iteration and writes the output to a tab-separated file that can be used to create nice charts to make your results more visual (using the bench2graph tool).

■ **Note** httperf can be obtained from Hewlett-Packard's web site free of charge or installed directly using your distribution's software management software, such as apt-get or yum.

Here you'll use httperf on a default, out-of-the-box installation of both Apache HTTP and nginx. No changes are made to the configuration files and both web services host the same file: a simple HTML file called index.html that contains 5011 bytes of data. You'll tell httperf to establish as many as 20,000 connections to the web server using the --num-conns parameter. In this example, the httperf package is executed from a local client to the web server Server02's index.html page that resides on the same subnet to prevent network bottlenecks.

```
$ httperf --server Server02 --uri /index.html --num-conns 20000 --add-header='Accept-Encoding:
gzip,deflate\n'
```

■ **Note** In order for httperf to properly handle compressed content, you will need to add additional header information using the --add-header option, as shown in this example.

These are the results for benchmarking the index.html file on an out-of-the-box Apache HTTP Server:

```
Maximum connect burst length: 1

Total: connections 20000 requests 20000 replies 20000 test-duration 30.041 s

Connection rate: 665.8 conn/s (1.5 ms/conn, <=1 concurrent connections)
Connection time [ms]: min 0.5 avg 1.5 max 25.4 median 1.5 stddev 0.7
Connection time [ms]: connect 0.6
Connection length [replies/conn]: 1.000

Request rate: 665.8 req/s (1.5 ms/req)
Request size [B]: 117.0

Reply rate [replies/s]: min 534.4 avg 665.7 max 794.8 stddev 92.2 (6 samples)
Reply time [ms]: response 0.8 transfer 0.0
Reply size [B]: header 283.0 content 1809.0 footer 0.0 (total 2092.0)
Reply status: 1xx=0 2xx=20000 3xx=0 4xx=0 5xx=0
```

```
CPU time [s]: user 2.52 system 27.52 (user 8.4% system 91.6% total 100.0%)
Net I/O: 1436.2 KB/s (11.8*10^6 bps)

Errors: total 0 client-timo 0 socket-timo 0 connrefused 0 connreset 0
Errors: fd-unavail 0 addrunavail 0 ftab-full 0 other 0
```

Here, the reply rate values are most relevant as they tells you about how many replies the web server is capable of sending back to the client per second. In this example, you can see it's capable of sending a minimum of 534.4 replies per second and a maximum of 794.8. Now, let's compare these values to those of nginx on the same server:

```
$ httperf --server Server02 --uri /index.html --num-conns 20000 --add-header='Accept-Encoding:
gzip,deflate\n'

Maximum connect burst length: 1

Total: connections 20000 requests 20000 replies 20000 test-duration 28.943 s

Connection rate: 691.0 conn/s (1.4 ms/conn, <=1 concurrent connections)
Connection time [ms]: min 0.7 avg 1.4 max 14.5 median 1.5 stddev 0.6
Connection time [ms]: connect 0.7
Connection length [replies/conn]: 1.000

Request rate: 691.0 req/s (1.4 ms/req)
Request size [B]: 117.0

Reply rate [replies/s]: min 612.5 avg 696.0 max 843.2 stddev 89.7 (5 samples)
Reply time [ms]: response 0.7 transfer 0.0
Reply size [B]: header 225.0 content 1925.0 footer 2.0 (total 2152.0)
Reply status: 1xx=0 2xx=20000 3xx=0 4xx=0 5xx=0

CPU time [s]: user 1.83 system 27.10 (user 6.3% system 93.6% total 100.0%)
Net I/O: 1529.8 KB/s (12.5*10^6 bps)

Errors: total 0 client-timo 0 socket-timo 0 connrefused 0 connreset 0
Errors: fd-unavail 0 addrunavail 0 ftab-full 0 other 0
```

When comparing the results, visible in Figure 8-1, you can see that there is a vast difference between the number of replies between the two web services: Apache's out-of-the-box installation is capable of sending a maximum of 794.8 replies per second but nginx is capable of sending as many as 843.2 replies per second. Indeed, merely switching web servers makes a great difference!

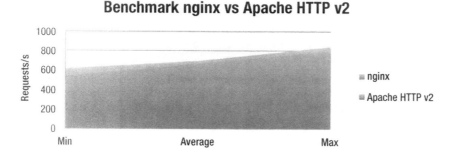

Figure 8-1. A benchmark comparison of nginx vs. Apache HTTP v2

Accelerating Apache HTTP

Now that you know your web server's performance, it's time to speed things up! Before applying techniques such as load balancing, there is actually a great deal of reconfiguration that can be done to speed up your web service. This not only includes changes made to the overall operating system (such as implementing memcached, which was discussed in Chapter 3) but especially to the web service itself.

Disabling Unneeded Modules

Apache HTTP is a modular program, which means the server administrator can choose to extend the program's capabilities by loading additional modules, or DSO (Dynamic Shared Object) modules, by modifying the server's httpd.conf configuration file in version 1.x or adding/removing symlinks in Apache's mods-enabled/ directory in version 2.x. By default, many of these additional modules are either statically compiled into the Apache core or loaded automatically as a DSO. Many of these DSO modules may not be required, however, and are best disabled to reduce the overall memory footprint and thus increase performance.

Each module is loaded using the LoadModule command, and you can easily find an entire list of the ones that are loaded on a default, out-of-the-box installation of Apache HTTP v2 by listing the mods-enabled directory, like so:

```
LoadModule alias_module /usr/lib/apache2/modules/mod_alias.so
LoadModule auth_basic_module /usr/lib/apache2/modules/mod_auth_basic.so
LoadModule authn_file_module /usr/lib/apache2/modules/mod_authn_file.so
LoadModule authz_default_module /usr/lib/apache2/modules/mod_authz_default.so
LoadModule authz_groupfile_module /usr/lib/apache2/modules/mod_authz_groupfile.so
LoadModule authz_host_module /usr/lib/apache2/modules/mod_authz_host.so
LoadModule authz_user_module /usr/lib/apache2/modules/mod_authz_user.so
LoadModule autoindex_module /usr/lib/apache2/modules/mod_autoindex.so
LoadModule cgi_module /usr/lib/apache2/modules/mod_cgi.so
LoadModule deflate_module /usr/lib/apache2/modules/mod_deflate.so
LoadModule dir_module /usr/lib/apache2/modules/mod_dir.so
LoadModule env_module /usr/lib/apache2/modules/mod_env.so
LoadModule mime_module /usr/lib/apache2/modules/mod_mime.so
LoadModule negotiation_module /usr/lib/apache2/modules/mod_negotiation.so
LoadModule reqtimeout_module /usr/lib/apache2/modules/mod_reqtimeout.so
```

```
LoadModule setenvif_module /usr/lib/apache2/modules/mod_setenvif.so
LoadModule status_module /usr/lib/apache2/modules/mod_status.so
```

Most of these modules are self-explanatory once you get to know Apache HTTP a little better. For example, mod_alias is used for creating a mapping between a URL to certain filesystem paths. mod_auth_basic can be used for providing basic authentication (username/password) on specific folders using a .htaccess file, and the mod_cgi module can be used to execute CGI scripts. Some of these may not be required and are best left as disabled if this is the case. Which one you should or shouldn't disable really depends on your configuration of Apache, however, so check if you can disable them safely before doing so.

Disabling DNS Lookups

Another method to reduce latency time is to ensure that DNS lookups are disabled. DNS lookups are not always done, however, except when you are using the Allow from or Deny from options to restrict access to specific web sites or folders. If you do decide to use these options, it's best to use IP addresses instead of a domain or hostname as the cumulative effect of DNS lookups imposes performance penalties every time your server receives a request from a client. In a similar fashion, DNS lookups are also performed when access logging is enabled in combination with the optional HostnameLookups. By default, however, HostnameLookups is disabled ever since Apache 1.3.

Note   If you do wish to log hostnames rather than IP addresses, it is considered best practice to use a post-processing program such as logresolve, which ships with Apache HTTP.

Using Compression

Another good method to speed up your web site's traffic is by using HTTP compression to compress your web site's content before sending it out to the client. In Apache HTTP v2, the mod_deflate module can be used to do this, which replaces the mod_gzip previously available in Apache HTTP v1.3. Using mod_deflate, file types such as HTML, text, PHP, XML, and other MIME types can be compressed to approximately 20 or 30 percent of their original size, thereby saving your server a great deal of traffic.

The best part about this is that the clients receiving this compressed data don't need any specific client software, as today's modern browsers natively know how to handle compressed content. Even when an old browser is used, such as Netscape, the browser will first negotiate with the web server to see if it can receive the content; otherwise, it requests the data be sent uncompressed instead.

Warning   Keep in mind that compressing data doesn't come effortlessly: in fact, it causes a slightly higher load on the server as the specified content needs to be compressed. Generally this is compensated by the decrease in the client's connection times, which tends to be the bottleneck. Formal benchmarking is suggested to verify the facts, which differ in each specific situation.

mod_deflate is enabled by default in Apache HTTP v2, and generally there is little that needs to be done to its configuration file (mod_deflate.conf) as several commonly used MIME types are already set to be compressed (HTML, XML, CSS, JavaScript, RSS, ECMAScript, and plain text files). The configuration can be easily altered, however, to specify which MIME types should or shouldn't be compressed. But be careful with this: some MIME types are already compressed, so you don't want attempt to compress these again with mod_deflate because there is little point in doing so. Examples of such file types are graphic files, music files, ZIP files, video files, and PDF files, to name a few.

■ **Note** Be careful when choosing what MIME types to compress. Certain types are already in a compressed state and would only cause additional CPU overhead while making little difference. Generally you only want to compress text-based files (such as HTML, JS, CSS, XML, and so on). When a specific web site contains a high number of small text files in these formats, you should also reconsider enabling compression as the time required to transfer the uncompressed files might be shorter than the time required to compress and transfer the files.

In order to check if mod_deflate is loaded successfully, apache2ctl can be used, which is included in Apache's installation. To check, open up a console and type

```
# apache2ctl -t -D DUMP_MODULES
```

This will show an entire list of modules currently loaded. If you see the deflate module listed there, you'll know it's loaded.

```
# apache2ctl -t -D DUMP_MODULES
Loaded Modules:
 core_module (static)
 [..]
 deflate_module (shared)
Syntax OK
```

Note that (static) behind the module name implies the module is statically compiled into the Apache core, where (shared) implies the module can be loaded or unloaded.

If the module isn't listed, you can load the module manually by using the LoadModule function in your web site's configuration file (httpd.conf for the entire web site, or your virtual host's specific configuration file in the sites-available/ directory). To load the module for your entire web site, you can simply create a symlink in the mods-enabled/ folder pointing to the mods-available/deflate* files using the ln command, like so:

```
# ln -s /etc/apache2/mods-available/deflate.* /etc/apache2/mods-enabled/
```

When you only wish to load the module for a certain virtual host, use the LoadModule function instead.

```
LoadModule deflate_module /usr/lib/apache2/modules/mod_deflate.so
```

FollowSymLinks and SymLinksIfOwnerMatch

The FollowSymLinks option can be used within a <Directory> directive to ensure that symbolic links defined within the web site's configuration file can be accessed from that directory. In a similar fashion, SymLinksIfOwnerMatch can be used to follow such symbolic links only if the target file or directory is owned by the same user as the link itself, thus providing a higher level of security.

However, when the latter is set, Apache will need to verify whether the owner of the link and the target directory are identical using lstat, which requires additional system calls and adds to the overall latency. In contrast, when the FollowSymLinks option is not set, Apache will need to issue some additional system calls when accessing a file because it has to check whether the file is a "real file" or a symbolic link.

■ **Note** Apache doesn't cache the results of these lstat operations; hence they need to occur on every single request, which drastically impacts the system's performance.

For the best performance, don't use the SymLinksIfOwnerMatch option and always enable FollowSymLinks in your Directory directives. The final results of the configuration modifications to Apache HTTP v2 can be seen in Figure 8-2.

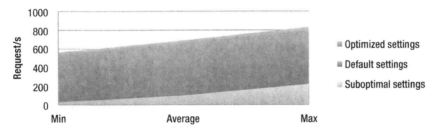

Figure 8-2: Benchmark comparison of different settings on Apache HTTP v2

Accelerating nginx

The out-of-the-box installation of nginx leaves little room for improvement. After all, nginx is designed for high performance, and it does an amazing job with the default settings already. There are a few tricks, however, that have more to do with fine-tuning the installation to match your server's hardware than, say, disabling modules as with Apache HTTP Server.

worker_processes and worker_cpu_affinity

The nginx configuration file (default: /etc/nginx/nginx.conf) lets you specify the worker_processes directive. Using this directive, you can tell nginx how many single-threaded processes can be created by nginx. For example, if nginx is performing CPU-intensive actions (such as compressing, encrypting, or executing code in the background) an additional worker process can be spawned (preferably on another CPU or core), thereby decreasing the web server's overall latency. The worker_processes directive is set to 1 by default.

```
worker_processes  4;
```

Note   For the best performance, you should set this option equal to the number of CPUs or cores in your server.

Chances are, however, that your operating system decides to bond the additional worker process on the same CPU/core on which the original process is already running. When needed, you can balance these processes appropriately across the system's cores using the worker_cpu_affinity option, which can be used to bind each worker process to a specific core/CPU.

The worker_cpu_affinity option takes the binary bitmask value from your CPU as an option, where the lowest order bitmask represents your first logical CPU and the highest order bit represents your last logical CPU. For example, if you have four CPUs on your system, you can set the affinity as such:

```
worker_processes 4;
worker_cpu_affinity 0001 0010 0100 1000;
```

If you have eight, the following would do the trick:

```
worker_processes 8;
worker_cpu_affinity 0001 0010 0100 1000 10000 100000 1000000 10000000;
```

After the changes have been made, you will need to restart nginx. You can use ps in combination with taskset to confirm which CPU each worker process is running on.

```
# ps ax | grep nginx
18996 ?         Ss      0:00 nginx: master process /usr/sbin/nginx
18997 ?         S       0:00 nginx: worker process
18998 ?         S       0:00 nginx: worker process
18999 ?         S       0:00 nginx: worker process
19000 ?         S       0:00 nginx: worker process

# taskset -p <pid id>
pid 18997's current affinity mask: 1
pid 18998's current affinity mask: 2
pid 18999's current affinity mask: 3
pid 19000's current affinity mask: 4
```

Note   Currently worker_cpu_affinity is only supported on Linux.

Gzip Compression

Just like Apache HTTP, nginx is also capable of compressing the data before sending it out to the visitor. It has two tricks for this: the gzip module and the gzip pre-compression module, both which can be enabled at the same time.

As is the case with Apache HTTP, you won't need to worry about any client-side software: modern browsers have full compatibility for compressed content, and those that don't can be explicitly disabled in the configuration file using the gzip_disable directive, which takes regular expressions for increased flexibility.

The gzip module is compiled by default, unless explicitly disabled during the package's configuration process using --without-http_gzip_module. The on-the-fly compression can be enabled in nginx's configuration file using the gzip directive under the http{} section.

```
http {
    gzip on;
}
```

The compression level can also be specified in the configuration file by using the gzip_comp_level directive. The gzip_comp_level directive takes an integer from a range of 1 to 9, where 1 represents the lowest level of compression (and thus the fastest) and 9 represents the highest level of compression (slower). By default, gzip_comp_level is set to 1.

```
http {
    gzip on;
    gzip_comp_level 3;
}
```

As is the case with Apache HTTP, you will need to find a good balance between the level of compression and what type of files you choose to compress and for which browsers. Keeping in mind that compression will add an additional load to your server, you want to avoid compressing files that have little to compress in the first place, like image, music, PDF files, etc.

By default, file types other than text/HTML aren't compressed. This can be changed, however, using the gzip_types directive where you can add additional MIME-types.

```
http {
    gzip on;
    gzip_comp_level 3;
    gzip_types application/javascript application/xml;
}
```

▦ **Note** Text/HTML MIME types are compressed by default. This doesn't need to be added to the list of gzip_types to compress.

As you've seen by now, the biggest conundrum of using compression is the additional server load created by the compression process. While this can generally be offset against the reduced connection times, the overall process can still be CPU intensive. That said, nginx provides an additional module called gzip_static, which allows nginx to look for an already compressed version of the data it wishes to send, thereby avoiding compressing the same data each time it is requested by a client.

The gzip_static module can be easily enabled using the gzip_static directive in nginx's configuration file under the http{} section.

```
http {
        gzip_static on
}
```

Once a request comes in, nginx will look for a .gz file in the same location as the original file and send it out instead. Of course, this does assume the file is there already, so you will need to create the .gz file yourself from the static data using gzip. Using this approach, nginx need only worry about serving the gzipped data itself, rather than compressing the original file each time it is being requested, causing additional load on the server.

Dynamic content stills need to be compressed on the fly, however, which can still be done using the gzip module. It's suggested that you use a lower compression level for this data to ensure your server's performance is not affected too much.

```
http {
        gzip on;
        gzip_static on;
        gzip_comp_level 2;
        gzip_types application/javascript application/xml;
}
```

The final results of the modification changes to nginx can be seen in Figure 8-3.

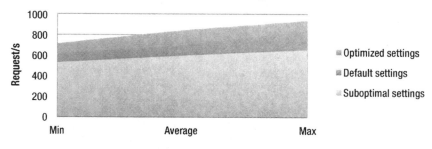

Figure 8-3. Benchmark comparison of different settings on nginx

Load Balancing Your Web Server

Now that you've seen how to improve your web server's overall performance, you can take it one step further and add load balancing to the equation. The idea of load balancing your web service is pretty simple: you distribute all incoming connections to your web site to a number of different web servers by using one or more load balancing servers. By doing so, you don't only reduce the overall load on the web servers, you also have good means of failover in case one of the web servers temporarily breaks down.

So, what do you need to set this up? Well, this depends on your wishes, really! The simplest setup requires at least two web servers and one load-balancing server. The load balancing server would generally require two network adapters with one connected to the Internet and the other connected to the same network segment to which the web servers are connected.

The Setup

In this example, you will assume a relatively simple setup as described earlier: two web servers running an optimized installation of either Apache or nginx on a Linux-based operating system (Ubuntu in this case) and one load balancing server running IPVS. IPVS, short for Internet Protocol Virtual Server, is the utility you'll be using to balance your server loads.

In the foreground, the load balancer (LoadBalancer) will be receiving all incoming connections. This means that if you use port forwarding, the connection needs to be redirected to this server. Likewise, people will be connecting to the external IP of the server LoadBalancer (1.2.3.4 in this case). The load balancer, or the Director, will be distributing the load across the web servers, or worker servers, using a weighted least connections (wlc) schedule.

■ **Note** There are several different methods available that IPVS can use for distributing the workload. All of these are described in Chapter 10, which also covers IPVS in greater detail than in this chapter.

Your load balancing server (LoadBalancer) will be using two network interface cards (or NICs): eth0 with the IP address 1.2.3.4, responsible for the incoming/outgoing traffic to the Internet and eth1 with the IP address 10.0.0.1 connected to a (virtual) network, which is where the workers also connected. Similarly, the workers (Server01 and Server02) will both be connected to the 10.0.0.x subnet, both with one NIC (eth0) with the IP address 10.0.0.2 and 10.0.0.3, respectively. These servers will not require any public IP address. An overview of the layout can be seen in Figure 8-4.

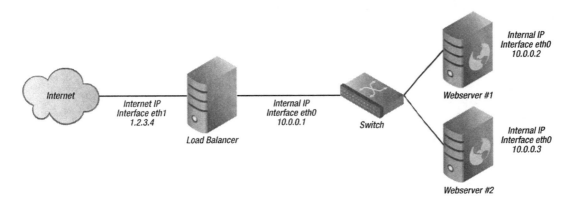

Figure 8-4. An overview of the setup

Preparing the Server

Now you're going to get your hands dirty. You will find that installing IPVS is a piece of cake, as it will be to configure your server and clients. The server might actually be the hardest, and even this is but a seven-step process! First, you'll have to confirm that your network settings are actually correct. On Linux, it is fairly easy to check what IP addresses your network adapters have been set to by using ifconfig.

```
# ifconfig
eth0      Link encap:Ethernet  HWaddr 02:00:b2:fa:35:e1
          inet addr:1.2.3.4  Bcast:1.2.3.255  Mask:255.255.255.0
          inet6 addr: fe80::b2ff:fefa:35e1/64 Scope:Link
          UP BROADCAST RUNNING MULTICAST  MTU:1500  Metric:1
          RX packets:124098 errors:0 dropped:0 overruns:0 frame:0
          TX packets:12181 errors:0 dropped:0 overruns:0 carrier:0
          collisions:0 txqueuelen:1000
          RX bytes:7818260 (7.8 MB)  TX bytes:4030566 (4.0 MB)

eth1      Link encap:Ethernet  HWaddr 00:1c:23:20:f4:53
          inet addr:10.0.0.1  Bcast:10.255.255.255  Mask:255.0.0.0
          inet6 addr: fe80::21c:23ff:fe20:f453/64 Scope:Link
          UP BROADCAST RUNNING MULTICAST  MTU:1500  Metric:1
          RX packets:8802179 errors:0 dropped:0 overruns:0 frame:0
          TX packets:7543819 errors:0 dropped:0 overruns:0 carrier:0
          collisions:0 txqueuelen:1000
          RX bytes:2613848314 (2.6 GB)  TX bytes:731286814 (731.2 MB)
          Interrupt:17
```

What you wish to see here is that eth0 is given a public IP address (1.2.3.4) and that eth1 is set to have an internal IP address (10.0.0.1) that can be used to connect to the web servers. You can use ping to confirm a connection can be established in both directions between load balancer and its workers.

```
# ping -c 1 10.0.0.2
PING 10.0.0.2 (10.0.0.2) 56(84) bytes of data.
64 bytes from 10.0.0.2: icmp_seq=1 ttl=64 time=0.316 ms

--- 10.0.0.2 ping statistics ---
1 packets transmitted, 1 received, 0% packet loss, time 0ms
rtt min/avg/max/mdev = 0.316/0.316/0.316/0.000 ms

# ping -c 1 10.0.0.3
PING 10.0.0.3 (10.0.0.3) 56(84) bytes of data.
64 bytes from 10.0.0.3: icmp_seq=1 ttl=64 time=0.342 ms

--- 10.0.0.3 ping statistics ---
1 packets transmitted, 1 received, 0% packet loss, time 0ms
rtt min/avg/max/mdev = 0.342/0.342/0.342/0.000 ms
```

Once you've confirmed that the network is working as it should, you're ready for the next step: modifying the load balancer's /etc/sysctl.conf with your favorite text editor (vim, nano, etc.). Using the /etc/sysctl.conf file, you can configure various kinds of networking and system variables. In this example, you will only need to uncomment one single line that, once done, allows you to forward any incoming IP packets (meant for the web servers) to your workers. Locate and uncomment the following line, or add it if it's not already there:

```
net.ipv4.ip_forward=1
```

Save the file, and close your text editor. Next, run sysctl -p to load in the modified configuration file, which will confirm the modification has been made.

```
#sysctl -p
net.ipv4.ip_forward = 1
```

Next, open and modify the file /proc/sys/net/ipv4/ip_forward so that it contains a 1. Optionally, you can use the echo command for this also.

```
# echo 1 > /proc/sys/net/ipv4/ip_forward
```

Once done, you are ready to install IPVS! Depending on your distribution of Linux, you can install IPVS using apt-get (debian/ubuntu), yum (CentOS, RHEL), or compile it yourself when needed. Here are the commands for apt-get and yum:

```
# apt-get install ipvsadm
# yum install ipvsadm
```

The installation should go smoothly and will install the required kernel module it needs to operate. For a more detailed guide on its installation and process specifics, please refer to Chapter 10.

Now, you will need to reconfigure IPVS so that it will run on boot up as a master-server and listen on eth0 for incoming connections to route. Don't worry; it sounds a lot harder than it is. You only need to run the following command to configure the package on Debian-flavored distributions:

```
# dpkg-reconfigure ipvsadm
```

Once prompted, all you will be required to do is answer the following questions accordingly:

```
Do you want to automatically load IPVS rules on boot? [Yes]
Daemon method: [master]
Multicast interface for ipvsadm: [eth0]
```

In order to do achieve the same in Red Hat-flavored distributions, use the ipvsadm command.

```
# ipvsadm --start-daemon=master --mcast-interface=eth0
```

Once done, the reconfiguration will close, and you're ready to configure your load balancer! The hardest part has already been done; from here on, it will only get simpler. Even simpler, you say? Yes, indeed. All you need to do next is create a new virtual service using the IPVSADM package. At the moment, the IPVS table is empty, which you can confirm by executing the ipvsadm command:

```
# ipvsadm
IP Virtual Server version 1.2.1 (size=4096)
Prot LocalAddress:Port Scheduler Flags
  -> RemoteAddress:Port              Forward Weight ActiveConn InActConn
#
```

Let's add the virtual service. You can do this using the -A parameter, followed by -t to specify that it concerns a TCP service. The syntax is as follows: 1.2.3.4 indicates the public IP address, and :80 is the port number your service should be listening on (usually :80 for web servers).

```
# ipvsadm -A -t 1.2.3.4:80
#
```

Once the service is created, you can add your workers to it to ensure any incoming connections on port 80 will be forwarded to the servers listed, regardless how many. Recall that you're using the weighted least connections schedule here, which directs the incoming connection to the worker with the lowest number of connections and the highest weight value. To add your workers, use the -a option, followed again by -t to specify that it concerns a TCP service, followed by the external IP address (identical to the virtual service's IP previously specified), its port number, the -r option to specify the real server's IP address and port number, and finally the -m option to use NAT (network address translation), which you previously enabled.

```
# ipvsadm -a -t 1.2.3.4:80 -r 10.0.0.2:80 -m
# ipvsadm -a -t 1.2.3.4:80 -r 10.0.0.3:80 -m
#
```

And that's it from the server side! To see your current IPVS table, just type ipvsadm on your terminal, which will also show you the number of active and inactive connections.

Preparing the Workers

Preparing the workers shouldn't take more than five minutes: it merely involves ensuring the web service (Apache, nginx, or any other web service listening on port 80) is running and modifying the worker's routing table. To be sure of the web server's status, you can simply request its status using the daemon on both servers.

```
# /etc/init.d/apache2 status
Apache is NOT running.

# /etc/init.d/nginx status
 * nginx is running
```

Be sure that the web service is running on both workers, however, and not just one of them. If so, the web site's performance might be degraded, if only a bit.

Once you got that covered, you can modify the systems' routing tables. The routing tables are a crucial part of the network's operation and allow you to specify how and where any outgoing traffic is sent in order to reach its final destination. For a more in-depth explanation of the routing table, please refer to Chapter 10. You will tell your servers' routing tables that any outgoing traffic coming from port 80 will be redirected to your load balancer or, in this case, your gateway. Note that you will need to specify the internal IP address from the load balancer followed by the NIC's identifier to use.

```
# route add default gw 10.0.0.1 eth0
```

To verify the route was added successfully, the route command can be executed once again, which will show you an overview of the known routes to the system.

```
# route
Kernel IP routing table
Destination     Gateway         Genmask         Flags Metric Ref    Use Iface
10.0.0.0        *               255.0.0.0       U     0      0        0 eth0
default         10.0.0.1        0.0.0.0         UG    0      0        0 eth0
```

And that's it. Voila, all done!

Testing the Load Balancer

So now that you've set up your load balancer as well as the workers, you can test that the setup works as expected by simply visiting the web site. However, if both web servers are, as intended, hosting the same data, it would be hard to tell what server you're actually visiting at the moment. A simple way to check is to use the ipvsadm command, which if you recall from earlier, shows you the number of active connections on the servers at that time. You can use the watch command to ensure the ipvsadm table is updated each second, so that you'll have a better view on this.

```
# watch -n 1 ipvsadm
Every 1.0s: ipvsadm

IP Virtual Server version 1.2.1 (size=4096)
Prot LocalAddress:Port Scheduler Flags
  -> RemoteAddress:Port           Forward Weight ActiveConn InActConn
TCP  1.2.3.4:www wlc
  -> 10.0.0.2:www                 Masq    1      0          418
  -> 10.0.0.3:www                 Masq    1      1          418
```

The ActiveConn field specifies the number of total active connections on each web server. As you can see in this example, the second web server with the IP address 10.0.0.3 currently has one active connection, and both have so far equally handled 418 connections each, as can be seen under the InActConns field (Inactive Connections).

Another more visual way of testing your load balancer is to generate a plain text file on each web server, specifying unique information. As is generally the case with your workers, they would host the same data, but creating one unique file on each would be a simple way of identifying the current worker. For example, you can create one file named id that contains but the hostname of the worker on each directory.

```
root@Server01# echo "Worker1" > /var/www/id
root@Server02# echo "Worker2" > /var/www/id
```

Now you can use a simple shell script in combination with lynx (a command-line browser) to print the /id file's output to the terminal itself, ten times in a row, from the web server itself or any other host.

```
# for i in {1..10}; do lynx -source 1.2.3.4/id; done
Server02
Server01
Server02
Server01
Server02
Server01
```

```
Server02
Server01
Server02
Server01
```

Thanks to the weighted least connection schedule used by IPVS, it should come as no surprise that both servers are now equally loaded with incoming connections.

Note   To ensure that the static data available to the web servers are always kept in sync, mirroring utilities such as rsync can be used to copy pieces of files that have changed.

Best of Both Worlds

Now that you've seen how load balancing can be applied to your web service using the IPVS package, you can take it another step further and separate dynamic from static content using nginx's reverse-proxy module. Using this, nginx is capable of redirecting any incoming requests for specific MIME types of a web site to another server. By doing so, you can, for example, use nginx on the foreground as the primary server serving the web site's static content such as HTML pages, image files, CSS files, and so on, and redirect any requests for dynamic data (such as PHP-generated content) to your high-end Apache server running at the back end. This way, you can reap the benefits of both: use nginx for handling pre-compressed static data, and use Apache for processing the web site's dynamic data. An overview of this setup can be seen in Figure 8-5.

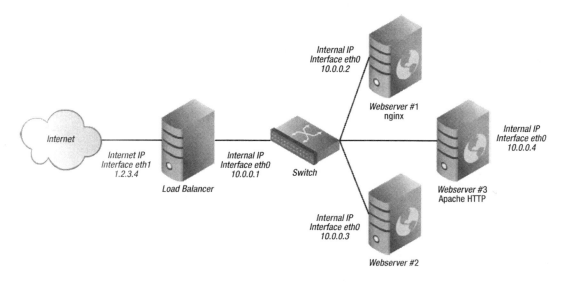

Figure 8-5. Adding an additional Apache HTTP server for dynamic content

The reserve-proxy module is relatively easy to configure. As a simple example, you will tell nginx to handle any requests itself other than the requests made for PHP pages, which generally contain dynamic content. Any request for a PHP document will be forwarded to your Apache HTTP server running on a third web server (Webserver #3 in this example). To do so, make sure Apache is up and running on the web server itself and readily accepting any incoming connections.

Note When using the reserve-proxy module to redirect traffic to a different web server for a specific MIME-type, that specific web server doesn't need to be reachable via a public IP because the outbound traffic will be sent via its front-end (nginx) server.

Once Apache HTTP is fully running on your web server and capable of handling PHP documents, you will tell nginx what to forward and to where by modifying the web site's specific configuration file using your favorite text editor. The default file that comes with nginx is called default and can be found under /etc/nginx/sites-enabled/default. In it, you will need to add the following under the server{} directive:

```
location ~ \.php$ {
        proxy_pass http://10.0.0.4;
        proxy_set_header X-Real-IP $remote_addr;
        proxy_set_header X-Forwarded-For $proxy_add_x_forwarded_for;
}
```

With this code, you are telling nginx to forward any request for any .php file on any location on the web site to the web server listening on the internal IP 10.0.0.4 using the proxy_pass directive. You're also telling nginx to modify some of the request header lines that will be send to the (Apache) web server using the proxy_set_header directive. That's all!

Once done, save the configuration file and reload nginx's settings.

```
# /etc/init.d/nginx restart
Restarting nginx: the configuration file /etc/nginx/nginx.conf syntax is ok
configuration file /etc/nginx/nginx.conf test is successful
nginx.
#
```

Warning If you've set up load balancing as previously shown, be sure you apply these changes on both nginx web servers.

Summary

Implementing load balancing to your web servers is a piece of cake: the installation of the IPVS software merely takes a few minutes. Configuring the load balancer as its worker is equally simple and takes just as long at best. The benefits of implementing load balancing on your web servers is easy to see: not only will the overall number of accepted incoming connections of your web site be increased, but your web site will also have a temporary fail-over in case one of the servers temporarily breaks down for whatever reason.

Several packages are available to perform load balancing, and some web services even offer their own solution, such as nginx with its proxy module, but the flexibility that IPVS has to offer with its vast set of balancing schedules makes it a very good choice indeed. Also, it can be considered an all-in-one load balancing solution, as the same approach can be used to load balance any other hosted service.

Of course, implementing load balancing is a great concept, but in order to make it successful you need to ensure that your web servers are also running in an optimal state. By reconfiguring the software—be it Apache HTTP, nginx, or any other web service application—you can generally speed up the service drastically. This is, therefore, a good place to start.

CHAPTER 9

Load Balancing Your Database

The previous chapter looked at load balancing the servers hosting your web site using nginx and the Apache HTTP server. We explained that while nginx is a high-performance web server for mostly static data, Apache HTTP is more efficient for handling dynamic data such as PHP pages. Today, the vast majority of web sites contain dynamically generated data—data that is stored on one or more databases. This data is then used to automatically generate one or more web pages whenever visited, without manual intervention. Indeed, it's clear to see why databases play a crucial role on today's World Wide Web.

In this chapter you'll be looking at load balancing your database. More specifically, you'll look at setting up and load balancing with MySQL Cluster. MySQL Cluster is an open source, high-performance, transactional database product that can be scaled linearly to match the needs of any service without having a single point of failure. MySQL Cluster can be obtained from `www.mysql.com/products/cluster/` and is maintained by the same team that brought us the more commonly known MySQL Server. As it is designed for high performance and fault tolerance, any data saved to one data node is automatically replicated and stored to the other data node(s) available, making it a network database (NDB). At the front end, the well-known MySQL Server is used for handling any SQL queries; it communicates to the NDB storage engine provided by MySQL Cluster that then requests the cluster's data nodes to process the queries and return the results to the MySQL server that first sent the request.

After you've set up MySQL Cluster, you will apply load balancing features to its MySQL Server nodes to ensure incoming connections will be equally distributed so that no one server will be overloaded with read/write operations. Finally, you'll test the setup by adding some data into your table and confirm that the incoming connections will be equally distributed.

Setting up the MySQL Cluster

Before you get started on applying load balancing to your servers and setting up the MySQL Cluster, let's look at your requirements for this setup. As mentioned, a MySQL Cluster will depend on several nodes working together: one or more cluster management nodes to manage, configure, and oversee your cluster, one (though commonly several) data nodes on which to store your data, and one or more MySQL nodes (traditional MySQL servers) that execute SQL queries.

In the presented setup, you will strip the required number of servers down to a total of three: one cluster management node also acting as your load balancer and two data nodes that will also be running the MySQL Server software. For now, you'll leave the load balancer out of the equation; however, you will set this up later in this chapter. An overview of your setup can be seen in Figure 9-1.

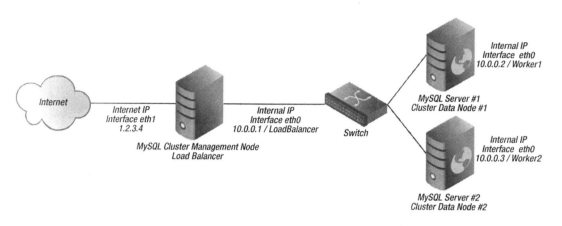

Figure 9-1. An overview of the setup

Your cluster management server, given the hostname LoadBalancer, will be responsible for running the cluster management server daemon. This process is responsible for distributing the cluster's configuration file to the data nodes in the cluster, starting and stopping data nodes, making backups, and monitoring the status of your cluster. For this, two processes will be used: ndb_mgmd (the cluster management server daemon) and ndb_mgm (the cluster management client).

As you will be performing load balancing on this server later on, the server is required to have two network interface cards (NICs). You will use eth0 as your Internet-facing network adapter (with a public IP address of 1.2.3.4), and eth1 to connect to your VLAN with a private IP address of 10.0.0.1. To prevent the IP address from constantly changing, it is recommended to manually configure the IP address for eth1, rather than obtaining an IP address using DHCP. To do this, you will use ifconfig with the following parameters to set eth1 up on your cluster management node:

```
LoadBalancer# ifconfig eth1 10.0.0.1 up
```

To confirm the changes were applied successfully, run ifconfig again.

```
LoadBalancer# ifconfig eth1
eth0      Link encap:Ethernet  HWaddr 00:1c:23:50:c4:d1
          inet addr:10.0.0.1  Bcast:10.0.0.255  Mask:255.255.255.0
          inet6 addr: fe80::21c:23ff:fe50:c4d1/64 Scope:Link
          UP BROADCAST RUNNING MULTICAST  MTU:1500  Metric:1
          RX packets:359593 errors:0 dropped:0 overruns:0 frame:0
          TX packets:628790 errors:0 dropped:0 overruns:0 carrier:0
          collisions:0 txqueuelen:1000
          RX bytes:53678741 (53.6 MB)  TX bytes:52946581 (52.9 MB)
          Interrupt:17
```

At this stage, you want to configure your other nodes to also be on the same subnet. As your other nodes don't require to be facing the Internet directly, these will only require one network interface card, and as such will be given a private IP address on their eth0 adapter.

```
Worker1# ifconfig eth0 10.0.0.2 up
Worker2# ifconfig eth0 10.0.0.3 up
```

For now, this is all you need to do on the worker nodes, so you can leave these alone for the time being. Once you've checked (using ping) that each node is successfully connected to your VLAN and can communicate with the others, you can proceed to install the actual cluster management software.

Installing the Management Software

The installation of the MySQL Cluster management software is much simpler than one might suspect. As mentioned, the MySQL Cluster manager needs only two binaries (or applications) in order to operate: the cluster management server daemon and the cluster management server client. Other than this, you will also be creating one configuration file that you will use to tell the daemon which data nodes and SQL servers to accept incoming connections from.

To start off, you will need to obtain a copy of the MySQL Cluster software. This can be downloaded free of charge from the aforementioned MySQL Developers' web site (www.mysql.com/downloads/cluster/) for platforms varying from Microsoft's Windows to Mac OS to Solaris. For this example, the generic 32-bit Linux version will be downloaded (Linux – Generic), which is currently at version 7.1.15 and around 223MB.

Note MySQL Cluster differs from the regular MySQL Server that is commonly installed. MySQL Cluster is a version that uses the NDBCLUSTER storage engine, allowing several MySQL Servers to run as a single cluster to form a high-availability and high-redundancy network database.

To download, use the command-line utility called wget or any web browser of choice.

```
# wget http://www.mysql.com/get/Downloads/MySQL-Cluster-7.1/mysql-cluster-gpl-7.1.15-linux-
i686-glibc23.tar.gz
```

Once downloaded, the archive can be extracted using tar on the command-line or a tar utility providing a graphical interface, such as TAR GUI. In this example, the command-line utility will be used as it comes pre-installed on most Linux distributions:

```
# tar xzf mysql-cluster-gpl-7.1.15-linux-i686-glibc23.tar.gz
```

Once the package is fully extracted, the result will be a directory named similarly to the archive. For the cluster management server you merely require two binaries. Other than these files, you don't need to install or copy anything else. To move the binary files that you require, you can use the mv command and specify the file names and their final destination, which will be the system's /usr/bin directory.

```
# cd mysql-cluster-gpl-7.1.15-linux-i686-glibc23
# mv bin/ndb_mgm /usr/local/bin/
# mv bin/ndb_mgmd /usr/local/bin/
```

After the files have been moved, you need to ensure they can be executed by changing their file modes using chmod's +x parameter.

```
# chmod +x /usr/local/bin/ndb_mg*
```

Configuring the Management Software

Now that the binaries are in place, you can proceed to configure your cluster and define how it will look using merely one configuration file on your cluster manager (hostname LoadBalancer). The file that you will be writing your cluster's global configuration settings in will be called config.ini and will be placed in the /var/lib/mysql-cluster directory. As you've downloaded the binaries yourself, however, rather than having used packet management software such as apt-get or yum, you will need to create this folder using the mkdir command. You will also create the /usr/local/mysql directory at the same time, as the cluster management software will be storing its configuration cache there later.

```
# mkdir /var/lib/mysql-cluster
# mkdir /usr/local/mysql/
```

Once the directories have been created, you can proceed with setting up your cluster's global configuration file, config.ini, using your favorite text editor (vim, nano, etc.).

```
# nano /var/lib/mysql-cluster/config.ini
```

There are several sections that you'll need to add to the configuration file. The first section you'll add is called [NDBD] and is used to define each data node and its individual settings, such as hostname or IP address, data memory size, and index memory size. However, as there are some settings that you wish to apply to each data node belonging to your cluster, you will add the word DEFAULT to the section name. By doing so, the settings listed will be applied to each [NDBD] section automatically, without needing to specify them again.

```
[NDBD DEFAULT]
DataMemory=512M
IndexMemory=18M
NoOfReplicas=2
```

The DataMemory parameter is used to specify the total amount of storage used (in megabytes) in the data node's memory for storing database records and indexes. This is set to 80MB by default, accepts a minimum of 1MB, and has no theoretical upper limit. The upper limit has to be set according to the system's total amount of memory available. The IndexMemory parameter is used to specify the total amount of storage available to the system for storing its hash indexes. The NoOfReplicas parameter is one of the few mandatory parameters in the configuration file and is used to define the total number of replicas available for each table stored in your cluster. This parameter must always be set under the [NDBD DEFAULT] section, even if nothing else is written there.

The next section you'll be adding is the [MYSQLD] section. This section is used to define the behavior of your cluster's MySQL servers. None of the parameters within this section are mandatory, however, and thus the section can be left blank so that the default settings will be used. Similar to the [NDBD] section, you will add the word DEFAULT to indicate these settings are the default to all your MySQL nodes connected, so you don't need to define them again on each individual node.

```
[MYSQLD DEFAULT]
```

You will add one more DEFAULT section to your cluster's configuration file. This is the NDB_MGMD section. The NDB_MGMD section is used to specify the cluster's management servers' behavior. For example, you can specify the port number of the cluster management node using the PortNumber parameter or specify where the cluster will log its information using the LogDestination parameter. As you want all your cluster management nodes to use the default settings unless otherwise specified, the word DEFAULT will be added to the section's name.

```
[NDB_MGMD DEFAULT]
```

Next, you will add the individual settings for each of your cluster's management nodes. As you only have one in this example, the section only needs to be specified once. If you had several nodes that you used for cluster management, you would need to add one section for each.

```
[NDB_MGMD]
HostName=10.0.0.1
```

Using the HostName parameter, you will specify your cluster management server's IP address or hostname. In this case, it will be the IP address of the current machine (LoadBalancer) that you're working on.

Moving on, you'll add an additional section called [NDBD] for each individual data node your cluster contains. Most of the options specified here can also be specified under the [NDBD DEFAULT] section or omitted to use the software's default values. If you want, you can also add parameters here to overwrite those specified in the [NDBD DEFAULT] section.

```
[NDBD]
HostName=10.0.0.2
DataDir=/var/lib/mysql-cluster
```

```
[NDBD]
HostName=10.0.0.3
DataDir=/var/lib/mysql-cluster
DataMemory=1024M
```

The parameters and their values should be self-explanatory: using the HostName parameter you can specify either the hostname or IP address of your data node, and using the DataDir parameter you can specify where the data node should place any output files from the management server, such as cluster log files (unless otherwise specified using the LogDestination parameter under the [NDB_MGM] section), process output files, and the daemon's process ID file.

Finally, you will specify the [MYSQLD] section to open up a "slot" for each MySQL server available to your cluster. The MySQL servers will be used to establish connections and perform queries on your database, so it's crucial that you open up the right number of slots for the number of MySQL servers you have. In your example, you have two such MySQL Servers available (also running on your cluster's data nodes), so you will want to add the section twice without specifying any parameters.

```
[MYSQLD]
[MYSQLD]
```

Once the sections and their appropriate parameters have been defined, you can save and close your text editor to end up with the configuration file shown in Listing 9-1.

Listing 9-1. The Cluster Management Server's config.ini File

```
[NDBD DEFAULT]
DataMemory=512M
IndexMemory=18M
NoOfReplicas=2

[MYSQLD DEFAULT]
[NDB_MGMD DEFAULT]
```

```
[NDB_MGMD]
HostName=10.0.0.1

[NDBD]
HostName=10.0.0.2
DataDir=/var/lib/mysql-cluster

[NDBD]
HostName=10.0.0.3
DataDir=/var/lib/mysql-cluster
DataMemory=1024M

[MYSQLD]
[MYSQLD]
```

Now that you've installed the cluster management server's binaries and have prepared its configuration file, you can start the cluster management server daemon by executing the **ndb_mgmd** command. The first time you execute the daemon you will need to specify the **--initial** flag, ensuring the configuration data from the **config.ini** file will be reloaded and bypassing any configuration cache already known to the daemon. You will also need to specify the **-f** flag to specify your configuration file's name and location.

```
# /usr/local/bin/ndb_mgmd -f /var/lib/mysql-cluster/config.ini --initial
MySQL Cluster Management Server mysql-5.1.56 ndb-7.1.15
```

That's all you need to do for now on your cluster management server. Next, you'll look at setting up your cluster's data nodes.

Preparing the Cluster's Data Nodes

Now that the cluster management server is running and waiting for incoming connections from your data nodes, you'll have a look at setting these up next. The process involves several steps. First, you prepare the server by adding a specific user and group for MySQL, create a directory, and set the permissions straight. Then you'll install the data node software as well as the MySQL Server software (as they will both be running on the same servers), configure the data nodes to connect them to the cluster, and finally ensure all is working well by making some test connections.

Note You may require to install glibc on all of your cluster's data nodes if not already available.

Before you install any of the MySQL Cluster software, you'll create the appropriate directories on your servers and ensure that MySQL can be executed using a separate user account called mysql for security reasons. The user will also be a member of the group called mysql which you'll also create using the groupadd function.

```
# groupadd mysql
```

Once the usergroup has been created, you proceed by creating your user called mysql, making it a member of the usergroup mysql previously created.

```
# useradd -r -g mysql mysql
```

■ **Note**   All the steps shown here should be executed on all data and MySQL server nodes available to your cluster.

Now, you can create the directory where your cluster management server will be writing its output files. Note this directory will need to match the location set on the cluster management server's `config.ini` file.

```
# mkdir /var/lib/mysql-cluster
```

Once created, you'll change the directory's permissions so that the mysql user previously created can write data to it using the `chown` command.

```
# chown root:mysql /var/lib/mysql-cluster/
```

Installing the MySQL Server and NDB Daemon

Once your data nodes are prepared you can continue to download and install the required software on them. The software package required for these nodes is identical to the one used on your cluster management server, so it might not be necessary to redownload it from the MySQL web site.

First, you extract the package using the `tar` command in a shell or by using a graphical interface, such as TAR GUI. The command line syntax is as follows:

```
# tar xzf mysql-cluster-gpl-7.1.15-linux-i686-glibc23.tar.gz
```

When extracted, you will move the entire directory to your system's `/usr/local` directory, used to store your system's local applications. Again, you need to ensure this is done on all data and MySQL nodes available to your cluster.

```
# mv mysql-cluster-gpl-7.1.15-linux-i686-glibc23 /usr/local/
```

After the directory has been moved to the `/usr/local` directory, you'll create a link to the `/usr/local/mysql` directory for faster access. For this, the `ln` command can be used using the `-s` parameter to specify the link should be a symbolic one. Optionally, you can also rename the folder, but as this would remove the version information available in the folder's name, creating a symbolic link is preferable.

```
# ln -s /usr/local/mysql-cluster-gpl-7.1.15-linux-i686-glibc23/ /usr/local/mysql
```

Once done, you can start the MySQL installation script from the `/usr/local/mysql` directory, which will generate new MySQL privilege tables and initialize the MySQL data directory used by the MySQL server application (mysqld) later on. Additionally, you'll specify the `--user` parameter to ensure any files and directories created by mysqld will be owned by the specified user. In your case, you'll specify the user mysql that was previously created.

```
# cd /usr/local/mysql
# scripts/mysql_install_db --user=mysql
Installing MySQL system tables...
OK
Filling help tables...
OK
```

After the installation script has finished setting up the system tables, you'll modify the permissions of the MySQL directory (/usr/local/mysql) to ensure the newly created mysql user and group can write to it, using chown -R, specifying all subdirectories should also be adjusted accordingly.

```
# chown -R root:mysql /usr/local/mysql
# chown -R mysql /usr/local/mysql/data
```

Now, you can proceed with adding MySQL's binary directory (/usr/local/mysql/bin) to your system's $PATH variable, so you can execute the commands provided by MySQL without needing to specify the full filepath. In order to do this, you first need to know what your current $PATH variable is set to, so use the echo command.

```
# echo $PATH
/usr/local/sbin:/usr/local/bin:/usr/sbin:/usr/bin:/sbin:/bin:/usr/games
```

Next, copy the information printed by echo; then add a colon and MySQL's binary directory (/usr/local/mysql/bin). Use the export command to update the system variable.

```
# export
PATH="/usr/local/sbin:/usr/local/bin:/usr/sbin:/usr/bin:/sbin:/bin:/usr/games:/usr/local/mysql
/bin"
```

That's it! You're done with the installation of the MySQL Server and data node software, so you can proceed to configure the settings for MySQL and the data nodes.

Configuring the NDB Daemon

Now that the MySQL Server and MySQL Cluster data node software is installed and available on your system, you can proceed with the data node's configuration to ensure it will become part of the MySQL cluster. To configure your data node, all you need to do is create the system's /etc/my.cnf file using a text editor, adding the following content:

```
[MYSQLD]
ndbcluster
ndb-connectstring=10.0.0.1

[MYSQL_CLUSTER]
ndb-connectstring=10.0.0.1
```

The first section titled [MYSQLD] will be used to enable the ndbcluster storage engine, followed by your cluster management server's IP address specified under the ndb-connectstring parameter. In the second section titled [mysql_cluster], you will specify the IP address of your cluster management server once more, for settings to be read and used by all MySQL Cluster executables available on this node.

Once done, save the file (/etc/my.cnf) and close the text editor. Everything has now been configured, and you're almost ready to start using MySQL Cluster.

Starting the Cluster Node's Services

Before you can start your services, you need to do just one more thing: add a start/stop script for your new services to the system's /etc/init.d directory. For MySQL Server, the script has been pre-built and is included in the download package under support-files/mysql.server, which you can simply copy to your /etc/init.d directory as such:

```
# cp /usr/local/mysql/support-files/mysql.server /etc/init.d/
```

Once copied, you'll need to change the script's file mode bits to ensure it can be executed using chmod's +x option:

```
# chmod +x /etc/init.d/mysql.server
```

Next, you'll execute the update-rc.d command to ensure your startup script is also executed at system startup. You'll specify the script's name, followed by the defaults option, to ensure the script is executed in runlevel 2, 3, 4, and 5. In Debian, you use the update-rc.d function to accomplish this.

```
# update-rc.d mysql.server defaults
 Adding system startup for /etc/init.d/mysql.server ...
   /etc/rc0.d/K20mysql.server -> ../init.d/mysql.server
   /etc/rc1.d/K20mysql.server -> ../init.d/mysql.server
   /etc/rc6.d/K20mysql.server -> ../init.d/mysql.server
   /etc/rc2.d/S20mysql.server -> ../init.d/mysql.server
   /etc/rc3.d/S20mysql.server -> ../init.d/mysql.server
   /etc/rc4.d/S20mysql.server -> ../init.d/mysql.server
   /etc/rc5.d/S20mysql.server -> ../init.d/mysql.server
```

■ **Note** When running a Red Hat-based distribution, chkconfig --add mysql.server can be used instead.

Next, you'll do the same for your NDBD service; your cluster data node's daemon is used to handle all the data in your tables using the NDB Cluster storage engine. For this, however, there is no out-of-the-box script available that you can copy, so you'll need to create it yourself. This can be very easily done by creating a new file in the /etc/init.d directory and writing the application's name in it. For this, you'll use the echo command.

```
# echo '/usr/local/mysql/bin/ndbd' > /etc/init.d/ndbd
```

As you did with the mysql.server script, you'll change this script's file mode bits, also ensuring it can be executed, and add it to the system's startup list using the update-rc.d command on Debian-based distributions.

```
# chmod +x /etc/init.d/ndbd
# update-rc.d ndbd defaults
Adding system startup for /etc/init.d/ndbd ...
   /etc/rc0.d/K20ndbd -> ../init.d/ndbd
   /etc/rc1.d/K20ndbd -> ../init.d/ndbd
   /etc/rc6.d/K20ndbd -> ../init.d/ndbd
   /etc/rc2.d/S20ndbd -> ../init.d/ndbd
   /etc/rc3.d/S20ndbd -> ../init.d/ndbd
```

```
/etc/rc4.d/S20ndbd -> ../init.d/ndbd
/etc/rc5.d/S20ndbd -> ../init.d/ndbd
```

> **Note** This particular step doesn't work on Red Hat-based distributions. For these you need to use a third-party script instead.

Once everything is fully in place, you can initialize your services and start using them. Starting the MySQL Server as well as the NDBD service can be done using the scripts added to the /etc/init.d directory earlier. First, start the MySQL service.

```
# /etc/init.d/mysql.server start
Starting MySQL
... *
```

When MySQL has started, you can proceed to initialize the NDB daemon on your cluster data nodes using the /etc/init.d/ndbd script also. For the NDB daemon you'll need to specify the --initial option to perform an initial startup, which will clean up any recovery files available from previous instances of the application and recreate logfiles.

```
# /etc/init.d/ndbd --initial
2011-08-08 12:16:59 [ndbd] INFO      -- Angel connected to '10.0.0.1:1186'
2011-08-08 12:16:59 [ndbd] INFO      -- Angel allocated nodeid: 3
```

> **Warning** When ndbd is unable to connect, ensure the worker's firewall is adjusted accordingly.

Updating MySQL's Root User

Now that all your services have been started, the first thing you'd want to do is change your MySQL Server's root user password on both servers, which currently is still blank. Then you'll want to ensure the root user can also connect to these servers from your load balancer, which isn't permitted by default.

To modify your root user's password, you can use the mysqladmin client software, which allows you to perform various kinds of administrative operations to your MySQL Server(s). For example, you can use it to create and delete (or "drop") databases, view the server's status, shut down the system, and so forth. In order for you to change the password on each server, the following command can be used (where newpassword represents the root user's new password):

```
# mysqladmin -u root password newpassword
```

When done, you can use the mysql client software to connect to your local database using the root user with the new password set and update its access settings using the **grant** command:

```
# mysql -u root -p
Enter password:

mysql> use mysql;
mysql> grant all on * to root@'10.0.0.1' identified by 'newpassword';
Query OK, 0 rows affected (0.00 sec)
```

Once done, quit the MySQL console using the quit; command, which will bring you back to the server's console.

```
mysql> quit;
Bye

#
```

___

■ **Warning** Be sure that each MySQL Server contains a user account with an identical username and password to ensure incoming connections can be established to each server successfully.

___

Testing the Installation

Now that you've set up your MySQL Cluster, it's time to test if it all works! The simplest way to do so is to go back to your cluster management server and use the ndb_mgm tool that you installed previously; it allows you to oversee exactly how your cluster is doing, start backups, and perform other administrative tasks. To execute, type ndb_mgm on the shell, which will open up a command-line interface that you can use to execute further commands.

```
# /usr/local/bin/ndb_mgm
-- NDB Cluster -- Management Client --
ndb_mgm>
```

Once there, you can use the show; command to see the nodes currently connected to your cluster. In the following output, you will see that one of your worker nodes (10.0.0.2) is connected (both the network database daemon as the MySQL server) while the other one is stopped for demonstration purposes (10.0.0.3).

```
ndb_mgm> show;
Cluster Configuration
---------------------
[ndbd(NDB)]     2 node(s)
id=2    @10.0.0.2  (mysql-5.1.56 ndb-7.1.15, Nodegroup: 0, Master)
id=3 (not connected, accepting connect from 10.0.0.3)

[ndb_mgmd(MGM)] 1 node(s)
id=1    @10.0.0.1 (mysql-5.1.56 ndb-7.1.15)

[mysqld(API)]   2 node(s)
id=4    @10.0.0.2  (mysql-5.1.56 ndb-7.1.15)
id=5 (not connected, accepting connect from any host)
```

Finally, add some data to your database using one of the MySQL servers (Worker1) to see if the data is indeed instantly replicated across all data nodes available to the cluster. For this example, you'll first create a database named PLB on your cluster, which will contain a table named test, and insert an integer value in it. (We won't go too much into detail on the SQL itself, as that lies outside the scope of this book.)

First, connect to your database using the root user without specifying any database name.

```
root@Worker1:/# mysql -u root -p
Enter password:
Welcome to the MySQL monitor.  Commands end with ; or \g.
Your MySQL connection id is 2
Server version: 5.1.56-ndb-7.1.15-cluster-gpl MySQL Cluster Server (GPL)

Copyright (c) 2000, 2010, Oracle and/or its affiliates. All rights reserved.
This software comes with ABSOLUTELY NO WARRANTY. This is free software,
and you are welcome to modify and redistribute it under the GPL v2 license

Type 'help;' or '\h' for help. Type '\c' to clear the current input statement.
```

Once connected, you'll create the database using the create database command, followed by the name of your database.

```
mysql> create database PLB;
Query OK, 1 row affected (0.04 sec)
```

After the database has been created, you will switch to the PLB database via the use command and create a new table called test, which will store integer values in its rows. Note that you will need to specify the engine type used when creating the table by adding ENGINE=NDBCLUSTER to your query if you wish to ensure the table is replicated in your cluster.

```
mysql> use PLB;
Database changed
mysql> create table test (number INT) ENGINE=NDBCLUSTER;
Query OK, 0 rows affected (0.67 sec)
```

Finally, add a row into your test table using the insert command, after which the select function can be used to confirm the data was added as expected on this node.

```
mysql> insert into test () values (100);
Query OK, 1 row affected (0.01 sec)

mysql> select * from test;
+----------+
| number |
+----------+
|    100   |
+----------+
1 row in set (0.00 sec)

mysql>
```

You've now added one record to your PLB database using the MySQL Server running on Worker1 and verified the data was available from that node. Now let's have a look at your cluster's database using Worker2 to confirm if indeed the data inserted was automatically replicated there also. You'll use the same syntax to open a connection to the MySQL server; from there it will search for the record immediately using the select command.

```
root@Worker2:/# mysql -u root -p
Enter password:
Welcome to the MySQL monitor.  Commands end with ; or \g.
Your MySQL connection id is 26
Server version: 5.1.56-ndb-7.1.15-cluster-gpl MySQL Cluster Server (GPL)

mysql> use PLB;
Database changed

mysql> select * from test;
+---------+
| number |
+---------+
|   100   |
+---------+
1 row in set (0.00 sec)

mysql>
```

As you can see, your data is readily available to your second cluster data node also. You've successfully set up your MySQL Cluster!

Applying Load Balancing

Now that you've successfully set up your MySQL Cluster, it's time to do a little load balancing! At this stage, any incoming connections will still need to be established to one of your MySQL servers (Worker1 or Worker2). As you can imagine, this can easily go wrong. What if one of your MySQL servers breaks down? Or even worse, what if Worker1 is fully booked performing all sorts of queries on your database, and Worker2 is just idling there if none of the applications you've told to connect to that database are actually being used?

This is where your load balancer comes in handy. By setting up your load balancer on one of your Internet-facing servers (LoadBalancer in this case), you will ensure that incoming connections made by any application (such as web servers) will be established to the load balancing server rather than one of the MySQL servers directly. Next, the load balancer will look at the number of open connections on your MySQL servers (Worker1 and Worker2) and route the connection onwards to the server best fit for the job at that moment.

At the same time, if one of the MySQL servers shuts down unexpectedly, there is no need to worry about any data loss either: you've previously set up your MySQL cluster, which automatically ensures that all data is replicated and available on each cluster data node; therefore, even when your MySQL server runs on the same server as your data cluster node, there is nothing to worry about.

Note   In larger environments, it is likely that more than three servers should be used, and it is a best practice to separate the MySQL server from the cluster data node. In this setup, the two of them are combined on a single host to reduce the number of servers to a minimum.

The Setup

As described earlier in this chapter, you'll be using three servers for your setup: two cluster data nodes named Worker1 and Worker2 (also running the MySQL Server software) and one cluster management server that will also be used as your load balancer. Your load balancer (named LoadBalancer) will have two network interface cards (NICs), with eth0 connected to the Internet (IP address 1.2.3.4) for public accessibility (if desired) and eth1 connected to your internal VLAN with the IP address 10.0.0.1. An overview of the setup can be seen in Figure 9-1.

The load balancer package that you'll be using for this set up is called IPVS. IPVS, short for Internet Protocol Virtual Server, can be used to implement transport-layer load balancing inside the Linux kernel, so that incoming requests can be forwarded to your MySQL servers running at the back end. You'll ensure that IPVS uses the weighted least connections (wlc) schedule, which ensures incoming connections are distributed to those servers handling the least connections at that moment. There are several other schedules IPVS can use to distribute the load towards the servers, varying from a round robin schedule to a locality-based least connection schedule. More in-depth details on IPVS can be found in Chapter 10.

There is no need to install any other software on your load balancer; in fact, there is no need to install any other software at all! Your MySQL servers (also referred to as "workers" where the load balancer is also referred to as the "director") will only require their routing table to be updated to ensure any traffic sent back will go through your load balancer.

Setting up the Load Balancer

Now that you know what your setup will look like, continue setting up your load balancer. First, you'll make some basic changes to your load balancer's configuration to ensure packets can be correctly forwarded to your workers. To do this, you'll need to modify your load balancer's **/etc/sysctl.conf** file. Using this file, you can configure various kinds of system and networking variables on your system. Open up the file in your favorite text editor (vim, nano, etc.) and search for the following line of text:

```
#net.ipv4.ip_forward=1
```

Once found, uncomment the line by removing the hash (#) symbol in front of it to enable packet forwarding, after which you can save the file and close the text editor.

```
net.ipv4.ip_forward=1
```

Next, you'll need to run **sysctl -p** on your command line to ensure your modified kernel parameters will be read from the configuration file. When executed, you will also see the modification you've made earlier.

```
# sysctl -p
net.ipv4.ip_forward = 1
```

After this, you'll also need to modify your load balancer's /proc/sys/net/ipv4/ip_forward file to enable IP forwarding. The file will only need to contain the value 1, and as such you'll be using the echo command for this on the command line. Optionally, you can open the file with a text editor and make the modifications accordingly.

```
# echo 1 > /proc/sys/net/ipv4/ip_forward
```

Now you're ready to install the load balancing software, IPVS. Depending on the distribution of Linux, IPVS can be installed using its package management software, such as apt-get on Debian-flavored distributions or yum for Red Hat-flavored distributions. For example,

```
# apt-get install ipvsadm
# yum install ipvsadm
```

The ipvsadm package should now be installed, and you can use it to configure, maintain, and inspect the kernel's virtual server table that you'll use to perform the load balancing. For a more in-depth explanation on IPVS' workings, please refer to Chapter 10. Once installed, you will need to configure IPVS to ensure it has started on system bootup and a few other things. To do so, use the dpkg --reconfigure package on Debian, specifying the application's name.

```
# dpkg --reconfigure ipvsadm
```

Once started, the package configuration tool will ask a set of questions, which need to be answered accordingly to ensure that IPVS is started at system bootup, that the load balancer will act as a master server, and that it will listen for incoming connections on eth0.

```
Do you want to automatically load IPVS rules on boot? [Yes]
Daemon method: [master]
Multicast interface for ipvsadm: [eth0]
```

In order to do achieve the same in Red Hat-flavored distributions, use the ipvsadm command.

```
# ipvsadm --start-daemon=master --mcast-interface=eth0
```

When done, the reconfiguration will close, and you can get started on configuring your load balancer using the ipvsadm command. When executing the ipvsadm command without specifying any parameters, you can view the current IPVS table, which should still be empty at this stage.

```
# ipvsadm
IP Virtual Server version 1.2.1 (size=4096)
Prot LocalAddress:Port Scheduler Flags
  -> RemoteAddress:Port           Forward Weight ActiveConn InActConn
```

To add your virtual service to IPVS, use the -A parameter, followed by the -t parameter to indicate a TCP service, and finally the IP address and port where incoming connections will be received on, which will be 1.2.3.4:3306.

```
# ipvsadm -A -t 1.2.3.4:3306
```

Once the virtual service is created, you can add your workers to it using the same ipvsadm tool, followed by a set of additional parameters. Recall that the IP addresses specified here need to match the (internal) IP addresses of the actual MySQL servers you've got running on your cluster. In this example, these are 10.0.0.2 for the MySQL Server running on Worker1 and 10.0.0.3 running on Worker2. To add each worker, use the -a option to add the entry to your table; followed by the -t option to specify that it involves a TCP service; followed by the external IP address and port of your load balancer as previously specified (1.2.3.4:3306); then the -r option to specify the worker's IP address and port number; and finally the -m option to use NAT (network address translation).

```
# ipvsadm -a -t 1.2.3.4:3306 -r 10.0.0.2:3306 -m
# ipvsadm -a -t 1.2.3.4:3306 -r 10.0.0.3:3306 -m
```

When finished, you can verify if the workers were added successfully by viewing the IPVS table by running the ipvsadm command without any additional parameters. This will also tell you the current number of active connections on each worker under the ActiveConn field.

```
# ipvsadm
IP Virtual Server version 1.2.1 (size=4096)
Prot      LocalAddress:Port       Scheduler     Flags
  ->        RemoteAddress:Port                       Forward Weight ActiveConn InActConn
TCP     1.2.3.4:mysql             wlc
  ->        10.0.0.2:mysql                           Masq    1       0          0
  ->        10.0.0.3:mysql                           Masq    1       0          0
```

Preparing the Workers

Now that you've successfully set up your load balancer, you can proceed with setting up your workers, or MySQL servers. Admittedly, there is little to be done to the MySQL servers in order to apply load balancing to them. They are already operational and happily accepting any incoming requests to their MySQL service. All you need to do is to ensure your outgoing connections will be made via your load balancer.

To do so, you will need to modify the workers' routing tables by using the route command and tell the system that your load balancer should be used as the default gateway for outbound connections. On each node, execute the following command:

```
# route add default gw 10.0.0.1 eth0
```

To verify the route was added successfully, the route command can be executed on each node to get an overview of the known routes to the system.

```
# route
Kernel IP routing table
Destination     Gateway         Genmask         Flags Metric Ref    Use Iface
10.0.0.0        *               255.0.0.0       U     0      0        0 eth0
default         10.0.0.1        0.0.0.0         UG    0      0        0 eth0
```

That's all you need to do! Your load balancer is now operational.

Testing the Load Balancer

Finally, let's make a small test to confirm your incoming SQL connections are indeed balanced across your workers. To do so, you can establish a connection to your cluster via another separate host on the subnet using the mysqladmin package or telnet. At the same time, you'll use the watch command to monitor your load balancer and ensure the data is updated every second.

```
# watch -n 1 ipvsadm
```

```
Every 1.0s: ipvsadm
IP Virtual Server version 1.2.1 (size=4096)
Prot      LocalAddress:Port       Scheduler     Flags
  ->        RemoteAddress:Port                       Forward Weight ActiveConn InActConn
```

```
TCP      1.2.3.4:mysql              wlc
  ->         10.0.0.2:mysql                        Masq    1     0        0
  ->         10.0.0.3:mysql                        Masq    1     0        0
```

Next, open up a terminal or command prompt on the host and run a simple script to request your MySQL server's status approximately ten times. When doing so, your load balancer ensures that five of the connections will be send to your first data node and the other five to the other. Keep in mind that the password needs to be set accordingly and that there is no space in between the -p option and the actual password.

```
# for i in {1..10}; do mysqladmin -u root -pnewpassword status -h 10.0.0.1; done
```

■ **Note** Be sure to allow incoming connections from the host's IP address, as otherwise the test will fail. This can be achieved by using MySQL's grant command.

Optionally you can use telnet to connect to the Load Balancer's MySQL port, 3306, from another host on the subnet. This connection will then be forwarded to one of the workers.

```
# telnet 10.0.0.1 3306
Trying 10.0.0.1…
Connected to 10.0.0.1.
Escape character is '^]'.
```

To see if your test went well, you need to switch back to the terminal where ipvsadm is running; you should now be able to see your servers handling five connections each.

```
Every 1.0s: ipvsadm
IP Virtual Server version 1.2.1 (size=4096)
Prot     LocalAddress:Port       Scheduler     Flags
  ->         RemoteAddress:Port                       Forward Weight ActiveConn InActConn
TCP      1.2.3.4:mysql              wlc
  ->         10.0.0.2:mysql                        Masq    1     0        5
  ->         10.0.0.3:mysql                        Masq    1     0        5
```

Your MySQL cluster is now fully operational, and incoming connections are being equally distributed to your MySQL servers using IPVS.

Summary

This chapter showed you how to set up and configure a very powerful database software package: MySQL Cluster. Each MySQL cluster consists of several parts: a cluster management node, a set of data nodes, and a set of MySQL servers. After setting up the MySQL cluster, you confirmed that any data added to one data node gets automatically replicated to the other node(s) available in your cluster, making it a high-availability package indeed.

After the MySQL cluster was set up, you looked at how to apply load balancing to the cluster's MySQL servers using IPVS to ensure not only one server would be fully loaded handling all connections; rather, thanks to IPVS, every incoming connection will be equally distributed across your MySQL servers, thereby providing a high-performance setup.

The next chapter focuses on network load balancing and provides a more detailed look at IPVS' capabilities and options.

CHAPTER 10

Network Load Balancing

This chapter will cover the concepts involved with network load balancing. Network load balancing involves spreading the load of processing a web site out over multiple servers in a network. After this chapter you should be familiar with

- TCP/IP

- Basic routing

- Basic network connectivity testing

- Installation and administration of the IPVS application

- Common task scheduling methods, their advantages, disadvantages, and uses

Sharing the Workload

So, you have configured your servers and set up load balancing on your HTTP web servers and your database. You can connect to your web server and you can see the loads increasing on both the server and the database. Your servers are live but occasionally you load your web site and it's slow. Yes, the load optimization you have performed is working. The issue is not with your software—it's your hardware! Having balanced your HTTP servers and your databases, you have set up your system to function well but it's still not enough.

It's time to add new hardware.

New hardware means another server to share the load with your existing server, to share the work. The problem is how do you share this workload? How do you tell one server to take a connection while the other doesn't? To understand, it's best to start looking at the process of a user connection as a whole. The process flows like this:

- A user sends a connection to your server.

- The load balancer receives the connection and then fires another connection to the appropriate HTTP server.

- The HTTP server processes this request.

- If needed, the server connects to the database.

- If connected, the database responds.

- The HTTP server forms a response.

- The response is sent out to the initial recipient.

Looking at these steps, you can see what you have and have not load balanced. In this instance, you have modified the HTTP connections and the database connections to spread the system load.

This leaves you with two portions of the connection left to be balanced: the user's connection in and the data transmission out that need to be configured to share load. To do this, you will add another server to the mix to divvy up the work and efficiently organize who will be doing what. But before you add this server, you should look more deeply at the connections that are being made to your server so you can understand exactly what's going on when you start shuffling these connections around.

TCP/IP

TCP/IP refers to a pair of protocols that represent the most common stream of organized traffic over the Internet. In order to load balance data being transmitted by this protocol set, you should understand the two subprotocols that combine to form it.

TCP

Network load balancing (NLB) distributes network traffic across a number of servers to enhance scalability and availability of applications. For the purpose under discussion, NLB is about distributing the incoming connections that are made so that no single server of yours becomes overloaded. As part of load balancing any system, it is important to understand exactly what it is you are balancing. This means an investigation into the networking of the Internet!

Across the Internet all messages are broken up into tiny fragments called *packets*. This allows a much higher level of control over how the packets are transmitted and how they reach their destination; it also provides a very high level of redundancy. Moreover, since the Internet is so heavily diverse in the number of pathways it contains, having small packets instead of large ones allows for changes in the path a connection takes between a client and a server.

Imagine trying to send a file that will take three hours to send internationally over an Internet connection. Then imagine trying to send it in one big hit with no breaks. Add to that the risk that if any points of connection between you and your destination drop out, your entire connection is lost! You can see the advantages of using a method like packet switching.

However, packets are simply the way to fragment information to make it easier. What about managing these connections as a whole? The Internet uses many, many protocols for information sharing, but for HTTP web servers the connections use TCP (Transmission Control Protocol). TCP connections are the primary and most common connection established on the Internet.

TCP connections work like this:

- A client sends an initial message to a server requesting a connection.

- The server responds; the client and server perform a "handshake," which allows the client and server to set up the rules of their communication.

- Following the handshake, the client and server enter the data transmission state, where they transfer data between them.

The other primary protocol in use over the Internet is UDP (User Datagram Protocol).The primary difference between the two is that UDP is a stateless protocol, while TCP is a stateful protocol.

A *stateful* protocol is one that manages the state of the connection. In the case of TCP, this is the connection control performed via handshake and the connection controlled by these states. UDP is a *stateless* protocol, which has no handshaking and little (if any) control.

At this point, I imagine you are asking, "Why do we use TCP when it sounds like UDP is much faster?" Yes, UDP is so much faster; the problem is that the speed of UDP comes at a cost—one of accuracy. UDP transmissions have little control over their packets since there is no mechanism (state) to control how they are transmitted and track if they need to be retransmitted. TCP allows for all this because the parameters of the connection and how they are established during its handshake (as well as issues with even a single packet) are handled by the transmission of an error state message.

To put it into an analogy, TCP is akin to two people having a conversation and establishing that they have both understood what each other has said. Many questions are asked and answers given. UDP, on the other hand, is two people yelling at each other and simply hoping that the other person receives the message they are trying to convey.

Now that you understand TCP, you need to understand how servers are able to establish a destination for the packets and how these packets are able to traverse the Internet to this destination.

IP

The method used to establish and transmit TCP packets over the Internet is called IP. IP stands for Internet Protocol and is the standard protocol for providing addressing and transmission of traffic over the Internet to its intended destination; this is called *routing*. IP addresses are assigned to every device connected to a network, to every device attached to the Internet, and for Internet devices assigned by your ISP. As it stands today, there are two versions of IP running over the Internet, IPv4 and IPv6.

IPv4 is the primary Internet protocol, which due to its limit of 4,294,967,296 (2^{32}) addresses, is being phased out and replaced with IPv6, which has 2^{128} addresses. An IPV4 address takes the form of four sets of numbers from 0-255 separated by a period. Probably the most common IP address in the world is 127.0.0.1, which is automatically assigned to every Internet-capable device as a self-reference IP address. IP addresses represent a unique identifier for each Internet-enabled device and thus provide an easy way of addressing each device from the Internet.

So how we have not run out of addresses already, given that everyone seems to have a desktop at home, a desktop at work, a laptop, and an Internet-enabled phone—not to mention all the servers on the Internet? Surely that's more than the four billion addresses available under IPv4? Yes, that is correct; the world has been running out of IP addresses since the mid 1990s but it was seen as infeasible for four billion people to upgrade to IPv6 at once.

A stop-gap solution to this problem came in the form of a system called PAT (Port Address Translation). PAT is a form of Network Address Translation (NAT) and is often referred to as such allow one Internet-enabled device (commonly a router) to share its Internet connection among many hosts. It does this by creating an internal network of sorts that allows all the hosts within its internal network to share a slice of its Internet. It is this routing and the creation of an internal network, with one computer providing Internet access for another, that you will be employing to provide load balancing for your server!

Routing

Routing, as mentioned, is the method by which IP packets are able to be transmitted to their destination. In modern packet switched networks, such as the Internet, routing is performed by each device carrying a routing table, which carries a list of known ways to get to certain destinations—even if that destination is simply another hop down the trail on its journey.

It is important to be aware of routing and its implications when constructing a network—as you are now—but it's even more important when dealing with network load balancing, where packets need to be returned in a specific manner. For example, look at the default routing table on your web server using the route command.

```
root@Server1:~# route
Kernel IP routing table
Destination     Gateway         Genmask         Flags Metric Ref    Use Iface
178.250.53.0    *               255.255.255.0   U     0      0        0 eth0
192.168.1.0     *               255.255.255.0   U     0      0        0 eth1
default         178-250-53-254. 0.0.0.0         UG    100    0        0 eth0
```

In this case you can see that there are three known routes, the first two are for specific networks and the third is a default route (the one to take when no other route is available). The lines of the route table are broken down as such:

- The destination (be that a network, signified by a 0 on the end of the destination, or a single address)

- The gateway, which is the address to send this message

- The genmask, which represents the class of network

- Any special flags such as

    - U (route is up)

    - H (target is a host)

    - G (use gateway)

    - R (reinstate route for dynamic routing)

    - D (dynamically installed by daemon or redirect)

    - M (modified from routing daemon or redirect)

    - A (installed by addrconf)

    - C (cache entry)

    - ! (reject route)

- The metric, which signifies the cost in using that route (lower values means more efficient route). Metric values can be used to direct traffic more efficiently.

- The Ref value (which is no longer used by the Linux Kernel)

- The Use value, which is the number of times this route has been looked up

- The Iface, which states the interface that this traffic should be sent out from

As part of configuring the load balancing system you will need to modify the default routes of the web servers so that all traffic will be sent back via your load balancer. To do this, you need to create some entries in the routing table.

■ **Caution** Be warned! You can seriously change the way your system interacts with a network using the route command.

Before making any changes, be sure you make a copy of your existing working route table by entering the route command and copying the whole config. If you follow the instructions here and if you are using SSH to access and modify your server, you will need to SSH to it from your load balancing server, rather than access it directly.

Now that you've been thoroughly warned, let's continue.

The routing table is modified with the route command. The basic syntax is as follows:

```
root@Server1:~# route add default gw 192.168.1.4 eth1
```

In this command you are telling route to add a default route, then you set the gateway to 192.168.1.3, and you provide an interface for this connection, which is eth1. This command will make all traffic (other than that specified directly by other routes) be sent via 192.168.1.4, which is your web server. To remove a route, simply invoke the same command in delete mode with - route del.

```
root@Server1:~# route del default gw 192.168.1.4 eth1
```

These routes will not remain in your system beyond a reboot, so to keep them you need to add them in a more permanent manner. In Ubuntu, you create these permanent routes by modifying the file /etc/network/interfaces and add the word up, then the route command to the bottom of the file, like so:

```
root@Server1:~# up route add default gw 192.168.1.4 eth1
```

You might encounter permission issues when trying to edit the file. If this is the case, use the following command:

```
root@Server1:~# sudo nano /etc/network/interfaces.
```

You can test this by either rebooting your system or executing the following command (note: it will restart your networking, as its name implies):

```
root@Server1:~# /etc/init.d/networking restart
```

Then run route to check the routing table. Now that you understand the basics of routing, you can set the default routes of your web servers!

The Load Balancer

In order to accomplish the aim of having one Internet address but have the workload of this one server spread over a number of servers, you need to introduce something specialized to take connections from one access point and spread them over a number of servers. To do this, you will be placing a load balancing application in front of the other servers; however, in order to facilitate these connections, you need to have these servers networked in a fashion that will allow for all your interconnection.

The most obvious way to do this is to create a back-end network; that is, have one server act as a receiver or gateway and have all the other servers connected to a network where they can be accessed by the gateway server. The following setup is a good example of what we're talking about: one server with two network connections, one to the Internet and the second to your network switch (this server will be your gateway). To the network switch you have a HTTP server, which will function as the content server that houses and delivers the actual content of your web site.

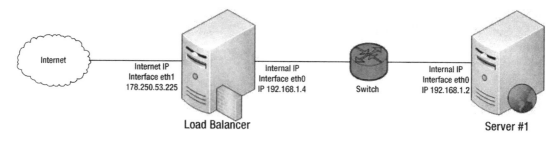

Figure 10-1. *Single server setup*

Figure 10-1 details the initial setup with a single server and a load balancer attached to the Internet. Once you have a setup like this, you need to confirm connectivity between the load balancer and the content server. In this case, use ping for simple connectivity testing. Ping is a simple utility available on all computers that sends a basic packet to a computer and then waits for a response. It is by far the world's most universal connectivity testing tool.

Ping is invoked by simply typing ping then the IP address you wish to test into the console, like so:

```
root@LoadBalancer:~# ping 192.168.1.2
PING 192.168.1.2 (192.168.1.2) 56(84) bytes of data.
64 bytes from 192.168.1.2: icmp_seq=1 ttl=64 time=10.0 ms
64 bytes from 192.168.1.2: icmp_seq=2 ttl=64 time=0.399 ms
64 bytes from 192.168.1.2: icmp_seq=3 ttl=64 time=0.360 ms
64 bytes from 192.168.1.2: icmp_seq=4 ttl=64 time=0.418 ms
64 bytes from 192.168.1.2: icmp_seq=5 ttl=64 time=0.556 ms
64 bytes from 192.168.1.2: icmp_seq=6 ttl=64 time=0.423 ms
^C
--- 192.168.1.2 ping statistics ---
6 packets transmitted, 6 received, 0% packet loss, time 4998ms
rtt min/avg/max/mdev = 0.360/2.036/10.061/3.589 ms
```

As you can see, I have successfully been able to receive packets from the server I tested against. Note the return packet size, the sequence numbers, the time-to-live of the packet, and finally the amount of time it took to get a response (the round trip time). This information tells you the availability of a server, and it can be used to tell you how steady the connection is by checking the trip times.

In this example you can see that the initial packet took much longer than the subsequent responses, meaning it probably took a moment for the system to wake up. This could be due to a couple of things:

- Delay in finding initial patching of routes both to and from the server.

- Server delay in organizing the response.

- Initial delay on the router.

Finally, having confirmed connectivity, you need to configure IP forwarding, which will allow your load balancing server to forward IP packets to other servers. To do this, you need to modify the /etc/sysctl.conf file and add (or uncomment) the following line:

```
net.ipv4.ip_forward = 1
```

After adding this line, you need to execute

```
root@Server1:~# sysctl -p
net.ipv4.ip_forward = 1
```

and then execute

```
root@Server1:~# echo "1" > /proc/sys/net/ipv4/ip_forward
```

Now you have confirmed your network connectivity and configured your IP forwarding, so you can proceed to set up your routing. To configure routing, login to the HTTP server and set the default route to transmit to the internal network address of your gateway server, since it will be the face of your system. Here is my initial routing table:

```
root@Server1:~# route
Kernel IP routing table
Destination     Gateway          Genmask          Flags Metric Ref    Use Iface
178.250.53.0    *                255.255.255.0    U     0      0        0 eth0
192.168.1.0     *                255.255.255.0    U     0      0        0 eth1
default         178.250.53.254   0.0.0.0          UG    100    0        0 eth0
```

Now you add the default route, like so:

```
root@Server1:~# route add default gw 192.168.1.4 eth1
```

And here is the result:

```
root@Server1:~# route
Kernel IP routing table
Destination     Gateway          Genmask          Flags Metric Ref    Use Iface
178.250.53.0    *                255.255.255.0    U     0      0        0 eth0
192.168.1.0     *                255.255.255.0    U     0      0        0 eth1
default         192.168.1.4      0.0.0.0          UG    0      0        0 eth1
default         178.250.53.254   0.0.0.0          UG    100    0        0 eth0
```

As you can see, nothing is removed; you have simply added a single default route with a 0 (highest) metric. Once again, you should confirm the connectivity between these servers with ping to make sure you didn't accidently enter the wrong route. Now that you have confirmed connectivity and set up the routing, you can install software to perform the gateway function!

IPVS

The utility you will be using to balance your server loads is called IPVS, short for Internet Protocol Virtual Server. The primary purpose of IPVS is to provide one single "face" for your web server and to handle incoming requests. These requests are then sent to each of the individual HTTP servers for processing and response. IPVS itself is an application embedded within the Linux kernel itself, which allows it to function with little overhead and increase performance.

IPVS functions by setting up one or a series of Virtual Services, assigning worker servers to this service and creating a Linux Director for each service. The Linux Director takes incoming requests to the server and then distributes the workload of each request to one of the many worker servers it maintains as part of the Virtual Service. These workers then perform the tasks required; the more worker servers added to the Virtual Service, the less each individual server has to do as the Director assigns requests.

IPVS Scheduling

Probably one of the most important parts of IPVS is its scheduling; that is, how it decides which of its worker servers will receive the next request. IPVS contains a number of different methods that you can use to schedule the distribution of jobs. While at a high level each of these schedulers will do basically the same thing—send jobs to the server with the aim of getting the work done the fastest—there are some significant differences that can drastically change the way your servers' load is handled.

The reason for the large variety of scheduling methods is because now two servers will (realistically) have the same load pattern, so different situations can arise where one different method may provide a significant advantage over another. With that in mind I'm sure you would agree that in addition to being familiar with the method of each and its strengths and weaknesses, there is nothing better than experimenting to find the correct algorithm for your needs!

The following sections cover the five most common scheduling systems used by IPVS.

Round-Robin Based Schedules

These connections will distribute connections in a rotational pattern among its servers.

Round-Robin

Acronym: rr

How it Works: The default scheduling algorithm, it works by simply creating a sequence of servers, then going through them in order.

Advantages: Simple to understand and works effectively.

Disadvantages: Doesn't consider server load, so potentially one server may be overloaded with high volume requests while another high-capacity server sits idle.

Best Used: When you have known equally complex requests, so no request places an undue load on a server.

Weighted Round-Robin

Acronym: wrr

How it Works: Servers are pre-assigned a weight value. Servers with a higher weight are assumed to be able to handle more load, and the scheduler proceeds with round-robin, adding more loads to the higher weighted servers in sequence.

Advantages: Uses the same simple round-robin method, but adds to this the ability assign more loads to specific servers.

Disadvantages: Requires user-driven weights, which require manual intervention to change; fails to take into account that different connections may require different amounts of load.

Best Used: When you have equally complex requests and also have knowledge of the request processing capability of each server, so that weights can be assigned efficiently and server loads are distributed more effectively.

Least-Connections Based Schedules

These connections will distribute connections to the servers that have the least active connections being distributed to them.

Least-Connections

Acronym: LC

How it Works: Server that has the least number of connections receives the next connection.

Advantages: Balances based on the actual number of connections to the servers, which limits the potential liability of one single server having a number of longer active connections.

Disadvantages: Doesn't take into account the processing capability of each server; also has a higher overhead, as the number of connections to a server needs to be counted and connection state monitored.

Best Used: When you have equally complex requests and also have knowledge of the request processing capability of each server, so that weights can be assigned efficiently and server loads are distributed more effectively.

Weighted Least-Connections

Acronym: wlc

How it Works: Server that has the least number of connections and the highest weight in ratio receives the next connection. This sets the algorithm "Number of Connections" divided by "Weight Value."

Advantages: Balances based on the actual number of connections to the servers, which limits the potential liability of one single server having a number of longer active connections and allows for a level of configurability by allowing servers to be assigned weights.

Disadvantages: Like all weighted scheduling algorithms, it requires manual intervention to change the weighting; it also has a significant overhead in calculating where to send the next connection.

Best Used: When you have equally complex requests and also have knowledge of the request processing capability of each server, so that weights can be assigned efficiently and server loads are distributed more effectively.

Locality-Based Scheduling

This one works based on the principle that sharing cache between servers needs to be minimized and thus avoids loading servers.

Locality-Based Least-Connection

Acronym: lblc

How it Works: Assigns jobs that are for the same end user to the same server, so long as that server is not overloaded and available. Otherwise it assigns to the server with the fewest jobs.

Advantages: Avoids creating further server-side load by allowing users from the same source IP to connect to one host, meaning that any cached data used by these users doesn't need to be replicated among the web servers.

Disadvantages: Due to NAT, there can be very large numbers of users behind a single IP address, which could lead to stress on a single server.

Best Used: When having multiple connections from one IP that shares data would cause significant load between servers, say in the case of large cookies or a large volume of session data.

IPVS Installation on Ubuntu

To begin with, let's install the IPVS system on an Ubuntu 10.04 LTS Natty Narwhal server. Start with apt-get to download and install the IPVS package.

```
root@ubuntu:~# apt-get install ipvsadm
Reading package lists... Done
Building dependency tree
Reading state information... Done
Suggested packages:
  heartbeat keepalived ldirectord
The following NEW packages will be installed:
  ipvsadm
0 upgraded, 1 newly installed, 0 to remove and 183 not upgraded.
Need to get 47.3 kB of archives.
After this operation, 205 kB of additional disk space will be used.
Get:1 http://us.archive.ubuntu.com/ubuntu/ natty/main ipvsadm amd64 1:1.25.clean-1ubuntu1
[47.3 kB]
Fetched 47.3 kB in 1s (27.8 kB/s)
Preconfiguring packages ...
Selecting previously deselected package ipvsadm.
(Reading database ... 133617 files and directories currently installed.)
Unpacking ipvsadm (from .../ipvsadm_1%3a1.25.clean-1ubuntu1_amd64.deb) ...
Processing triggers for man-db ...
Processing triggers for ureadahead ...
```

```
ureadahead will be reprofiled on next reboot
Setting up ipvsadm (1:1.25.clean-1ubuntu1) ...
update-rc.d: warning: ipvsadm start runlevel arguments (2 3 4 5) do not match LSB Default-
Start values (2 3 5)
 * ipvsadm is not configured to run. Please run dpkg-reconfigure ipvsadm
```

IPVS should now have been installed as a kernel module. Test to see that it is installed correctly by using lsmod to confirm that all the kernel modules are loaded.

```
root@ubuntu:~# lsmod | grep ip_vs
ip_vs                 137211  0
```

Configure the package; in this case, let's go with the defaults by using the following answers to the dpkg's questions:

- Yes to loading on boot, which means that IPVSADM will start with the sever.

- Create a master server, which says this server is the master of a cluster (even your little cluster of 1).

- Use the eth0 interface for multicast; this setting says which interface to communicate with the rest of its cluster.

```
root@LoadBalancer:~#  dpkg-reconfigure ipvsadm
 * ipvsadm is not configured to run. Please run dpkg-reconfigure ipvsadm
 * Clearing the current IPVS table...
[ OK ]
update-rc.d: warning: ipvsadm start runlevel arguments (2 3 4 5) do not match LSB Default-
Start values (2 3 5)
 * Clearing the current IPVS table...
[ OK ]
 * Loading IPVS configuration...
[ OK ]
 * Starting IPVS Connection Synchronization Daemon master
```

As the response from this command shows, you have started the daemon; do your own checks to confirm using ps.

```
root@LoadBalancer:~# ps -ef | grep ipvs
root      2009    2  0 19:46 ?        00:00:00 [ipvs_syncmaster]
```

IPVS Installation on Centos

Let's look over an installation of IPVS on the new Centos 6 release. Begin by telling yum to fetch and install ipvsadm.

```
[root@centos ~]# yum install ipvsadm
Loaded plugins: fastestmirror, refresh-packagekit
Loading mirror speeds from cached hostfile
 * base: mirror.optus.net
 * extras: mirror.optus.net
 * updates: mirror.optus.net
Setting up Install Process
Resolving Dependencies
```

```
--> Running transaction check
---> Package ipvsadm.x86_64 0:1.25-9.el6 set to be updated
--> Finished Dependency Resolution

Dependencies Resolved

================================================================================
 Package            Arch            Version            Repository     Size
================================================================================
Installing:
 ipvsadm            x86_64          1.25-9.el6          base           41 k

Transaction Summary
================================================================================
Install       1 Package(s)
Upgrade       0 Package(s)

Total download size: 41 k
Installed size: 74 k
Is this ok [y/N]: y
Downloading Packages:
ipvsadm-1.25-9.el6.x86_64.rpm
|  41 kB      00:00
Running rpm_check_debug
Running Transaction Test
Transaction Test Succeeded
Running Transaction
  Installing      : ipvsadm-1.25-9.el6.x86_64
1/1

Installed:
  ipvsadm.x86_64 0:1.25-9.el6
```

Complete! IPVS should now be installed as a kernel module. Test to see that it is installed correctly by using lsmod to confirm all the kernel modules are loaded.

```
[root@centos ~]# lsmod | grep ip_vs
ip_vs                  108205  0
```

This command shows you that the IPVS module is installed in the kernel and ready to go. You have set up your IPVS system and you can begin using it.

IPVSADM

Now that you have IPVS running, you need to tell it what to do. Configuring a Linux daemon that contains tables to dictate its function can be very daunting at first; I personally have fond memories of configuring a DHCP daemon. The basic principal with IPVSADM is that you want to create your virtual server to collect all your incoming requests, and then distribute them out over your worker HTTP servers. So, let's start simple, with one load balancer working with a single virtual server, and work upwards from there.

First, you create the virtual server. To do this you need to know the Internet-facing IP of your server. The command you will use is

```
root@LoadBalancer:~# ipvsadm -A -t 178.250.53.225:80
```

where 178.250.53.225 is the web-facing IP address of your server.

This command uses -A to add a new virtual server and -t to set the mode to TCP, and it then gives the IP address followed by: 80, which represents the port on that address (80 as the standard HTTP port). Now that you have created a virtual server, let's add a worker. To do so, use this command:

```
root@LoadBalancer:~# ipvsadm -a -t 178.250.53.225:80 -r 192.168.1.2:80 -m
```

This command uses the -a to add a new host reference for the Virtual Server, the -t to set TCP, the IP, and port of the virtual server you're working with. The -r is used to specify that you will be using the -r flag followed by the IP and port of the local server you will be sending to. Finally, you have -m, which says that you will be using "masquerade mode," which means that your Virtual Server will be masquerading as the actual web servers using NAT—this is the most simple and straightforward way to achieve your goals.

So, now that you have added your servers and run ipvsadm, let's check out its routing table!

```
root@LoadBalancer:~# ipvsadm
Prot LocalAddress:Port Scheduler Flags
  -> RemoteAddress:Port           Forward Weight ActiveConn InActConn
TCP  178-250-53-225.rdns.melbourn wlc
  -> 192.168.1.2:www              Masq   1      0          0
```

This table shows that TCP connections bound for 178.250.53.225 will be routed to the server 192.168.1.2:www using weighted least-connection as its scheduling algorithm (this is the default) and that it will be a masqueraded connection. The Weight, ActiveConn, and InActConn show the weight value assigned to the server (in this case 1), the number of active connections to the server, and the number of previously active (now inactive) connections.

Now for the real test: to ensure your HTTP server is running and that IPVS is running, you can ping your HTTP server from your load balancer and see that your HTTP server has its default route set to that of your load balancer. Open your browser and direct it to your web server. Your web page should appear.

If not, go over your settings.

- Check that your web server and IPVS are running (use ps -ef to check the list of running processes).

- Check that your servers can communicate between each other (use ping to test both directions).

- Check that your default routes are good on your HTTP server (use route and go over the table).

- Check that you enabled IP forwarding with the modification to the command and created the file /proc/sys/net/ipv4/ip_forward with the value 1 inside.

- Check that your IPVS tables are correct (view them with ipvsadm, check the IPs, the port [80 or www are what you used], the mode [masquerading], etc.).

- If you aren't using the standard 80 HTTP port (say you're using 8080 or 443), make sure you adjusted your IPVS settings accordingly.

- If all else fails, remove all the settings, get your system working as it was before, and then try again!

- Check the ActiveConn and InActConn values for your link via ipvsadm. If they are increasing, it's likely that your web server isn't sending back to your load balancer. Remember to set the default route to the load balancers internal address on your web server.

Congratulations! You have successfully got IPVS working to load balance your web server!

Expanding IPVS

Adding one server provides little in the way of load balancing; now you want to add a second?

Well, fire up ipvadm and add it!

Additional servers can readily be added by connecting them to the switch, then using a tool like ping to confirm connectivity. Figure 10-2 shows where this new server—and all new servers like it—can be added.

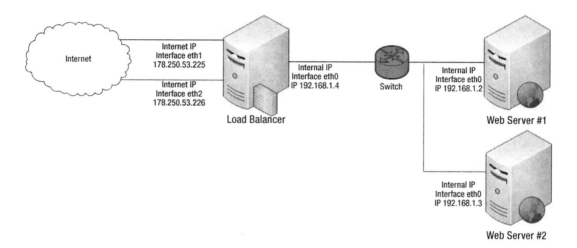

Figure 10-2. Multiple server setup

Once you have added the server and confirmed connectivity you will again need to set the net IPV4 forwarding; you will also need to modify the routing table. You then need to follow the steps you used earlier to install IPVS on this system. However, once that's done, it's a simple job to add the new server to your IPVS server.

```
root@LoadBalancer:~# ipvsadm -a -t 178.250.53.225:80 -r 192.168.1.3:80 -m
```

Now that you have your second server added, confirm its connectivity and routing, then direct it to your web page; yep, just as before. But checking the IPVS tables, as you can see here, I have had one connection to EACH of my servers, showing that they are working correctly.

Pressing refresh doesn't change which server you are using right away. You need to wait for the connection state to close (removed from the list of inactive but remembered connections) and then load again.

```
root@LoadBalancer:~# ipvsadm
Prot LocalAddress:Port Scheduler Flags
  -> RemoteAddress:Port          Forward Weight ActiveConn InActConn
TCP  178-250-53-225.rdns.melbourn wlc
  -> 192.168.1.2:www             Masq    1      0          1
  -> 192.168.1.3:www             Masq    1      0          1
```

We found that a good way to test this is to modify each server's default index page to show something slightly different. In our case, we added the following HTML to each of the pages displayed to show me which server we were on, just above the final body tag:

```
<p>Server #[x]</p>
</body>
```

Adding this line and giving each server a different number allows you to refresh your browser when your connection closes; you should see a different page. If this doesn't work, try it a few times more or, if possible, use a web-based proxy service to display your page while you have it open on your browser, as the proxy will show up as an entirely new connection. Try loading via one of the many free proxies at www.proxy.org.

Failing this, inspect the routing table. If the new server isn't being routed to, or you see the count only incrementing for one server, you should perform all the connectivity tests you performed previously for confirming a single server!

Advanced IPVS

Now that you know the basics of IPVS, let's look at performing some more complex changes to your system to enhance your load balancing. The features are setting and changing scheduling algorithms, setting and changing weight values, changing which protocols are transmitted, and changing which ports are used. You will also look at how you can set up multiple different virtual servers within one physical server, such as an HTTP version and a HTTPS version of the same application. Once you understand how all these portions of the configuration are modified, the sky is the limit as to what you will be able to configure.

Changing Scheduling Algorithm

As discussed in an earlier portion of this chapter, there are several different scheduling algorithms that can be used to change the way in which IPVS distributes connections. We have covered the most commonly used algorithms within IPVS and how to build an IPVS configuration. Let's expand on this initial system by changing the scheduling algorithm to better adapt your servers to your situation.

Start by removing your current setup and adding a new one that specifies the scheduling algorithm to round-robin. First, execute an ipvsadm command to remove your existing configuration. To do this you will execute ipvsadm with a -D for delete virtual server; then you will specify -t and the configuration information for your virtual server.

```
root@LoadBalancer:~# ipvsadm -D -t 178.250.53.225:80
root@LoadBalancer:~# ipvsadm
IP Virtual Server version 1.2.1 (size=4096)
```

```
Prot LocalAddress:Port Scheduler Flags
  -> RemoteAddress:Port            Forward Weight ActiveConn InActConn
```

Now that you have cleaned your config, let's add back the same server in round-robin mode. Then add back your two servers from before. The change to this command from the one executed originally is the addition of the –s flag and the rr symbol, which corresponds to the round-robin algorithm you will now be using!

```
root@LoadBalancer:~# ipvsadm -A -t 178.250.53.225:80 -s rr
root@LoadBalancer:~# ipvsadm -a -t 178.250.53.225:80 -r 192.168.1.2:80 -m
root@LoadBalancer:~# ipvsadm -a -t 178.250.53.225:80 -r 192.168.1.3:80 -m
root@LoadBalancer:~# ipvsadm
IP Virtual Server version 1.2.1 (size=4096)
Prot LocalAddress:Port Scheduler Flags
  -> RemoteAddress:Port            Forward Weight ActiveConn InActConn
TCP  178-250-53-225.rdns.melbourn rr
  -> 192.168.1.2:www               Masq    1      0          0
  -> 192.168.1.3:www               Masq    1      0          0
```

Now you can see your server is again up and running. The difference is subtle, but you can see that where previously your server's IP was followed by the code wlc, it's now followed by rr, which tells you it is operating in round-robin mode.

Although it's good to be able to change these configurations, it's a real pain to need to delete and re-create the entire table for every minor change. So let's look at performing an edit using ipvsadm -E to switch the scheduling algorithm over to weighted round-robin. This command is structured identically to the add and delete commands, with the –t flag representing TCP, the IP, and Port as your servers' identifiers, and the upgraded algorithm. This is the execution and result, which speaks for itself:

```
root@LoadBalancer:~# ipvsadm -E -t 178.250.53.225:80 -s wrr
root@LoadBalancer:~# ipvsadm
IP Virtual Server version 1.2.1 (size=4096)
Prot LocalAddress:Port Scheduler Flags
  -> RemoteAddress:Port            Forward Weight ActiveConn InActConn
TCP  178-250-53-225.rdns.melbourn wrr
  -> 192.168.1.2:www               Masq    1      0          0
  -> 192.168.1.3:www               Masq    1      0          0
```

As you can see, the scheduling algorithm is again changed, this time from rr to wrr; this was done without the need to delete the existing entries first.

Assigning Weight Values

You have just changed the scheduling algorithm you were using from weighted least-connections to round-robin and finally to weighted round-robin. You are now using a weighted algorithm but you haven't given your servers any weight values to take advantage of it. So let's add weight values.

Start by first deleting and adding a new entry with a weight value, just as you did with the scheduling algorithms.

```
root@LoadBalancer:~# ipvsadm -d -t 178.250.53.225:80 -r 192.168.1.3:80
root@LoadBalancer:~# ipvsadm
IP Virtual Server version 1.2.1 (size=4096)
Prot LocalAddress:Port Scheduler Flags
  -> RemoteAddress:Port            Forward Weight ActiveConn InActConn
```

```
TCP  178-250-53-225.rdns.melbourn wrr
  -> 192.168.1.2:www              Masq    1      0          0
root@LoadBalancer:~# ipvsadm -a -t 178.250.53.225:80 -r 192.168.1.3:80 -m -w 2
root@LoadBalancer:~# ipvsadm
IP Virtual Server version 1.2.1 (size=4096)
Prot LocalAddress:Port Scheduler Flags
  -> RemoteAddress:Port          Forward Weight ActiveConn InActConn
TCP  178-250-53-225.rdns.melbourn wrr
  -> 192.168.1.2:www              Masq    1      0          0
  -> 192.168.1.3:www              Masq    2      0          0
```

As you can see, you can delete entries for real servers in a similar manner to that of deleting whole virtual servers; however, this time you use the lowercase -d, which specifies you are working with a real server within a virtual server—rather than a virtual sever as a whole. The syntax used is the -d followed by the same identifiers for the virtual server you used in its creation. Following this, you use the -r, which identifies the individual real server within the virtual server. This will delete it. Also note that the -m you used to specify masquerading is not needed when you are performing a delete.

The add command is the same as when you added this real server to the virtual one. The change this time is the specification of the -w flag with a weight. In this case I have specified a weight of 2, which sets this server "below" the 192.168.1.2 server; as such, it will receive a lower priority.

You can now perform an edit in this same manner, using the -e flag.

```
root@LoadBalancer:~# ipvsadm -e -t 178.250.53.225:80 -r 192.168.1.2:80 -w 3
root@LoadBalancer:~# ipvsadm
IP Virtual Server version 1.2.1 (size=4096)
Prot LocalAddress:Port Scheduler Flags
  -> RemoteAddress:Port          Forward Weight ActiveConn InActConn
TCP  178-250-53-225.rdns.melbourn wrr
  -> 192.168.1.2:www              Route   3      0          0
  -> 192.168.1.3:www              Masq    2      0          0
```

From this you can see that while I was able to modify the weight with the -w tag, I left out the -m tag. This had the unintended consequence of changing the forwarding method from masquerading to routing. Another simple modify command will be needed to repair this oversight—this time with the -m in place!

```
root@LoadBalancer:~# ipvsadm -e -t 178.250.53.225:80 -r 192.168.1.2:80 -m -w 3
root@LoadBalancer:~# ipvsadm
IP Virtual Server version 1.2.1 (size=4096)
Prot LocalAddress:Port Scheduler Flags
  -> RemoteAddress:Port          Forward Weight ActiveConn InActConn
TCP  178-250-53-225.rdns.melbourn wrr
  -> 192.168.1.2:www              Masq    3      0          0
  -> 192.168.1.3:www              Masq    2      0          0
```

You can see us executing the correct edit command, which contains the -m for masquerading mode. It is important to remember that when performing an edit, the only things that should be changed are those that you wish to be changed; otherwise the application will treat these as a desire to edit the system to return to the defaults.

Protocol and Multiple Virtual Servers

Now that you have the ability to quickly modify the settings and configurations, let's talk about some of the other options. You have been working with your current virtual servers using only TCP protocol; you can also set up IPVS to work with UDP. By switching protocol, you can allow UDP traffic through; however, this doesn't mean that IPVS will being treating TCP traffic as UDP traffic, but it allows you to work with other forms of content, such as video traffic.

In the following example you will set up a new virtual server to work with traffic on port 443 (HTTPS). I will also assign it to work with the two existing physical servers. The point is to illustrate that you can share multiple forms of traffic from one single virtual server linked with many different kinds of physical servers.

```
root@LoadBalancer:~# ipvsadm -A -t 178.250.53.225:443 -s wrr
root@LoadBalancer:~# ipvsadm -a -t 178.250.53.225:443 -r 192.168.1.2:443 -m
root@LoadBalancer:~# ipvsadm -a -t 178.250.53.225:443 -r 192.168.1.3:443 -m
root@LoadBalancer:~# ipvsadm
IP Virtual Server version 1.2.1 (size=4096)
Prot LocalAddress:Port Scheduler Flags
  -> RemoteAddress:Port          Forward Weight ActiveConn InActConn
TCP  178-250-53-225.rdns.melbourn wrr
  -> 192.168.1.2:www             Masq    3      0          0
  -> 192.168.1.3:www             Masq    2      0          0
TCP  178-250-53-225.rdns.melbourn wrr
  -> 192.168.1.2:https           Masq    1      0          0
  -> 192.168.1.3:https           Masq    1      0          0
```

This setup allows you to have two servers, one running a www configuration and another running HTTPS. The key to these functions are that IPVS will simply relay traffic as it's instructed; it will simply direct traffic flow. Now let's look at modifying the way this traffic flow is structured. You will modify the port 80 entries to forward back to port 443, in effect treating all incoming HTTP traffic as HTTPS traffic. Unfortunately, you can't simply modify these entries as it will result in an error.

```
root@LoadBalancer:~# ipvsadm -e -t 178.250.53.225:80 -r 192.168.1.2:80 -m
No such destination
```

To make this change you will need to add new entries and delete the old ones. In this instance you add two new connections directing traffic that is incoming to 178.250.53.225 on port 80 to

```
root@LoadBalancer:~# ipvsadm -a -t 178.250.53.225:80 -r 192.168.1.2:443 -m
root@LoadBalancer:~# ipvsadm -a -t 178.250.53.225:80 -r 192.168.1.3:443 -m -w 2
root@LoadBalancer:~# ipvsadm -d -t 178.250.53.225:80 -r 192.168.1.2:80
root@LoadBalancer:~# ipvsadm -d -t 178.250.53.225:80 -r 192.168.1.3:80
root@LoadBalancer:~# ipvsadm
IP Virtual Server version 1.2.1 (size=4096)
Prot LocalAddress:Port Scheduler Flags
  -> RemoteAddress:Port          Forward Weight ActiveConn InActConn
TCP  178-250-53-225.rdns.melbourn wrr
  -> 192.168.1.2:https           Masq    1      0          0
  -> 192.168.1.3:https           Masq    2      0          0
TCP  178-250-53-225.rdns.melbourn wrr
  -> 192.168.1.2:https           Masq    1      0          0
  -> 192.168.1.3:https           Masq    1      0          0
```

This modification shows that you have successfully directed all port 80 traffic on your first entry over to port 443 on your existing servers. The downside of this is that IPVS will maintain separate queues for each of these traffic streams, meaning that IPVS will perform a weighted round-robin calculation for each incoming port 80 connection, independent of any connections made to port 443. The reasoning for this is that even though you have made these connections to the same server, IPVS makes no correlation between real devices or virtual servers.

The final portion of this chapter will concern protocols, specifically configuration for UDP protocol. You have currently configured two virtual servers with both of these servers taking connections to the IP 178.250.53.225 on ports 80 and 443, then directing these to 192.168.1.2 and 192.168.1.3 on port 80 via TCP protocol.

Now let's say you want to add a video portion to your server using UDP protocol on port 554, which is Real Time Streaming Protocol (RTSP)—similar to what popular streaming video sites on the Internet use. So let's create a UDP virtual server. Just as before, you use ipvsadm -A but you substitute the -t flag with -u representing UDP.

```
root@LoadBalancer:~# ipvsadm -A -u 178.250.53.225:554 -s wrr
root@LoadBalancer:~# ipvsadm -a -u 178.250.53.225:554 -r 192.168.1.2:554 -m
root@LoadBalancer:~# ipvsadm -a -u 178.250.53.225:554 -r 192.168.1.3:554 -m
root@LoadBalancer:~# ipvsadm
IP Virtual Server version 1.2.1 (size=4096)
Prot LocalAddress:Port Scheduler Flags
  -> RemoteAddress:Port           Forward Weight ActiveConn InActConn
TCP  178-250-53-225.rdns.melbourn wrr
  -> 192.168.1.2:https            Masq    3      0          0
  -> 192.168.1.3:https            Masq    2      0          0
TCP  178-250-53-225.rdns.melbourn wrr
  -> 192.168.1.2:https            Masq    1      0          0
  -> 192.168.1.3:https            Masq    1      0          0
UDP  178-250-53-225.rdns.melbourn wrr
  -> 192.168.1.2:rtsp             Masq    1      0          0
  -> 192.168.1.3:rtsp             Masq    1      0          0
```

As you can see, you invoke the ipvsadm -A command the same as you did to add a virtual server in the past, but in this instance you simply changed the -t with a -u. The same is true for adding the references to your real server, since you need to identify the protocol because you can have the same ports in different protocols. As it stands now, you have three virtual servers created that use three different ports over two protocols.

Another IP Address

Up to this point you have been working with only a single IP address for your IPVS server; it's now possible to duplicate your load balancing further by adding a secondary IP address. This will work in the same fashion as adding other IPVS entries. Look at Figure 10-3 to see how this network will be laid out. The only change is the addition of a new Internet connection and its IP address.

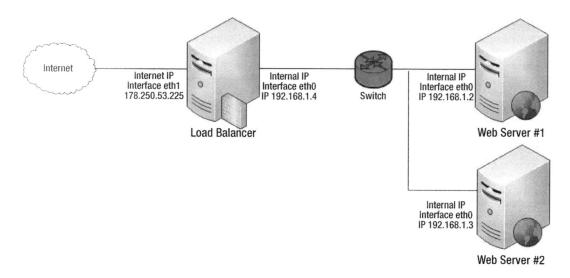

Figure 10-3. *New Internet connection*

In Figure 10-3 you have added a new Ethernet device. Fortunately, since you have already set this server up, no real configurations need to be changed beyond allowing traffic that is addressed to 178.250.53.226 to be load balanced and routed to your servers. You'll do this in the same manner. These are the commands you should issue to IPVS to duplicate your setup to this new address:

```
root@LoadBalancer:~# ipvsadm -A -t 178.250.53.226:80 -s wrr
root@LoadBalancer:~# ipvsadm -a -t 178.250.53.226:80 -r 192.168.1.2:443 -m -w 3
root@LoadBalancer:~# ipvsadm -a -t 178.250.53.226:80 -r 192.168.1.3:443 -m -w 2
root@LoadBalancer:~# ipvsadm -A -t 178.250.53.226:443 -s wrr
root@LoadBalancer:~# ipvsadm -a -t 178.250.53.226:443 -r 192.168.1.2:443 -m
root@LoadBalancer:~# ipvsadm -a -t 178.250.53.226:443 -r 192.168.1.3:443 -m
root@LoadBalancer:~# ipvsadm -A -u 178.250.53.226:554 -s wrr
root@LoadBalancer:~# ipvsadm -a -u 178.250.53.226:554 -r 192.168.1.2:554 -m
root@LoadBalancer:~# ipvsadm -a -u 178.250.53.226:554 -r 192.168.1.3:554 -m
root@LoadBalancer:~# ipvsadm
IP Virtual Server version 1.2.1 (size=4096)
Prot LocalAddress:Port Scheduler Flags
  -> RemoteAddress:Port          Forward Weight ActiveConn InActConn
TCP  178-250-53-225.rdns.melbourn wrr
  -> 192.168.1.2:https           Masq    3       0          0
  -> 192.168.1.3:https           Masq    2       0          0
TCP  178-250-53-225.rdns.melbourn wrr
  -> 192.168.1.2:https           Masq    1       0          0
  -> 192.168.1.3:https           Masq    1       0          0
UDP  178-250-53-225.rdns.melbourn wrr
  -> 192.168.1.2:rtsp            Masq    1       0          0
  -> 192.168.1.3:rtsp            Masq    1       0          0
TCP  178-250-53-226.rdns.melbourn wrr
  -> 192.168.1.2:https           Masq    3       0          0
  -> 192.168.1.3:https           Masq    2       0          0
```

```
TCP  178-250-53-226.rdns.melbourn wrr
  -> 192.168.1.2:https          Masq    1       0           0
  -> 192.168.1.3:https          Masq    1       0           0
UDP  178-250-53-226.rdns.melbourn wrr
  -> 192.168.1.2:rtsp           Masq    1       0           0
  -> 192.168.1.3:rtsp           Masq    1       0           0
```

This output shows the creation of three new IPVS entries that relate to content coming into your new IP address. I have configured this to work in the exact same manner as the previous entries by simply combining all of the entries you made previously into one single set of entries. This allows you to make a bulk change to the IPVS table. Testing this is as simple as directing a connection towards the new Internet-facing IP 178.250.53.226; the server should display as expected.

Making It Stick

You have made a large number of config changes to your system over this period, but none of them have actually been written out to a file to be saved for posterity. This means that nothing you have done (except the IPV4 forwarding you enabled) will be saved. Now that you have a working configuration, it's a good idea to save it so you can use it again. On Ubuntu this is accomplished by executing

```
/etc/init.d/ipvsadm save
```

Given that you told Ubuntu to save the configuration to be used on boot, this method is most effective. It saves the IPVS table to /etc/ipvsadm.rules where you can view it.

In Centos the most ideal method for your purposes is to add the IPVS table entries to /etc/sysconfig/ipvsadm; this will enable them to be run on boot. Additionally, each of the changes that have been made to each of the real servers for routing purposes will need to be saved into these files. For your servers, add the following to your /etc/sysconfig/ipvsadm file. If you are fully satisfied that you want to write these commands out directly, you can try the following:

```
ipvsadm-save | sed 's/^/ipvsadm /' > /etc/sysconfig/ipvsadm
```

This command will output your current IPVS table to the screen and then redirect it to sed, which will append the ipvsadm command to the front; finally it will write it to the file and remove any previous configurations. The following are the printed contents of your full ipvsadm table from the system you have configured here:

```
ipvsadm -A -t 178.250.53.225:80 -s wrr
ipvsadm -a -t 178.250.53.225:80 -r 192.168.1.2:443 -m -w 3
ipvsadm -a -t 178.250.53.225:80 -r 192.168.1.3:443 -m -w 2
ipvsadm -A -t 178.250.53.225:443 -s wrr
ipvsadm -a -t 178.250.53.225:443 -r 192.168.1.2:443 -m
ipvsadm -a -t 178.250.53.225:443 -r 192.168.1.3:443 -m
ipvsadm -A -u 178.250.53.225:554 -s wrr
ipvsadm -a -u 178.250.53.225:554 -r 192.168.1.2:554 -m
ipvsadm -a -u 178.250.53.225:554 -r 192.168.1.3:554 -m
ipvsadm -A -t 178.250.53.226:80 -s wrr
ipvsadm -a -t 178.250.53.226:80 -r 192.168.1.2:443 -m -w 3
ipvsadm -a -t 178.250.53.226:80 -r 192.168.1.3:443 -m -w 2
ipvsadm -A -t 178.250.53.226:443 -s wrr
ipvsadm -a -t 178.250.53.226:443 -r 192.168.1.2:443 -m
ipvsadm -a -t 178.250.53.226:443 -r 192.168.1.3:443 -m
```

```
ipvsadm -A -u 178.250.53.226:554 -s wrr
ipvsadm -a -u 178.250.53.226:554 -r 192.168.1.2:554 -m
ipvsadm -a -u 178.250.53.226:554 -r 192.168.1.3:554 -m
```

Summary

This chapter covered quite a large amount of content. You learned about network load balancing and some basic networking tenants to ensure that you can establish interconnection between your servers. By now you should be familiar with the networking protocols and how they work. In addition, you should understand what IPVS does and how to install and configure it. Finally, you should be familiar with the basic scheduling algorithms that IPVS uses. From these humble beginnings you should have the ability to fully create an IPVS server through which you can balance out the network connections and distribute load to servers over a network.

## CHAPTER 11

SSL Load Balancing

This chapter on SSL load balancing aims to provide you with an understanding of

- SSL and TLS: what they are and what they do.

- The advantages and disadvantages of encryption.

- What public-key cryptography is and how it relates to encryption online.

- Why there is a need for TLS load balancing.

- How to load balance a TLS connection.

TLS is an important part of the infrastructure of the Internet. And with the ever-increasing focus on security and privacy it is essential to be able to provide this for your users while minimizing the impact to your web site. After all, what good is a web site that is so secure you can't use it?

This chapter will provide you with a good working knowledge of SSL so that you can offer security and privacy to your users. You'll also learn how to configure a SSL system to negate some of the performance impacts of providing SSL to your user base.

What are SSL and TLS?

First you need to understand TLS and SSL! TLS stands for Transport Layer Security and refers to the protocol that is used to provide secure connectivity over the Internet. SSL is the predecessor protocol to TLS and stands for Secure Socket Layer. Given that TLS is the more modern protocol, you might be wondering why we called this chapter "SSL Load Balancing."

This is one of those Internet history moments: in this instance I'm not referring to the TLS protocol but the most popular implementation of TLS called OpenSSL. This historic throwback also appears in many systems that still refer to their TLS implementation as an SSL implementation. Now that you understand the naming and background, we can begin in earnest.

TLS as a security protocol is an implementation of public-key cryptography; it aims to provide secure communications and the ability to validate that a given message comes from the indented sender (this last part is called *non-repudiation*). TLS as a protocol sits on top of TCP and UDP (for information on TCP and UDP please see Chapter 10 on network load balancing) to provide security to the communications that are occurring over them.

This is extremely important as neither TCP nor UDP provide any security; they are, by design, simply data transportation protocols. TLS and SSL as forms of secure communications rely on the security of public-key cryptography, which provides you with the ability to secure communications and validate senders. To understand how a TLS connection is established and functions, you need to understand public-key cryptography.

Public-Key Cryptography

Public-key cryptography, or *asymmetric cryptography*, is a form of mathematically derived encryption. That's a lot of terms all at once, so I'll start from the beginning. The purpose of this type of cryptography is to create a key (think password) that is used to change the content of a given message so that you can't change it back without knowing the key.

The use of one secret key to alter (encrypt) the content of a message is called symmetric key encryption because the key used to encrypt and decrypt is the same. Asymmetric key cryptography differs from symmetric key cryptography because, as you would expect given the names, it uses two different keys: one to encrypt and another to decrypt.

The big jump here is that only the decryption key is secret (called the private key); the other key is made "public," thus the name. This means that anyone can create a message, secure it, and send it with the knowledge that only the intended recipient will be able to read it—and all using publically available information. The reason all this is possible is that the two keys are mathematically related, with the public key being derived from the private key. It is this relationship that makes the private key the only thing that can decrypt messages encrypted with the public key.

We will not go into the particular mathematics involved—that would take more than a full chapter—but public-key cryptography uses number factorization and discreet logarithm problems to create keys that are linked; knowing the public key will not allow someone to readily divine the private key. Figure 11-1 shows how public-key cryptography works at a high level.

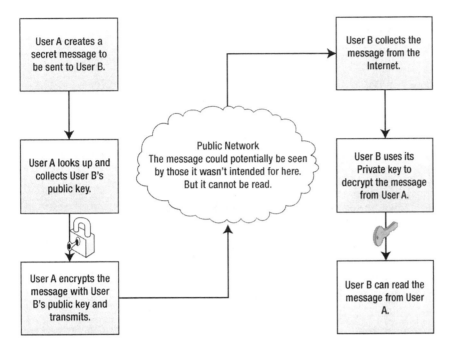

Figure 11-1. *Public key cryptography overview*

Trust and Certificate Authorities

At this point, you have established that you can create a secure one-way communication using a public key. The duplication of having two of these sets of communications at once would allow you to have secure two-way communication. However, even if you exchange one set of keys over the secure channel—say you collect a public key from an end user after establishing a connection—how can you be certain that the person you are sending the message to is indeed the person you WANT to send it to— and not just some impersonator who has released a public key and says they are the one with whom you wish to communicate?

This is where trust comes in. Trust is the basis on which the secure portion of the Internet works.

The concept is similar to a spider's web. To begin with, you start with highly trusted groups called certificate authorities (CAs, for short). These CAs are trusted third parties and act to vouch that the owner of a web site is the one whose key you have by issuing them a digital certificate that contains the web site name and public key. These CAs issue what are called root certificates that are installed into your browser's cache of certificates.

When you wish to make a connection via TLS with a web site, you download its certificate, ensure it is the certificate for the site you are visiting, validate that it comes from a known and trusted certificate authority, and then establish a secure connection.

TLS Encryption

Now that you have an understanding of public-key cryptography, you can look at TLS encryption.

- TLS establishes its connections by performing a secure handshake, like that used by TCP, where cryptographic protocols are set and keys exchanged.

- The handshake begins with the client sending a request along with a list of the common cryptographic systems that are available to it.

- The server picks the strongest cryptographic system available from the list and informs the client of the decision.

- The server sends back its digital certificate as a form of ID. The certificate normally contains the server name, the server's public encryption key, and a trusted authority who can vouch for the certificate.

- The client may contact the server that issued the certificate (the trusted CA, as above) and confirm the validity of the certificate before proceeding.

- In order to generate the session keys used for the secure connection, the client encrypts a random number with the server's public key and sends the result to the server. Only the server should be able to decrypt it with its private key.

- From the random number, both parties generate key material for encryption and decryption.

This handshake will last for the duration of the connection and provides both ends of the connection with the ability to communicate securely, knowing only the other party can see the contents of their conversation.

TLS Load Balancing

Now that you understand what goes into encrypting something using TLS, you can see that it adds a significant layer of complexity to a normal HTTP connection. The complexities exist both in the establishment and in the effort spent to encrypt and decrypt a transaction. Thus the load placed on a normal HTTP server can be significantly increased with the added overhead of a TLS layer of communications.

This means that there is real benefit in load balancing the TLS portion of a communication as it will alleviate a significant amount of stress from your servers. The unfortunate thing about SSL load balancing is that it introduces a requirement that each connection needs to continue using one certificate and one session, meaning you can't readily divert SSL traffic between servers. Given the above, there are two ways that you can continue working on SSL going forward. These methods are called SSL acceleration and SSL termination.

SSL termination refers to setting a termination point for an SSL connection and then setting these connections to be passed to your web servers. There are several ways to manage this, but the most common is the use of a reverse proxy, which is simply a server that acts as the secure face of your web site, deals with the SSL portion of the connections, and forwards normally insecure connections back to your site.

In short, you can create a point to terminate all SSL to your web site before sending it to your servers, which means they simply don't have to deal with it.

SSL acceleration, on the other hand, involves specialized hardware. It means adding a specialized cryptographic processing card to your server and then directing all the SSL processing to be done by this piece of hardware. These two systems have several implications between them that you need to be aware of when choosing which path to go down.

Both require that on top of ensuring that your traffic is load balanced, you need to establish connection persistence to allow one client to be constantly connect with the server providing its SSL connection.

SSL termination implications include the following:

- It creates an insecure area between your end user and your server, which needs to be taken into account.

- Depending on your setup, it can require more or less hardware; it will always require an additional server at minimum.

SSL acceleration implications are more cut and dry.

- You will need an SSL accelerator per server that you wish to work with.

- Your web server will need to support the particular web server you are working with.

Configuring SSL on Your Web Server

In order to use SSL on your server, you need to have configured your server to use a set of digital certificates and to accept incoming HTTPS connections. The following steps will allow you to create your own self-signed certificate.

▓ **Warning** A self-signed certificate provides no validity to users that you are who you say you are. It will show SSL warnings with regard to your web site on your client's browsers. If you wish to avoid these, you need to purchase a digital certificate and install it in the same manner used to install the self-signed certificates (discussed next).

To begin, you will need to have OpenSSL installed; this can be done with your favorite package manager. To start creating an SSL certificate, perform the following and answer all the questions the application puts to you:

```
openssl genrsa -des3 -out private.key 1024
openssl req -new -key private.key -out private.csr
cp private.key private.key.bkp
openssl rsa -in private.key.bkp -out private.key
```

Note You can change the number of bits encryption by modifying the 1024 at the end; you simply need to use a factorial of 2 such as 512, 1024, 2048, etc.

The previous code has created a private.key file and a private.csr file, which are your private key and your certificate signing request. The .key file uses a 1024-bit number as the encryption key. It has also removed the password you added upon generation. This is very useful when adding it to a web server because you will be asked for the key on a restart of your web server.

Now that you have created the key, you will need to create a certificate. The following command will create a certificate valid for 365 days:

```
openssl x509 -req -days 365 -in private.csr -signkey private.key -out private.crt
```

Here is our example execution of the steps to create a new key:

```
root@loadbalancer:~# openssl genrsa -des3 -out private.key 1024
Generating RSA private key, 1024 bit long modulus
.....................++++++
.++++++
e is 65537 (0x10001)
Enter pass phrase for private.key:
Verifying - Enter pass phrase for private.key:
root@loadbalancer:~# openssl req -new -key private.key -out private.csr
Enter pass phrase for private.key:
You are about to be asked to enter information that will be incorporated
into your certificate request.
What you are about to enter is what is called a Distinguished Name or a DN.
There are quite a few fields but you can leave some blank
For some fields there will be a default value,
If you enter '.', the field will be left blank.
-----
Country Name (2 letter code) [AU]:
State or Province Name (full name) [Some-State]:
Locality Name (eg, city) []:
Organization Name (eg, company) [Internet Widgits Pty Ltd]:
Organizational Unit Name (eg, section) []:
Common Name (eg, YOUR name) []:
Email Address []:

Please enter the following 'extra' attributes
to be sent with your certificate request
A challenge password []:
An optional company name []:
root@loadbalancer:~# cp private.key private.key.bkp
root@loadbalancer:~# openssl rsa -in private.key.bkp -out private.key
Enter pass phrase for private.key.bkp:
writing RSA key
root@loadbalancer:~# ls
private.csr  private.key  private.key.bkp
```

```
root@loadbalancer:~# openssl x509 -req -days 365 -in private.csr -signkey private.key -out
private.crt
Signature ok
subject=/C=AU/ST=Some-State/O=Internet Widgits Pty Ltd
Getting Private key
root@loadbalancer:~# ls
private.crt  private.csr  private.key  private.key.bkp
root@loadbalancer:~#
```

Now that you have created a certificate, you can install it into your Apache config. On Ubuntu this means executing

```
sudo mv privkey.key /etc/ssl/private/
sudo mv private.crt /etc/ssl/certs/
```

On Centos this means executing

```
mkdir -p /etc/ssl
ln -s /etc/pki/tls/private/ /etc/ssl/private/
mv private.key /etc/ssl/private/
mv private.crt /etc/ssl/certs/
```

Note Centos differs slightly from Ubuntu but still maintains a /etc/ssl/certs directory. For consistency's sake, we have simply created the second link for the /etc/ssl/private directory.

Now that you have added your keys, you can begin using them.

Apache

Within Apache you need to modify your server configuration by creating a virtual host entry for a HTTPS server. Here is a short example:

```
<IfModule mod_ssl.c>
<VirtualHost *:443>
    DocumentRoot /var/www/example.com
    ServerName example.com
    SSLEngine on
    SSLCertificateFile /etc/ssl/certs/private.crt
    SSLCertificateKeyFile /etc/ssl/private/private.key
</VirtualHost>
</IfModule>
```

Note that there is an IfModule command, which says if you have loaded mod_ssl.c you will create this virtual host. Please check that your httpd.conf loads mod_ssl by searching for

```
LoadModule ssl_module modules/mod_ssl.so
```

If this doesn't exist, you need to install mod_ssl using either
Centos:

```
yum install mod_ssl
```

then add the LoadModule line to your httpd.conf
or Ubuntu:

```
ln -s /etc/apache2/mods-available/ssl.conf /etc/apache2/mods-enabled/ssl.conf
ln -s /etc/apache2/mods-available/ssl.load /etc/apache2/mods-enabled/ssl.load
```

Following all this, restart your Apache server and check your log file. You should see something resembling

```
Apache/2.2.17 (Ubuntu) PHP/5.3.5-1ubuntu7.2 with Suhosin-Patch mod_ssl/2.2.17 OpenSSL/0.9.8o
configured
```

The mention of mod_ssl shows that it has been added successfully.

Nginx

Within nginx, you simply need to add the following directive into your nginx config:

```
server {
  listen 443 default_server ssl;
  server_name localhost;
  root html;
  index index.html index.htm;

  ssl on;
  ssl_certificate       /etc/ssl/certs/private.crt;
  ssl_certificate_key   /etc/ssl/private/private.key;
}
```

It is also important to remember that if you are downloading nginx from your package manager to use one of the more complete bundles that includes SSL (such as nginx or ngnix-full). If you are compiling from source, be sure to add --with-http_ssl_module when you execute ./configure to begin your build, as this will compile the module.

SSL Acceleration

It's time to start working with SSL acceleration. SSL acceleration in this context requires additional specialized hardware to perform specialist cryptographic processing and thus give accelerated performance. We won't instruct you on how to install an SSL accelerator card, nor will we recommend any particular brands. There are more than a dozen brands; each has its own specific installation instructions and each will perform better at specific functions. To demonstrate how to configure SSL acceleration, we have found that there is a SSL accelerator included within the CPU of one of the test servers.

From this point, we will assume you have successfully set up the hardware and the web server of your choice. Next you'll learn how to enable an SSL accelerator within Apache and then in nginx.

Apache

Adding an SSL accelerator to Apache is relatively simple. Open your web site's Host or VirtualHost entry and add the following:

```
SSLCryptoDevice <Device>
```

Nginx

Adding an SSL accelerator to nginx is just as simple as in Apache. Open your web site's Server entry within the nginx config and add

```
ssl_engine <Device>
```

The Device directive is simply the device identifier that OpenSSL knows your SSL accelerator as. If your new device has not come with an OpenSSL device name, run the following:

```
root@ubuntu:/var/log# openssl engine
(aesni) Intel AES-NI engine (no-aesni)
(dynamic) Dynamic engine loading support
```

This lists the device names that your current OpenSSL configuration allows for. (In our case, we would probably use the aesni engine because Dynamic is a reserved name that allows for the specific loading of other modules dynamically without need for a re-initialization.)

The aesni engine is a SSL accelerator on board certain Intel processors that allows increased processing speed to AES transactions. (From this point, you can aesni to your config as the SSL device of your choice and your web server will use it to accelerate its SSL processing.)

SSL Termination

SSL termination represents the use of a server to act as your SSL endpoint. You set this up to process all your SSL connections before they reach your web servers (meaning they won't need to perform any of the SSL processing we have suggested and will simply function as normal HTTP web servers). The concept here is to create a de-militarized zone (or DMZ) behind your SSL server, as shown in Figure 11-2.

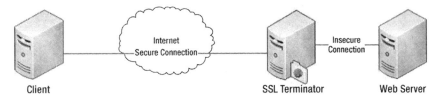

Figure 11-2. SSL terminator diagram

As you can see, there is a DMZ behind the SSL terminator where all the HTTPS traffic is decrypted. This means that you must have a secure environment within your DMZ or else some or all of the secure traffic you are sending can be intercepted. For your purposes, you will be using a piece of software called reverse proxy, which acts as a transparent pass-through. The reverse proxy strips the TLS off the packets and passes them forward, leaving everyone none the wiser of its actions.

The easiest reverse proxy to install is, in fact, nginx. We have found the setup and configuration of nginx to be incredibly straightforward and simple. Moreover, reusing the same pieces of software keeps it simple! To begin, install nginx.

Configuring Nginx

Now you will configure nginx in the vein of Figure 11-2. The configuration is relatively simple; you just need to add a new (or replace the existing) server config.

In Ubuntu, this is /etc/nginx/sites-enabled/default.

In Centos, this is /etc/nginx/nginx.conf.

Reminder Do a backup before proceeding.

Open your nginx config and add the following (ensure that this is the only server listing for this host on port 443):

```
server {
        #Basic server information
        listen          443;
        server_name     memcache.plb.membrey.hk;
        #Enable SSL and set the details
        ssl             on;
        ssl_certificate         /etc/ssl/certs/private.crt;
        ssl_certificate_key     /etc/ssl/private/private.key;
        keepalive_timeout       60;

        #Logfiles
        access_log      /var/log/ssl-access.log;
        error_log       /var/log/ssl-error.log;

        location / {
         #setup the Proxy for our server
         #ADD THE WEB SERVERS LOCAL IP BELOW
                proxy_pass  http://192.168.1.2;
```

```
        #Timeout if the real server is dead
                proxy_next_upstream error timeout invalid_header http_500 http_502 http_503;

                # Basic Proxy Config
                proxy_set_header Host $host;
                proxy_set_header X-Real-IP $remote_addr;
                proxy_set_header X-Forwarded-For $proxy_add_x_forwarded_for;
                proxy_set_header X-Forwarded-Proto https;
                proxy_redirect       off;
        }
}
```

This config specifies a basic nginx web server that will take connections on port 443. It enables SSL with the certificates you have made and set up earlier. Finally, you set the root location (location /) as a proxy to your actual web server and use the HTTP protocol.

You then set the basic proxy configuration so it can send the default headers, and you also set the proxy to timeout if the back-end server is dead with the correct HTTP return codes.

Now that this is done, you can restart your nginx server with /etc/init.d/nginx restart.

Testing the SSL

Now it's time to test your SSL connection. Trying to telnet to port 443 is out, as telnet doesn't support SSL directly, so you need to use the OpenSSL application to test. Execute the following command (but change the hostname to your server's hostname):

```
openssl s_client -showcerts -connect memcache.plb.membrey.hk:443
```

■ **Note** Press Ctrl+C to exit OpenSSL.

You should see something like this:

```
root@loadbalancer:~# openssl s_client -showcerts -connect memcache.plb.membrey.hk:443
CONNECTED(00000003)
depth=0 /C=AU/ST=Some-State/O=Internet Widgits Pty Ltd
verify error:num=18:self signed certificate
verify return:1
depth=0 /C=AU/ST=Some-State/O=Internet Widgits Pty Ltd
verify return:1
---
Certificate chain
 0 s:/C=AU/ST=Some-State/O=Internet Widgits Pty Ltd
   i:/C=AU/ST=Some-State/O=Internet Widgits Pty Ltd
-----BEGIN CERTIFICATE-----
MIICATCCAWoCCQDgobNIdJnMPzANBgkqhkiG9w0BAQUFADBFMQswCQYDVQQGEwJB
VTETMBEGA1UECBMKU29tZS1TdGF0ZTEhMB8GA1UEChMYSW50ZXJuZXQgV2lkZ2lo
cyBQdHkgTHRkMB4XDTExMDgxMDEyMTAxMVoXDTEyMDgwOTEyMTAxMVowRTELMAkG
A1UEBhMCQVUxEzARBgNVBAgTClNvbWUtU3RhdGUxITAfBgNVBAoTGEludGVybmV0
```

IFdpZGdpdHMgUHR5IExoZDCBnzANBgkqhkiG9w0BAQEFAAOBjQAwgYkCgYEAvioR
IXxpypoKKsrtx9Co20630ean+Wg+GQO1pH1TQIYKfIwYRpoGZ+92ABLYOz9ckIzc
PWTizr9ND15VseUKFtFOCTnnSdIfRDzKCjGPO+n5fTDvRT6TM82AZkCC9t+aOa7v
KFCX/s8wave19C/3FVJnhlHiXTyg21PJxgzSfwMCAwEAATANBgkqhkiG9w0BAQUF
AAOBgQC4arPPO69h1m9uRbZCeUwvgRNrsmLXvDGriE/LGZhrc7YdvSrSzSiwJJvE
0sJL2knIDOpceLdqppF/6IjUjOXcbD2jn1v/qk2KcQZlsf727f2vjJVtcjipPxce
wYvo3U6jjTJiON+TBQDJS3oPsRg2CGEHLP3v4ecQTRFx9TLzQQ==
-----END CERTIFICATE-----

Server certificate
subject=/C=AU/ST=Some-State/O=Internet Widgits Pty Ltd
issuer=/C=AU/ST=Some-State/O=Internet Widgits Pty Ltd

No client certificate CA names sent

SSL handshake has read 1088 bytes and written 319 bytes

New, TLSv1/SSLv3, Cipher is DHE-RSA-AES256-SHA
Server public key is 1024 bit
Secure Renegotiation IS supported
Compression: NONE
Expansion: NONE
SSL-Session:
    Protocol : TLSv1
    Cipher   : DHE-RSA-AES256-SHA
    Session-ID: A9DED7E88A5C30F9404749A0DF28DE526F1DE12F34999E76ED2BB6F6D6EA6EBC
    Session-ID-ctx:
    Master-Key:
015446465E9F9F95FA03DC4442ADD4EF34EA7B31F96133C859AFA7C2030643C1EAFF183CE6030EC3B6F451BE26FF4C
65
    Key-Arg   : None
    Start Time: 1313017806
    Timeout   : 300 (sec)
    Verify return code: 18 (self signed certificate)
---
^C
root@loadbalancer:~#

Looking through it you can see all of the details of the certificate you added when you created it (in our case the defaults). If you are getting any errors, try the following:

- Go back over your configs; you may have mistyped something.

- Check and re-create your certificates and their storage location.

- Check that nginx has booted correctly and look over its logs for any errors.

Now you can try the next trick: loading your page.

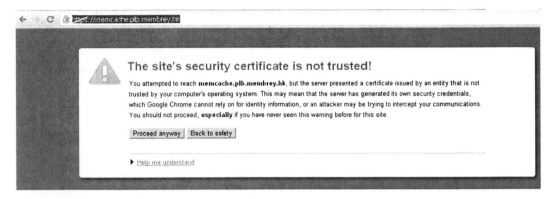

Figure 11-3. *The greatest warning message ever (browser depending)!*

The error in Figure 11-3 is an SSL error because you are using an untrusted self-signed certificate. This is great because it shows that TLS is WORKING!

If we press the proceed button, it will load the page of our web server. Everything works!

If it doesn't, check the following:

- That your web server is running and available on port 80 at the IP you specified.

- Ping testing between your SSL terminator and your web server.

- That your SSL connections are working as expected.

- If necessary, add the basic nginx web site into your config and attempt to connect to this via normal HTTP. If you can view it, this confirms your nginx is working and that the issue is with your web server.

- If your web site is using specialist headers (such as other CGIs), you may need to modify the proxy_set_header entries or add a new one.

Further Configurations

Now that you have set up the basic SSL terminator, you can add some additional features to improve its performance. These commands can be used in either Apache or nginx; both versions are shown here.

Engine

You can now combine the SSL accelerator settings from earlier into your SSL terminator, which is a great way to improve performance of your terminator. This can be enabled with the following:

Nginx: `ssl_engine <Device>`

Apache: `SSLCryptoDevice <Device>`

And, just as in the section on SSL acceleration, your currently available devices can be found with

```
openssl engine
```

Caching

You can allow browsers to reuse the same SSL session over a period, which cuts down on session establishment. But it does add the risk that those sessions can be reused or taken over after the initial user has closed off. To limit the potential for problems, you can also set a time limit on the life of these sessions.

Nginx

`ssl_session_cache <options>`

Within the `ssl_session_cache` command there are a number of options: off, none, builtin, and shared.

- *Off* means that you aren't offering SSL caching to clients.

- *None* means you lie; you offer SSL caching but actually perform a recalculation every time.

- *Builtin* means you use the built-in cache within a single OpenSSL worker. After the built-in, you need to provide a size such as builtin:1000, which provides a kilobyte.

- *Shared* means you use a shared cache over all of the OpenSSL worker processes. In this case, you need to provide a name for this shared cache and a size. OpenSSL suggests that 1MB of memory can support 4,000 simultaneous connections in cache, such as (*shared:SSL:10m*), which says you are creating a shared cache called SSL that will provide 10m of memory (approx 30,000 connections).

You can also combine built-in and shared memory by adding them together, such as (`ssl_session_cache builtin:1000 shared:SSL:5m`). The timeouts of these cached sessions are set with

`ssl_session_timeout <time>`

This can be set to something like `ssl_session_timeout 600` or `ssl_session_timeout 5m`, which sets the timeout to 10 and 5 minutes, respectively. It is also important to note that the defaults for these parameters (if they are left unset) are

```
ssl_session_cache off
ssl_session_timeout 5m
```

Apache

`SSLSessionCache <options>`

Within `SSLSessionCache` you can set one of three options: none, dbm, or shm.

- *None* means session caching is unavailable.

- *dbm* means that to use a database file to cache all the sessions, the dbm is followed by a : and the name of a file to be used. This caching uses a hard disk file to store its cache so it's limited by your hard disk's speed.

- *shm* is a high performance mode of DBM that creates a file handle but stores the cache in RAM (which is much faster). This caching isn't supported on all platforms and you will need to check beforehand. The file is configured by a : and the filename; an optional size limit in bytes can be added after in brackets (), like so: `SSLSessionCache shm:/var/tmp/ssl_cache(1024000)`

Timeouts are controlled with a time limit value with `SSLSessionCacheTimeout` and a value in sessions.

```
SSLSessionCacheTimeout <time>
```

The defaults for these options are

```
SSLSessionCache none
SSLSessionCacheTimeout 300
```

Protocols

You can limit the particular protocols that can be used to establish a TLS or SSL session to your SSL terminator with the `ssl_protocols` option. This command allows you to specify which protocols you wish to use and can therefore remove older protocols that may have weaknesses. (See the breaking of the Enigma cipher in World War II for a real life example!) The command simply requires you to specify the protocols you wish to support.

This command allows for all the protocols to be used:

Nginx: `ssl_protocols SSLv2 SSLv3 TLSv1`

Apache: `SSLProtocol SSLv2 SSLv3 TLSv1`
This command allows for only TLSv1 protocol to be used:

Nginx: `ssl_protocols TLSv1`

Apache: `SSLProtocol TLSv1`

Specific Ciphers

You can also limit the ciphers used (if, for example, you want to only use a specific set that works with your SSL accelerator). You can list the available ciphers to your OpenSSL implementation with

```
openssl ciphers
```

The specific lists of ciphers can be managed using `ssl_ciphers`.

Nginx: `ssl_ciphers <OpenSSL Cyperspec>`

Apache: `SSLCipherSuite <OpenSSL Cyperspec>`
The SSL cipher spec is a part of OpenSSL and is fairly complex. You can validate which spec you are using with the following command, which will list all the ciphers being used:

```
openssl ciphers -v '<OpenSSL Cyperspec>'
```

The basics of a cipher spec are ALL and cypher name, then the use of + to add and ! to remove. Finally, every item on this list is separated by a colon (:) so you can build them like this:
`ALL:!DES` which includes everything, except those that have DES as part of the cipher.

AES:+SHA which includes only the ciphers that are AES and SHA.

```
root@loadbalancer:~# openssl ciphers -v 'AES:+SHA'
ADH-AES256-SHA          SSLv3 Kx=DH        Au=None Enc=AES(256)  Mac=SHA1
DHE-RSA-AES256-SHA      SSLv3 Kx=DH        Au=RSA  Enc=AES(256)  Mac=SHA1
DHE-DSS-AES256-SHA      SSLv3 Kx=DH        Au=DSS  Enc=AES(256)  Mac=SHA1
AES256-SHA              SSLv3 Kx=RSA       Au=RSA  Enc=AES(256)  Mac=SHA1
ADH-AES128-SHA          SSLv3 Kx=DH        Au=None Enc=AES(128)  Mac=SHA1
DHE-RSA-AES128-SHA      SSLv3 Kx=DH        Au=RSA  Enc=AES(128)  Mac=SHA1
DHE-DSS-AES128-SHA      SSLv3 Kx=DH        Au=DSS  Enc=AES(128)  Mac=SHA1
AES128-SHA              SSLv3 Kx=RSA       Au=RSA  Enc=AES(128)  Mac=SHA1
```

AES:SHA, however, is very different; it includes both AES and SHA.

```
root@loadbalancer:~# openssl ciphers -v 'AES:SHA'
ADH-AES256-SHA           SSLv3 Kx=DH        Au=None Enc=AES(256)  Mac=SHA1
DHE-RSA-AES256-SHA       SSLv3 Kx=DH        Au=RSA  Enc=AES(256)  Mac=SHA1
DHE-DSS-AES256-SHA       SSLv3 Kx=DH        Au=DSS  Enc=AES(256)  Mac=SHA1
AES256-SHA               SSLv3 Kx=RSA       Au=RSA  Enc=AES(256)  Mac=SHA1
ADH-AES128-SHA           SSLv3 Kx=DH        Au=None Enc=AES(128)  Mac=SHA1
DHE-RSA-AES128-SHA       SSLv3 Kx=DH        Au=RSA  Enc=AES(128)  Mac=SHA1
DHE-DSS-AES128-SHA       SSLv3 Kx=DH        Au=DSS  Enc=AES(128)  Mac=SHA1
AES128-SHA               SSLv3 Kx=RSA       Au=RSA  Enc=AES(128)  Mac=SHA1
ADH-DES-CBC3-SHA         SSLv3 Kx=DH        Au=None Enc=3DES(168) Mac=SHA1
ADH-DES-CBC-SHA          SSLv3 Kx=DH        Au=None Enc=DES(56)   Mac=SHA1
EXP-ADH-DES-CBC-SHA      SSLv3 Kx=DH(512)   Au=None Enc=DES(40)   Mac=SHA1 export
EDH-RSA-DES-CBC3-SHA     SSLv3 Kx=DH        Au=RSA  Enc=3DES(168) Mac=SHA1
EDH-RSA-DES-CBC-SHA      SSLv3 Kx=DH        Au=RSA  Enc=DES(56)   Mac=SHA1
EXP-EDH-RSA-DES-CBC-SHA  SSLv3 Kx=DH(512)   Au=RSA  Enc=DES(40)   Mac=SHA1 export
EDH-DSS-DES-CBC3-SHA     SSLv3 Kx=DH        Au=DSS  Enc=3DES(168) Mac=SHA1
EDH-DSS-DES-CBC-SHA      SSLv3 Kx=DH        Au=DSS  Enc=DES(56)   Mac=SHA1
EXP-EDH-DSS-DES-CBC-SHA  SSLv3 Kx=DH(512)   Au=DSS  Enc=DES(40)   Mac=SHA1 export
DES-CBC3-SHA             SSLv3 Kx=RSA       Au=RSA  Enc=3DES(168) Mac=SHA1
DES-CBC-SHA              SSLv3 Kx=RSA       Au=RSA  Enc=DES(56)   Mac=SHA1
EXP-DES-CBC-SHA          SSLv3 Kx=RSA(512)  Au=RSA  Enc=DES(40)   Mac=SHA1 export
RC4-SHA                  SSLv3 Kx=RSA       Au=RSA  Enc=RC4(128)  Mac=SHA1
NULL-SHA                 SSLv3 Kx=RSA       Au=RSA  Enc=None      Mac=SHA1
```

In addition to these lists, you can use the HIGH, MEDIUM, and LOW keywords to list ciphers according to their strength.

Finally, as an example with our aesni engine, we want to use only AES ciphers so we can simply type 'AES' as our cipher suite; if we only want to use high-strength AES, we can type 'HIGH:+AES', like so:

```
root@loadbalancer:~# openssl ciphers -v 'HIGH:+AES'
ADH-DES-CBC3-SHA       SSLv3 Kx=DH    Au=None Enc=3DES(168) Mac=SHA1
EDH-RSA-DES-CBC3-SHA   SSLv3 Kx=DH    Au=RSA  Enc=3DES(168) Mac=SHA1
EDH-DSS-DES-CBC3-SHA   SSLv3 Kx=DH    Au=DSS  Enc=3DES(168) Mac=SHA1
DES-CBC3-SHA           SSLv3 Kx=RSA   Au=RSA  Enc=3DES(168) Mac=SHA1
DES-CBC3-MD5           SSLv2 Kx=RSA   Au=RSA  Enc=3DES(168) Mac=MD5
ADH-AES256-SHA         SSLv3 Kx=DH    Au=None Enc=AES(256)  Mac=SHA1
DHE-RSA-AES256-SHA     SSLv3 Kx=DH    Au=RSA  Enc=AES(256)  Mac=SHA1
DHE-DSS-AES256-SHA     SSLv3 Kx=DH    Au=DSS  Enc=AES(256)  Mac=SHA1
AES256-SHA             SSLv3 Kx=RSA   Au=RSA  Enc=AES(256)  Mac=SHA1
ADH-AES128-SHA         SSLv3 Kx=DH    Au=None Enc=AES(128)  Mac=SHA1
```

```
DHE-RSA-AES128-SHA    SSLv3  Kx=DH    Au=RSA  Enc=AES(128)  Mac=SHA1
DHE-DSS-AES128-SHA    SSLv3  Kx=DH    Au=DSS  Enc=AES(128)  Mac=SHA1
AES128-SHA            SSLv3  Kx=RSA   Au=RSA  Enc=AES(128)  Mac=SHA1
```

By now you can see the power you can add to your simple SSL terminator or SSL accelerator by fine-tuning the inner workings of your SSL system.

LVS and Your SSL Terminator

You have newly configured a SSL terminator. This terminator will provide your servers with a SSL face to the Internet. This means you will need to make some changes in order to allow you to link the new SSL terminator with your load balancer from before. The answer is actually very simple: you place the SSL terminator in front of the load balancer, as shown in Figure 11-4.

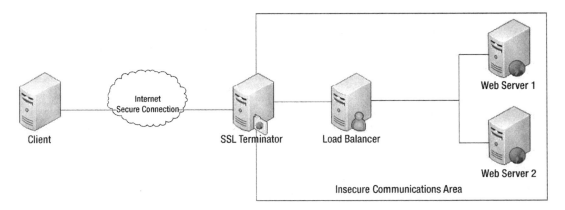

Figure 11-4. *SSL terminator and load balancer*

The only change you need to make is to let the SSL terminator be the face of your web site and ensure that the SSL terminator points to the load balancer. That's it. The connections will now flow transparently through each layer of your system, from SSL from the Internet to the terminator, and then it becomes a normal HTTP connection, just as the load balancer expects. An alternate way to structure this setup is to place the SSL servers between the load balancer and each web server, as shown in Figure 11-5.

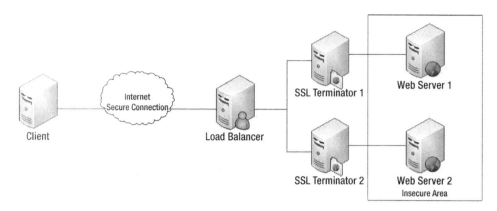

Figure 11-5. Multiple SSL terminators

The key different between the two approaches is the number of SSL servers available for processing. The tradeoff is simply the number of servers involved; by adding a new server you can increase your potential load—at a higher cost. To configure this, simply replace the web servers' addresses with the SSL terminators' addresses in your load balancer, and then point your SSL terminators towards your web servers.

With these two configurations you can deploy both a load balancer and an SSL terminator in a manner that will allow you to tailor your system to allow you to increase your SSL throughput. You can expand upon this by using a combination of SSL terminators and SSL accelerators to minimize cost and maximize throughput.

Integrated Load Balancer/SSL Terminator

It is possible to host both your SSL terminator and load balancer on one server. Just alter the following from the nginx config for an SSL terminator from earlier:

```
proxy_pass  http://127.0.0.1;
```

This will mean that any requests that come in as HTTPS are directed via the reverse proxy back to itself via the 127.0.0.1 on port 80 as HTTP traffic. From here, the load balancer will treat these as normal web connections and things can proceed as normal!

Summary

Over the course of this chapter you learned what SSL and TLS are, how they are valuable, and how they work. As part of this understanding you should also now be familiar with public-key cryptography and digital certificates. You should also now be able to generate your own self-signed digital certificates and then install them into your web server. Finally, you should be familiar with the SSL options available to you on a web server to increase performance, including SSL acceleration, and you should be able to configure an nginx server to work as a reverse proxy to accelerate an SSL connection.

CHAPTER 12

Clustering for High Availability

One of the most common measures applied to modern IT systems is the Service Level Agreement (SLA) for Availability — an agreement that an IT Service will be available for a certain amount of time per year. Commonly, this measure specifies how much of the time a server is available and working – its "uptime" - and is normally defined as a percentage over a year.

The three most common uptime targets are 99.9%, 99.99%, and 99.999%; or, as they are often expressed, three 9s, four 9s, and five 9s, respectively. These require a website to run uninterrupted for an entire year with downtime not exceeding

- Three 9s: 8.76 hours

- Four 9s: 52.56 minutes

- Five 9s: 5.26 minutes

There are agreements in place stipulating that a website must be available for an entire year with the amount of acceptable downtime allowed being under 5 and a half minutes.

Of course, that is a *very* high level of service to maintain because it provides time for no more than one reboot of the server per year. Moreover, it means that there is realistically not enough time to recover if the server has any problem whatsoever - because it can take more than 5 minutes to log in and diagnose basic issues with a server. Let alone the time needed to fix any of these issues.

While some of these SLAs may seem fantastic, they are not. Take, for instance, an online retailer (such as Amazon or Ebay) and imagine how much business it would lose if its servers were to go down for an hour – it could run into millions. Imagine a moderately sized bank's central transaction processing server going down. How much money would the bank lose? It is for these reasons that these fantastic SLA targets aren't just needed; they are mandatory. Because the world could end if some of these servers are down at the wrong moment.

But we hear you saying, "Downtime is unavoidable in practice! What about patching, maintenance, upgrades, hardware issues?" All true. These are also inescapable parts of having a server. The answer to these problems lies in two concepts: *clustering* and *High Availability*.

The aim of this chapter, therefore, is the following:

- Introduce you to the idea of High Availability, what it means and some methods of achieving it

- Introduce you to clustering, what it means and how it works

- Introduce you to the idea of single point of failure

- Give you the skills to identify a single point of failure and offer some common mitigation strategies

- Show you how to configure an LVS system to work in a clustered manner

So, with this in mind, let's begin.

High Availability

High Availability is just what it sounds like: it is the ability for servers to be nearly always available for use in their intended purpose. High Availability (as with most other IT products) also refers to the method used to create servers that have the capability to be called highly available.

More than a few software vendors have called their software that provides systems with high availability just that: High Availability (or HA for short). For you purposes, High Availability is much more pure — it is the ability for the web site to remain available and running at all times, meeting that lofty 5 nine target from before.

In order to achieve something of this magnitude, you need to first examine what you would need to do to achieve this.

The main reason why you would breach a given level of availability is through the time needed to recover from one of the components of the web server being unable to fulfill its function. This means that like any High Availability system, the goal is to be able to work despite the failure of one of the components of the system. The main way you are to achieve this is through redundancy - having a backup system to take over. And in more advanced cases, you can do this automatically. One of the key advantages of what you have been doing so far with Load Balancing is that you already have much of this redundancy available in the form of the systems you have set up to allow us to share load.

For example, have a look at the system you created earlier when you were working with IPVS in Chapter 11 to share the load between multiple servers in Figure 12-1 and Figure 12-2.

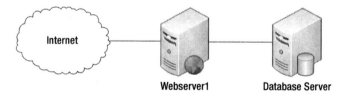

Figure 12-1. Basic web server configuration

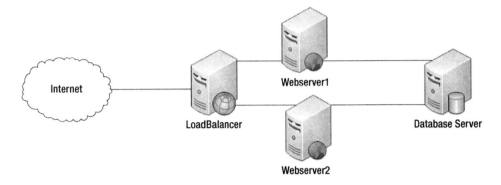

Figure 12-2. *LoadBalanced web server configuration*

From here, imagine that WebServer1 suffers a failure and need to be forcibly shut down and restarted. This process would take several minutes. Normally, if there is only WebServer1 (as in Figure 12-1) and it goes down, your site would be offline; however, in this instance, there are two servers that have been load balanced with IPVS (as in Figure 12-2).

The IPVS system means that if one of the servers goes down, you simply need to temporarily remove it from the list of servers within IPVS and you will be running fully again, but with a lower capacity. You can see that having the load balanced architecture provides a clear advantage over single server architecture. If one of the servers dies, you have the ability to continue that servers load on the other. This concept is called Fail Over and is one of the key principles involved in High Availability.

Now that you understand High Availability, you can learn more about how to achieve it.

Single Point of Failure

To achieve high availability in servers, you need to have the system configured so that all the systems are redundant. What you are looking to find in these examples is called single points of failure, which is one single system that if it becomes unavailable would stop the entire system from being able to function. This is simple enough in principle to achieve, but occasionally there are some caveats. Take the server setup in Figure 12-3.

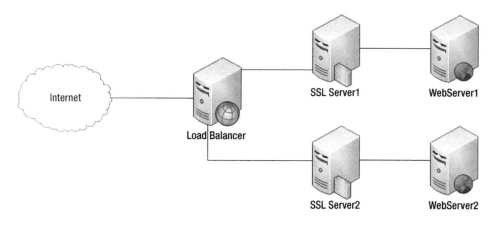

Figure 12- 3. *Twin SSL and web server layout*

In this instance, there is only one single point of failure: the Load Balancer because even if one SSL server or web server goes down, the other pair of servers can still function. Now look over the next design, shown in Figure 12-4.

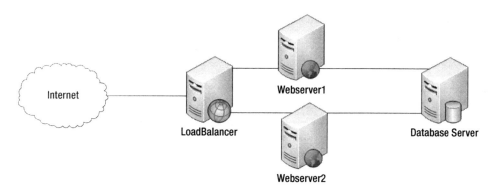

Figure 12-4. *Dual web server and database*

In this case, there are two Single Points of Failure: the Load Balancer as before and this time the database server. The reasoning for this is that if either of the web servers falls over, there is no problem. But if the DB server falls over neither of the web servers will function because the DB server feeds into both the web servers.

Single point of failure can go much deeper than simply redundancy for servers. More and more complex systems actually go so far as to have two full network routes and to have two fully independent power sources! Moreover, they expand beyond this by attempting to have these systems set up in a "physically dispersed" manner. They work to ensure that no two redundant sources of a critical resource share the same space: networking cables, power cables, and the like take different physical paths to get between their source and destination. Often this leads to having two totally different sets of cables running down each side of a building. Just in case by accident one set of cables gets cut, the others will still function as they are in a different place.

From all the above, you should now have the impression that much of what creates a High Availability environment is about creating a setup where the failure of no single point can stop it functioning. To this end, you look to create redundant systems that can take over or accept more load in the event of a failure. This concept of creating a group of servers that are capable of supporting each other in the event of a failure is called a *cluster*.

Clustering

Clustering is the creation of a group of servers that are designed to perform the same function: share load, and in the case of a failure of a cluster member, to have the remainder of the cluster assume its workload. Clustering can be simply one of a group of applications performing the same application function over a several servers, or several servers that aim to assume the full load of another in its group in the event of a failure.

As mentioned earlier, clustering is widely seen as one of the most effective methods of creating a High Availability environment. This is due to the fact that it uses already-running systems that are being used to share load to deal with the failure of one of its members. Moreover, because most clustered systems have automated or semi-automated methods for dealing with the failure of a member, these systems can continue functioning with little intervention – beyond, of course, the work required to either repair the server or reconfigure the cluster to remove the broken server permanently.

Clustering for High Availability differs from the other most common methods in that it aims to make use of the servers that are being used to provide High Availability.

The other common method of providing High Availability is called the Standby method, which involves having a spare server ready to assume the load of the original in the event of its failure. This server can be either cold (turned off, waiting to be activated and called for), warm (running, but needing to have the application systems it is to take over from enabled) or hot (working in parallel to the server it is to replace and ready to take over from exactly where it was at the moment it is needed). As you can imagine, cold standby servers are of less use than warm or hot standbys, but are significantly less costly. Although hot standbys are very useful when a failure occurs, it is very wasteful to allocate all that energy to a just-in-case server.

While there are some circumstances when having a server ready to take over is a distinct benefit, such as when you need to have a specific application at a specific IP address it is often much more efficient to have these servers in a position to perform some of the processing, instead of spending a huge amount of their time waiting in readiness. Having a cluster of servers that are all processing together provides a real advantage as you get both the surety that your application is available, and you also get the increased performance from having an extra server involved in the processing. While we initially described a cluster as a group of servers that are joined together sharing a workload and covering incase one should fail, clusters can be more complex.

Some clusters are built with a controlling application overseeing the distribution of the workload and ensuring that if one of the servers fails, its workload is covered. If this seems very familiar, you are quite correct. In Chapter 11, you began making a basic cluster using the IPVS application as the cluster controller. You added several servers that shared a processing load for a website and with only a small amount of human intervention, you can remove a problematic from the group and its processing will be shared among the remaining servers. While this is a good situation it is far from ideal, it would be best if we could introduce a way for IPVS to automatically detect a failed server and work around it.

IPVS Failover

To create this cluster, you need two things: you need an automated way to change which servers are being used by the virtual server to create a virtual server. There is a specialist daemon designed to work with IPVS in just this fashion; it is called ldirectord. Ldirectord works closely with the IPVS system implemented in Chapter 10 to modify the IPVS tables when a server fails or stops responding to HTTP (website) requests.

The second issue you may have spotted is that the load balancer being used by IPVS is a glaring single point of failure. If the load balancer stops functioning, you could not use the website.

The solution is to introduce a failover server that will take over the function of the load balancer in the event of its failure. In addition to creating a failover server, you need a mechanism that allows the secondary load balancer to detect a failure in the primary load balancer and take over. This application is called heartbeat, which works by having communications between both the load balancer servers and in the event of one failing, the second takes over.

This leaves us with a final issue that we have not mentioned yet. Having two load balancers means you have two load balancer IP addresses. While we list this as an issue, it is a very common part of a cluster because if the machine connecting outward at the time fails, the cluster becomes unreachable.

The solution to this problem is called a virtual IP address, where at any one time; one server within the cluster will have the virtual IP address which allows it to speak on the clusters behalf. This means that you can simply point all traffic to this virtual IP address, which is the permanent access point for the cluster. The setup you will make means you can create something akin to the setup shown in Figure 12-5.

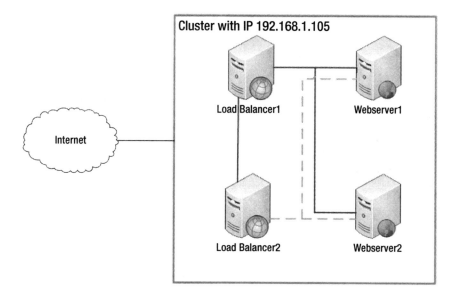

Figure 12-5. Cluster with load balancer

To begin, install ipvsadm, ldirectord, and heartbeat. Perform this on both your intended load balancers because they will be the ones that control the cluster and need to ensure that the load balancing system is running.

Install with Ubuntu

```
root@testbox:~# apt-get install ipvsadm ldirectord heartbeat
Reading package lists... Done
Building dependency tree
Reading state information... Done
The following extra packages will be installed:
  cluster-agents cluster-glue fancontrol gawk libauthen-radius-perl libcluster-glue
libconvert-asn1-perl libcorosync4 libcrypt-ssleay-perl libcurl3 libdbi-perl libdigest-hmac-
perl libdigest-sha1-perl libesmtp5 libheartbeat2
  libio-socket-inet6-perl libio-socket-ssl-perl libltdl7 libmail-pop3client-perl libnet-
daemon-perl libnet-dns-perl libnet-imap-simple-perl libnet-imap-simple-ssl-perl libnet-ip-perl
libnet-ldap-perl libnet-libidn-perl
  libnet-ssleay-perl libnet1 libnl1 libnspr4-0d libnss3-1d libopenhpi2 libopenipmi0
libperl5.10 libplrpc-perl libsensors4 libsnmp-base libsnmp15 libsocket6-perl libxml2-utils
libxslt1.1 lm-sensors openhpid pacemaker perl perl-base
  perl-modules
Suggested packages:
  keepalived dbishell libauthen-sasl-perl sensord read-edid i2c-tools perl-doc libterm-
readline-gnu-perl libterm-readline-perl-perl
The following NEW packages will be installed:
  cluster-agents cluster-glue fancontrol gawk heartbeat ipvsadm ldirectord libauthen-radius-
perl libcluster-glue libconvert-asn1-perl libcorosync4 libcrypt-ssleay-perl libcurl3 libdbi-
perl libdigest-hmac-perl libdigest-sha1-perl
  libesmtp5 libheartbeat2 libio-socket-inet6-perl libio-socket-ssl-perl libltdl7 libmail-
pop3client-perl libnet-daemon-perl libnet-dns-perl libnet-imap-simple-perl libnet-imap-simple-
ssl-perl libnet-ip-perl libnet-ldap-perl
  libnet-libidn-perl libnet-ssleay-perl libnet1 libnl1 libnspr4-0d libnss3-1d libopenhpi2
libopenipmi0 libperl5.10 libplrpc-perl libsensors4 libsnmp-base libsnmp15 libsocket6-perl
libxml2-utils libxslt1.1 lm-sensors openhpid pacemaker
The following packages will be upgraded:
  perl perl-base perl-modules
3 upgraded, 47 newly installed, 0 to remove and 75 not upgraded.
Need to get 10.6MB/21.5MB of archives.
After this operation, 36.2MB of additional disk space will be used.
Do you want to continue [Y/n]? y
addgroup: The group `haclient' already exists as a system group. Exiting.
Warning: The home dir /var/lib/heartbeat you specified already exists.
The system user `hacluster' already exists. Exiting.

Setting up lm-sensors (1:3.1.2-2) ...

Processing triggers for libc-bin ...
ldconfig deferred processing now taking place
Processing triggers for python-central ...
root@testbox:~#
```

Install with Centos

Unfortunately, the latest version of Centos hasn't had ldirectord and heartbeat ported to it. To install on an earlier version of Centos (such as 5) execute the following:

```
yum install heartbeat heartbeat-ldirector ipvsadm -y
```

Configure

Now that you have installed everything, ensure all these servers can reference each other by name. The /etc/hosts file has been modified to ensure that each server has the same reference name as every other server.

This function can also be performed by having a DNS server provide identities for each of your servers, but setting up a DNS is well beyond the scope of what is done here. You will need to use the name given by uname -n for each server as one of the recognizable hostnames for the cluster.

This is very important as heartbeat uses these names. So, I've added the following to our /etc/hosts file:

```
192.168.1.2 server1
192.168.1.3 server2
192.168.1.4 loadbalancer1
192.168.1.1 loadbalancer2
```

These entries provide the previous name aliases to all the servers we are currently working with. These entries need to be added to all servers to ensure consistency among them. Again, on both load balancers, you will need to enable IPv4 forwarding. Open /etc/sysctl.conf and set the following:

```
net.ipv4.ip_forward = 1
```

Then execute the following:

```
root@testbox:~# sysctl -p
net.ipv4.ip_forward = 1
root@testbox:~#
```

You should expect to see the ipv4 foward = 1, as this means that the particular part of the configuration has been loaded. Now that you have ipv4 forwarding and server names standard, you need to begin configuring heartbeat.

Heartbeat has three main configuration files:

File	Description
/etc/ha.d/ha.cf	The main configuration file
/etc.ha.d/authkeys	Contains authentication information
/etc/ha.d/haresources	The resource configuration file

These files must be configured before you can use heartbeat. Heartbeat will fail to start otherwise. Let's start by adding the heartbeat configuration at /etc/ha.d/ha.cf.

Following is the basic configuration we used:

```
logfacility local0
bcast eth1 # Linux
mcast eth1 225.0.0.1 694 1 0
auto_failback off
node loadbalancer1
node loadbalancer2
respawn hacluster /usr/lib/heartbeat/ipfail
apiauth ipfail gid=haclient uid=hacluster
```

Note `/etc/ha.d/ha.cf` needs to be the same on each load balancer.

There are quite a few configuration options setup there, so let's go over them.

The `mcast` and `bcast` Ethernet adapters are set to allow communications between the servers of your cluster. This is because these adapters will not send standard addressed IP packets, but will instead use broadcast (bcast) and multicast (mcast) packets, which give them more flexibility.

The auto failback is set to off, which means that in the event of a failure you will continue using the server you were on. This can be advantageous if one of your servers is having intermittent failures and to save on constantly failing back to the original server. You may, however, want to change this if your second load balancer is a failover server that lacks the power of the original.

We have also added the names of each of the load balancers as nodes to the cluster. At this point, it is *very* important for us to point out that you need to use the first name outputted by `uname -n` as the node names. This is the method that heartbeat uses to identify servers, so you will need to ensure that you are using these `uname -n` names and that each server knows how to contact the other via these names. This is the reason the `/etc/hosts` file on each server was set up.

Next, you need to modify `/etc/ha.d/haresources` to allocate some resources specifically for the cluster to use. Our configuration is the following:

```
loadbalancer \
ldirectord::ldirectord.cf \
LVSSyncDaemonSwap::master \
IPaddr2::192.168.1.105/24/eth1
```

This tells heartbeat to take over the IP address 192.168.1.105 using the subnet mask 24 and use eth1 as the device.

Note `/etc/ha.d/haresources` must be the same on each load balancer.

This specifies that you have to create on the load balancer (which will be your primary) an instance of lddirectord from `lddirector.cf`.

You will set this server up as the master of the cluster. And finally you need to create the special virtual IP address that will be the cluster's IP address. This command specifies the IP you will use, its netmask (the standard 24), the Ethernet adapter to which it will belong, and finally the network address for this adapter.

If you are using a different network setup, you need to adapt it accordingly.

Having set up the failover setup and allocated some resources to the cluster on the load balancers, you need to have a shared authentication method.

To set this up, create the following in /etc/ha.d/authkeys:

```
auth 3
3 md5 password1
```

■ **Note** /etc/ha.d/authkeys must be the same on each load balancer.

This creates an authentication mechanism to use an MD5 hashed password (one of the Internet standard authentication methods) and sets the password to the ever secure 'password1'. Once you have added this, you need to set authkeys to be read only by root. To do this, execute the following:

```
chmod 600 /etc/ha.d/authkeys
```

■ **Note** Remember to change the password to something other than 'password1'.

Finally, you need to add the ldirectord.cf mentioned earlier. This configuration file is to be found at /etc/ha.d/ldirectord.cf. Our configuration is as follows:

```
virtual=192.168.1.105:80
        real=192.168.1.2:80 masq
        real=192.168.1.3:80 masq
        fallback=127.0.0.1:80
        service=http
        request="index.html"
        receive="Welcome to nginx!"
        scheduler=wrr
        protocol=tcp
        checktype=negotiate
```

■ **Note** You will need tabs for each entry after the virtual! This lets ldirectord know they belong to the virtual above.

Many of these configuration options will seem familiar from Chapter 10, but let's go over them quickly. We provide the virtual IP address we have allocated and set up in the resources section. You then link two real servers to this virtual server and set yourself as the fallback address.

Now that you have the basics of the cluster set up, you need to specify how you are to check that the real servers are available. You specify the page they are to request and the response they are to expect. For this purpose, we have set the item expected to receive as the title of our nginx basic index page.

Finally, you need to set the scheduler that is to be used and the scheduler being used to perform it (for more in-depth information on schedulers, see Chapter 10).

Now that you have done the setup, you need to do some quick housework. You need to ensure that heartbeat starts on boot and ldirectord *doesn't!* You need to stop ldirectord from starting because heartbeat will call it depending on when it is needed - which avoids having two servers running it at once and consuming extra resources.

Execute the following to alter your boot configuration:

```
root@loadbalancer:~# update-rc.d heartbeat start 75 2 3 4 5 . stop 05 0 1 6 .
 System start/stop links for /etc/init.d/heartbeat already exist.
root@loadbalancer:~# update-rc.d -f ldirectord remove
 Removing any system startup links for /etc/init.d/ldirectord ...
   /etc/rc0.d/K20ldirectord
   /etc/rc1.d/K20ldirectord
   /etc/rc2.d/S20ldirectord
   /etc/rc3.d/S20ldirectord
   /etc/rc4.d/S20ldirectord
   /etc/rc5.d/S20ldirectord
   /etc/rc6.d/K20ldirectord
```

And now, you start the applications with the following:

```
/etc/init.d/ldirectord stop
/etc/init.d/heartbeat start
```

Common Config Problems

If you see errors similar to Unknown command real=X (as follows), you will need to add a tab to the start of each entry below the virtual in your /etc/ha.d/ldirectord.cf file:

```
root@loadbalancer:~# /etc/init.d/heartbeat start
Starting High-Availability services: \1 better written as $1 at
/etc/ha.d/resource.d/ldirectord line 1252.
\1 better written as $1 at /etc/ha.d/resource.d/ldirectord line 1252.
Error [354] reading file /etc/ha.d/ldirectord.cf at line 2: Unknown command
real=192.168.1.103:80 gate

 Heartbeat failure [rc=6]. Failed.

heartbeat[376]: 2011/08/21_02:21:38 ERROR: Cannot open keyfile [/etc/ha.d//authkeys].  Stop.
heartbeat[376]: 2011/08/21_02:21:38 ERROR: Authentication configuration error.
heartbeat[376]: 2011/08/21_02:21:38 ERROR: Configuration error, heartbeat not started.
```

When starting heartbeat, we ran into the following issue:

```
Starting High-Availability services: \1 better written as $1 at
/etc/ha.d/resource.d/ldirectord line 1252.
\1 better written as $1 at /etc/ha.d/resource.d/ldirectord line 1252.
```

The fix was to open /etc/ha.d/resource.d/ldirectord and modify line 1252 to the regular expression there so it looks like the following:

```
$addr =~ s/^\"([^"]*)\"$/\$1/;
```

This simply adds a $ sign in front of the number 1. This is likely due to a typo in the release we were using.

If you see the following, you will need to execute chmod 600 /etc/ha.d/authkeys. This is a security feature that is designed to limit anyone but root from having access to your shared authentication keys:

```
root@loadbalancer:~# /etc/init.d/heartbeat start
Starting High-Availability services:  Heartbeat failure [rc=6]. Failed.

heartbeat[715]: 2011/08/21_02:28:12 ERROR: Cannot open keyfile [/etc/ha.d//authkeys].  Stop.
heartbeat[715]: 2011/08/21_02:28:12 ERROR: Authentication configuration error.
heartbeat[715]: 2011/08/21_02:28:12 ERROR: Configuration error, heartbeat not started.
```

If you see the following, you may not have set the uname -n nodenames as the node entries in /etc/ha.d/ha.cf.

```
root@loadbalancer:~# /etc/init.d/heartbeat start
Starting High-Availability services:  Heartbeat failure [rc=6]. Failed.
heartbeat: baudrate setting must precede media statementsheartbeat[846]: 2011/08/21_02:32:30
WARN: Core dumps could be lost if multiple dumps occur.
heartbeat[846]: 2011/08/21_02:32:30 WARN: Consider setting non-default value in
/proc/sys/kernel/core_pattern (or equivalent) for maximum supportability
heartbeat[846]: 2011/08/21_02:32:30 WARN: Consider setting /proc/sys/kernel/core_uses_pid (or
equivalent) to 1 for maximum supportability
heartbeat[846]: 2011/08/21_02:32:30 info: Version 2 support: false
heartbeat[846]: 2011/08/21_02:32:30 ERROR: Current node [loadbalancer] not in configuration!
heartbeat[846]: 2011/08/21_02:32:30 info: By default, cluster nodes are named by `uname -n`
and must be declared with a 'node' directive in the ha.cf file.
heartbeat[846]: 2011/08/21_02:32:30 info: See also: http://linux-
ha.org/wiki/Ha.cf#node_directive
heartbeat[846]: 2011/08/21_02:32:30 WARN: Logging daemon is disabled --enabling logging daemon
is recommended
heartbeat[846]: 2011/08/21_02:32:30 ERROR: Configuration error, heartbeat not started.
```

If you have configured your system correctly you should simply expect to see this:

```
root@loadbalancer:~# /etc/init.d/heartbeat start
Starting High-Availability services: Done.
```

Confirming Your System

If all has started execute ip addr sh ethx on the primary server of your cluster, remembering to replace the Ethernet adapter in the text with the one you are using for your cluster (that is, replace ethx with eth0 or eth1). You should expect to see something akin to this:

```
inet 192.168.1.105/24 brd 192.168.1.255 scope global secondary eth1
```

This line contains a global IP address that references our new cluster IP address. If not, check your configs; the ha.cf and the haresources need to be identical on all servers. If this line doesn't appear below your Ethernet adapter, you should follow all the previous config steps, ensure that you have referenced your server names correctly, and are executing on the master. After this, the following are some common solutions we found to common problems and are extremely useful.

The first thing that has given us *endless* hours of problems was a missing LVSSyncDaemonSwap.

Check your /etc/ha.d/resources.d folder; if the LVSSyncDaemonSwap script doesn't exist within it, you will need to download from source. When doing this, we downloaded the source code from the Internet and extracted the LVSSyncDaemonSwap file from source and installed it into /etc/ha.d/resources.d.

If you are doing this, be sure to check that the line /etc/ha.d/shellfuncs is present because it is required for the script to execute correctly.

If all is working from here, you can start to test by executing this:

```
ldirectord ldirectord.cf status
```

It will list the status of the ldirectord server and the PID of its process on the primary server and will show it as being stopped on the failover server.

Execution on primary server:

```
root@loadbalancer:~# ldirectord ldirectord.cf status
ldirectord for /etc/ha.d/ldirectord.cf is running with pid: 10517
root@loadbalancer:~#
```

Execution on secondary server:

```
root@testbox:~#  ldirectord ldirectord.cf status
ldirectord is stopped for /etc/ha.d/ldirectord.cf
root@testbox:~#
```

If you see both ldirectords as stopped, you need to follow the same steps as if you saw no second IP address. Go over your configs, check the log files in /var/logs, and check your process table (ps -ef) to see that heartbeat (and by consequence) ldirectord are running.

Now that you have established that heartbeat and ldirectord are running, check your ipvsadm tables on the primary server and you should see something akin to this:

```
root@loadbalancer:~# ipvsadm
IP Virtual Server version 1.2.1 (size=4096)
Prot LocalAddress:Port Scheduler Flags
  -> RemoteAddress:Port           Forward Weight ActiveConn InActConn
TCP  192.168.1.105:www wrr
  -> server2:www                  Masq    1      0          0
  -> server1:www                  Masq    1      0          0
```

On the secondary server you should see this:

```
root@testbox:~# ipvsadm
IP Virtual Server version 1.2.1 (size=4096)
Prot LocalAddress:Port Scheduler Flags
  -> RemoteAddress:Port           Forward Weight ActiveConn InActConn
```

It shows that only the primary server, which has the virtual IP address, has the IPVS system running and has the configuration you loaded into the ldirectord.cf file.

If you see something like this, you need to check that both the servers are up, running and available from the load balancer and the IP addresses you specified:

```
root@loadbalancer:~# ipvsadm
IP Virtual Server version 1.2.1 (size=4096)
Prot LocalAddress:Port Scheduler Flags
  -> RemoteAddress:Port           Forward Weight ActiveConn InActConn
TCP  192.168.1.105:www wrr
  -> localhost:www                Local  1     0          0
root@loadbalancer:~#
```

You will also need to check that the file you have specified for the ldirectord daemon to load is present on both pages and contains the specified test string to search for. The preceding entry with localhost means that your remove servers are unavailable and it has gone to the failback server on localhost.

Testing

The first test you can do is reboot the load balancer on the primary server with /etc/init.d/heartbeat restart.

This will failover the server to the backup. You can test with your ipvsadm command, executed on both servers like before.

On the primary server, you will see this:

```
root@testbox:~# ipvsadm
IP Virtual Server version 1.2.1 (size=4096)
Prot LocalAddress:Port Scheduler Flags
  -> RemoteAddress:Port           Forward Weight ActiveConn InActConn
```

On the secondary server, you should see this:

```
root@loadbalancer:~# ipvsadm
IP Virtual Server version 1.2.1 (size=4096)
Prot LocalAddress:Port Scheduler Flags
  -> RemoteAddress:Port           Forward Weight ActiveConn InActConn
TCP  192.168.1.105:www wrr
  -> server2:www                  Masq   1     0          0
  -> server1:www                  Masq   1     0          0
```

This shows that your backup is working as expected and that you have failed over. To fail back, simply execute /etc/init.d/heartbeat restart on the secondary server, and the system will simply start again via the primary (assuming it's running, of course!)

You can also test the load balancing adaptation in the same manner. Simply stop your web server on one of the real servers. Here is an example of our system with our web server being stopped and restarted:

```
root@loadbalancer:~# ipvsadm
IP Virtual Server version 1.2.1 (size=4096)
Prot LocalAddress:Port Scheduler Flags
  -> RemoteAddress:Port           Forward Weight ActiveConn InActConn
TCP  192.168.1.105:www wrr
  -> server1:www                  Masq   1     0          0
  -> server2:www                  Masq   1     0          0
```

The preceding code shows the normal running state, just prior to the restart.

```
root@loadbalancer:~# ipvsadm
IP Virtual Server version 1.2.1 (size=4096)
Prot LocalAddress:Port Scheduler Flags
  -> RemoteAddress:Port           Forward Weight ActiveConn InActConn
TCP  192.168.1.105:www wrr
  -> server2:www                  Masq   1     0          0
```

The preceding code now shows our web server to be stopped and the unavailable server has been removed from the cluster.

```
root@loadbalancer:~# ipvsadm
IP Virtual Server version 1.2.1 (size=4096)
Prot LocalAddress:Port Scheduler Flags
  -> RemoteAddress:Port           Forward Weight ActiveConn InActConn
TCP  192.168.1.105:www wrr
  -> server1:www                  Masq   1     0          0
  -> server2:www                  Masq   1     0          0
```

Finally, after it powers back up, the server is visible again!

Web Server Specifics

Now that you have set everything up, you simply need to add a gateway entry for your IP addresses. This means that all connections outbound via these servers' local network connections should be passed via the virtual IP address.

To do this, you need to edit the networking configuration files per the config for your operating system.

Ubuntu

Open /etc/network/interfaces.

Add the following line to the end of the entry for your cluster network address gateway 192.168.1.105 E.G.

```
auto eth1
iface eth1 inet static
   address 192.168.1.2
   netmask 255.255.255.0
   gateway 192.168.1.105
```

Now reboot your network adapters with /etc/init.d/networking restart.

Centos

Open the network file for the Ethernet adapter you are working with within the folder /etc/sysconfig/network. For ourselves, we edited ifcfg-eth1 and added this:

```
GATEWAY=192.168.1.105
```

Now execute /etc/init.d/network restart to reboot your network adapters.

This should allow you to visit your servers via the virtual IP address and view your websites!

Advanced Config Options

The two primary files (ha.cf and ldirectord.cf) you used to configure the HA cluster. While we provided a working simple config in our examples, there are a number of other useful configuration options that can be used. We will go over these in some more depth here.

ha.cf

The following allow you to have much more granular control over the relationship between your primary load balancer and your secondary load balancer via heartbeat:

- logfile <filename> – As its name implies, it allows you to specify a log file for the heartbeat daemon to write, too

- keepalive <number> – The amount of time between checks that your real servers are alive

- deadtime <number> – The amount of time that a server needs to be unresponsive before it is declared dead

- auto_failback <on or off> - This allows you to toggle weather; following a failover your server will attempt to automatically switch back to having the original primary run the cluster.

Note   Remember that ha.cf needs to be the same on each load balancer.

---

ldirectord.cf

The following are all global directives and do not need to be tabbed in as the entries below a virtual server do. They allow for a higher level of control:

- checktimeout – The timeout given to a check of the real servers by ldirectord before it is declared dead

- checkinterval – The interval between checks that each real server is functioning

In addition, more virtual servers can be added to your ldirectord.cf, which should allow you to work with both the HTTP and HTTPS portions of your web page, for example. An example of this is the following:

```
virtual=192.168.6.240:80
        fallback=127.0.0.1:80
        real=192.168.1.2:80 masq
        real=192.168.1.3:80 masq
```

```
        service=http
        request="Welcome to nginx!"
        receive="Test Page"
        scheduler=wrr
        protocol=tcp
        checktype=negotiate

virtual=192.168.6.240:443
        fallback=127.0.0.1:443
        real=192.168.1.2:443 masq
        real=192.168.1.3:443 masq
        service=https
        request="index.html"
        receive="Welcome to nginx!"
        scheduler=wlc
        protocol=tcp
        checktype=negotiate
```

Web Server

In the previous configurations, we simply listed the contents of our index page. It is highly recommended to create a simple file with a known piece of text in it as your web server test. In our servers, we created a file called loadbalancer.html and added the simple text "Server Is Available" to our web servers' root.

This can be a real advantage when the content of your index page is dependent on some user information, or is dynamically generated and there are no concrete pieces of the page you can rely on.

Summary

This chapter discussed High Availability and how it can provide a significant advantage to your servers. You learned what clustering is and about the relationship between clustering and High Availability. You now have the ability to identify a single point of failure.

From here, you should be able to build a working High Availability cluster on Linux using ipvsadm, heartbeat, and ldirectord. Finally, you should be able to change the configuration of both to better suit your load balancing needs!

## CHAPTER 13

Load Balancing in the Cloud

Cloud computing is one of the newest developments in IT and is becoming more and more pervasive as time goes by. In view of its growing popularity and market presence, it is important to understand the impact of load balancing within the cloud.

This chapter aims to provide the following:

- A clear and concise definition of what cloud computing is!

- A ground up view of what comprises a cloud platform and cloud server.

- Methods for taking advantage of cloud computing to load balance your application loads.

- Common methods for load balancing the cloud itself.

- An overview of some of the specific implications of working within the cloud.

Cloud Computing

As with any new technology, there is a significant amount of conjecture about what exactly constitutes cloud computing. There are a number of definitions held by various people and the term *cloud* is used almost interchangeably by many different people.

While these definitions normally contain a measure of what true cloud computing is they often fail to provide many of the other characteristics that make cloud computing such a robust solution.

In our opinion the best definition of cloud computing platform is "a fully automated server platform that allows users to purchase, remotely create, dynamically scale, and administer system."

By this definition, a cloud computing platform is "fully orchestrated," which means that it functions without the need of its owner to perform basic business tasks. This means that the platform can - within reason, of course - operate without human intervention. Servers can be created, destroyed, modified, and users charged all by the system without the need for an administrator to intervene. In addition to this a cloud computing system is "elastic"; the amount of resources available to a server can be expanded and contracted with little or no intervention or downtime.

This is indeed a very broad definition, but covers the entirety of what it means to have cloud servers. While this definition provides some context, it lacks substance. Realistically, a cloud system is one that allows you as the customer to readily create a cloud server without needing the owner to perform any tasks. This server is in every way the same as a server physically owned by you, except that you have no responsibility for the hardware.

In addition, with little intervention you can change the resources available for your server to use. A cloud computer is simply a server that customers can scale to their needs and use exactly like one they purchase but without knowledge of the hardware and only accessible via the Internet.

As an example, you will see how to perform some of these modifications on the cloud platform provided by serverlove.com. First, before diving into using the system, you need to understand how server platforms like this function – you need to walk before you run. Serverlove uses a system called *virtualization* to provide a way for multiple users to take advantage of the resources of a cluster of servers. Given that virtualization introduces a significant amount of complexity into a server you should become familiar with it.

Virtualization

Virtualization is a method for creating what are called *virtual servers* that run on a cluster of a number of real servers. When you create these servers, you are allowing one very powerful server to emulate the function of several lesser servers.

While at a high level, this simply sounds like introducing a complex system to create fancy servers. Virtualization allows for a smaller number of high-powered servers to create a larger number of lesser servers while reducing the overall cost in space, power, and other infrastructure.

The real advantage of virtualized servers and hardware are that if one machine is at or near idle, others within its cluster can take advantage of its resources to perform their processing. This is the same in principle as clustered groups of servers, but virtualization allows for an even higher level of resource sharing.

The reason why this is so effective is that often a server will never use anywhere near its full capacity, so this excess capacity is shared with other servers until needed again. Even in situations in which you have heavily clustered your environment, there will still be some spare resources at any given moment.

This sharing of resources is what allows one high capacity server to host several virtualized servers all at once.

The way a virtualized server functions is that it introduces an abstraction layer between the hardware and the operating system. This abstraction layer is called the hypervisor.

Hypervisor

A *hypervisor* is a piece of software that acts as a resource allocation and hardware abstraction layer on a physical server.

This means that a hypervisor is software that slices up and shares the hardware resources of a single physical server among a number of virtual servers.

Figure 13-1 depicts the normal relationship between a server and an operating system (OS). A server hosts an OS, which in turn runs applications.

Figure 13-1. *Standard server*

Figure 13-2 depicts a hypervisor, which sits between the server and the OS and allows one server to host several operating system instances.

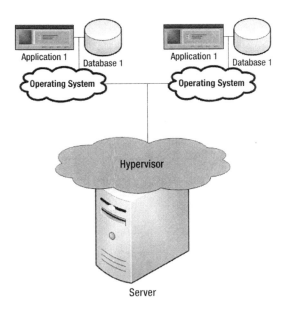

Figure 13-2. *Server with hypervisor*

There are two types of hypervisors (see Figure 13-3). The first is called a bare metal hypervisor, which is the basic hypervisor system that you have gone over above.

213

The second type is called a *hosted hypervisor*, which is not installed to the hardware itself, but within an operating system on the server, and thus is under the control of that operating system.

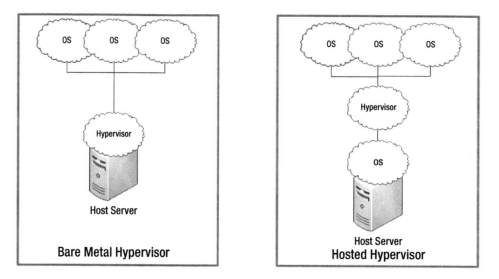

Figure 13-3. Bare metal hypervisor versus hosted hypervisor

The differences between the two hypervisors trade off flexibility in control against performance. The bare metal hypervisor has a significantly higher level of control over the resources available to it because it does not have to go through an intermediary to access the resources.

This comes at a cost since most bare metal hypervisors lack friendly user interfaces; some do not allow any user intervention at all. Hosted hypervisors, on the other hand, are limited by the operating system they are placed on; they can't allocate resources beyond what the parent operating system will provide them to use, and are governed by the resource control systems of the parent.

Hosted hypervisors are significantly easier to access, set up, and manage as they are normally able to take advantage of the parent operating systems graphical user interface to provide their own graphical management system.

Today there are a number of hypervisors on the market in both styles. The best known ones are these:

Bare metal

- VMware
- HyperV

Hosted

- VMware Player
- VirtualBox
- Xen

While hypervisors do give a significant advantage in allowing a large number of virtual servers to share resources, these setups are still limited by the resources available to the host server.

This means that only the amount of server resources on a host server is available for use, and if several servers at once try to use a significantly higher than expected amount of resources this can lead to the "starvation" of other servers.

For this reason many virtualization platforms employ a system of clustering to share resources whenever possible. However, before you go into examining how virtual clusters work, you should look at virtualized resources.

Virtualized Resources

Traditionally, a server's resources are limited to compute power, memory, physical storage, and network bandwidth. There are others, but those would be specialist resources that would be used depending on the situation.

Virtualization allows for these resources to be shared among a number of virtual servers. The first thing that you need to understand is how.

The first resource you will look at is storage. Storage is the long term storage attached to a server - for instance, the hard drive that contains the full working image of your operating system.

Storage is potentially one of the least virtualized resources available. Simply put, the virtual platform creates a section of its storage space and then allocates this aside for use by each virtual server. The issue here becomes whether a number of servers are trying to do a large volume of disk writes at the same time because this means that the amount of data pending to be written to disk continues to increase.

While these issues are extremely rare, they are normally solved by using higher performance disks, RAID arrays for speed, and network storage systems, which allow a much higher level of throughput. Allocation of these resources is straightforward and based on the ongoing full need of the server.

The second resource is *network bandwidth*. Bandwidth is like storage, in that is a simple resource that is easily split among several different virtual servers from a physical one. One 10Gbit link can be the same as 100 x 100Mbit links. In addition to this virtualization can begin to make a real advantage here, whereby 1x 10Gbit link could be shared as a gigabit connection over 20 virtual servers.

This is called *overprovisioning* and takes advantage of the fact that none of the virtual servers will be using the fill gigabit of bandwidth at all times.

The third resource involved in this case is Memory. Memory is a runtime dependant resource of a server and as such requires a significant amount of care to balance. RAM like disk and network is simply a shared resource that is split per physical server among all the virtual servers.

Each virtual server is given an allocation and can in theory consume memory up to that amount. While each server is allocated a maximum, it is rare for any machine to use anywhere near that amount. For example, the desktop we are using to write this is currently consuming only one-fourth of its available capacity, despite running several intensive applications in the background. Even if we ramp up and start running more applications, we only really reach a maximum of one-third of our capacity.

While this is a desktop and the applications we are running are not performing the kind of workload a complex business application would you should be able to see that it is not common for a computer to consume the entire amount of RAM available to it.

Finally, it is important to note that some hypervisors allow for "memory reclamation." This happens in times of crisis and is designed to reclaim RAM from each of the virtual servers to better balance the load and occurs by each virtual server having an application spawned by the hypervisor, which begins consuming RAM and then feeding this consumed RAM back to store data for other servers.

The final resource, CPU, is shared via the concept of time slicing, which means that all the current requests for processing are sliced up, and these are all shared between the various virtual servers.

This works the same as having multiple processes on a regular server; each of the processes queues until it can gain access to the CPU, process and then return to idle.

CPU is one of the hardest resources to share as the hypervisor not only needs to give a portion to each server but also needs to do so regularly, since CPU requests need to be attended to in a timely manner.

This introduces one of additional measures of a CPU, which is the "waiting time" measure. This measure tells how long a particular server has been sitting in the ready-and-waiting state before being able to gain access to the CPU to process.

A small measure of wait time for a CPU is expected; this occurs in all PCs when they are running, however, excessive wait times can cause serious issues with computers, their internal clocks and cause major issues with running applications.

While it is obviously impossible to have a constant level of 0 waiting time, if the levels get too excessive (say over a second), you can begin seeing real performance issues.

Managing Virtual Resources

Although for anyone who will be building a server in a public cloud there will be little scope for changing the resource allocation, there is still significant benefit in understanding how performance can be altered and potentially discussing with your cloud provider to see ways to improve performance.

So, let's start looking at managing resources from a hypervisor perspective.

To understand how to examine the performance of a virtual server, you will need to become familiar with the basic measures available to you within a hypervisor (when referring to the server with the hypervisor on it, you call it a *host*) and how each of them is sliced among the virtual machines.

To begin with, you should look at how your resources are shared among your servers. With networking resources, you normally allocate one of the basic forms of networking to a server (10Mbit, 100Mbit, 1Gbit, and so on); each represents either the whole of a physical adapter or a fixed portion of its available capacity.

Performance management of networking is really about ensuring that you have enough capacity to deal with the data you are looking to transfer. For metrics, network is the same as for a regular server proportion of bandwidth consumed over a time period.

Storage as a resource is similar to networking as mentioned earlier. Storage metrics are predominantly around the capacity. There are two metrics: how much is available to each individual virtual machine and how much is available to the host as a whole.

Running out of storage on your virtual machine can simply require you to expand the capacity available to it, which often requires as little as a few configuration changes and a restart. The host running out of space can be more troubling if the storage is hosted within it.

This would require that you purchase more storage capacity from the provider to add to the host and likely reboot it and all the virtual machines hosted on it. Finally, if storage is on a network device, that simply means expanding the amount available via the network device.

The other common measures you will see for storage are the throughput measures, which show how much data is being written to storage at any given time and often a *storage block* measure that shows the amount of time, if any, that your virtual machine has been waiting to write but has been unable to due to other machines using the disk.

Memory as a resource works in a similar fashion. You will have a current usage versus the total available capacity metrics that show the current usage, and both these measures are available for the host and for each virtual machine.

This should allow you to evaluate the current performance of your server and host. In addition to the usage metrics, you can have a memory reclamation measure. These reclamation measures are never a good sign as they are forcing the virtual machine operating system to work as if it were under extreme load.

To need to be using the reclamation measure, your host must be in need of memory that it doesn't have. This lack can occur during a period of peak processing or if your host is too far overprovisioned. One final measure you may see is the virtual memory measure.

With virtual memory, your computer uses a portion of its disk storage to act as longer-term memory; the problem is that the time taken to read and write to and from virtual memory is significantly higher than that of using normal RAM, which can cause delays.

Ideally, a computer will use some virtual memory, but using too much might be a sign that your virtual machine is under some strain and you should look to alter its allocation and increase the amount of memory available to it.

CPU is the final resource (and in our opinion the most important) because it is not being shared as simply portions of a fixed CPU; it represents a number of clock cycles offered to the virtual machine to process. The main CPU measures are like the previous measures: a proportion of the allocation CPU run time used per virtual server and a proportion of the total available processing resources consumed by all the virtual machines.

While CPU has both measures for consumption, it also has the waiting measure mentioned earlier. CPU waiting time can be a real problem for virtual machines because they are unusable while they are in the waiting state.

This makes it vital to ensure that an adequate amount of processing capacity is available to all servers. In times of high load, that you should either shut down unnecessary virtual machines or find a way to limit the amount of CPU these other machines use.

Now that you know the basic resources, you can look at how to balance these out to gain higher performance.

Balancing

There is a multitude of different systems and software that you can use to modify performance. As such, we cannot give specific application advice; what follows here is a series of steps and guidelines we have used to balance the performance of virtual machines on a virtual platform.

As with any form of load balancing, you should examine your performance beforehand, make the change, and then examine. You should be looking for improvements and aiming to make things more efficient.

If you cannot control which machines are running on a host, there is little you can do. However, gaining some background into how a virtual platform works will give you an edge in working with virtual machines.

The key concept on a virtual platform is to have enough servers running on the host that the resources are taxed, which minimizes waste, but are not overtaxed, which would lead to some of your servers being starved for resources.

One of the first things any virtualization software systems provisioning manual normally covers is the idea that you need to mix your virtual machines up; some will be performing nighttime processing, and some will perform daytime processing, for example. This way, you will have one doing heavy processing while the other rests. This can be advantageous for virtual machine owners to keep in mind because you can work to find some equilibrium as well.

So, with this in mind you need to ensure that the servers on your cluster are doing different forms of processing at different times. Mixing workloads will go a long way to leveling out the kinds of total workload you have.

Next is to look at allocations per virtual machine, which requires a measure of historical information about your server and will need for it to have been running for a time, the longer the better.

You need to look at the performance over this period and find the average and the maximum. If there are some significant spikes that don't occur regularly, you should look over your servers running logs and find out why these occur.

If you have found that you have need for excess capacity at a certain point during the day or week, you should look to arrange a flexible CPU amount overall, but set your allocation lower totally.

You should look to be running as high a CPU consumption as you can without affecting the performance of the application, depending on the OS, application, and so on. Under a good running workload, this can be 60% of your CPU allocation.

This theory runs completely contrary to the normal way people allocate resources: you add as much as you can to deal with growth and any extra need for processing power.

While this is advantageous in a virtual machine, it is a waste to have all that extra capacity sitting idle on your server. Moreover, in the cloud it actually costs you more to have this because in the cloud you pay for the resources you are given. (This is true for most of the resources you will have.) If you don't need the extra capacity, do not ask for it and get rid of it. While you are doing this, you should always be looking at not only your system performance but also your application performance. This is the ultimate balancing act.

Looking from a higher level at the host side of things, everything becomes more fixed. You cannot juggle the available resources to find that sweet spot as you would with a virtual machine.

Instead it becomes about ensuring that the collection of virtual machines is okay and able to function. This means that you are realistically monitoring all these resources to ensure that you don't have too many virtual machines on one host.

Examining the values for how much CPU and RAM are good beginning indicators, and like a virtual machine you will want these values to be high, but not full.

Storage ensures that you have enough disk space to continue running, and networking is the same: that you have enough to continue allowing all your servers to function. In addition to this disk space, storage also encompasses the input and output to storage devices, which is referred to as I/O. Beyond having enough capacity, it is also very important to ensure that your storage devices are not flooded with requests for storage. Having higher levels of storage I/O can cause major problems with storage as each server will need to wait longer and longer in a queue for its turn to store data.

Now beyond these basic raw consumption measures, you will have some other metrics, such as the CPU waiting time measure and the memory reclamation measure. These are very important measures as having any memory reclamation is a sign that your host is under load, and you need to remove some of the applications consuming memory.

This is not the same for the CPU waiting time because having a hypervisor introduces this by default, which means you will only be able to achieve a waiting time of 0 for all your servers at all times when you have less virtual machines that your host has logical processors. Having a small wait time on each server is normal and simply makes the server function at the same level as it would with physical resources. This is not to say that waiting time is a low-impact resource.

You must at all times ensure that waiting times for your servers are low, normally under one second; any more time that this and you run the risk of severely crippling the virtual machines running on the host. As with most of these resources, it is simply another measure that says you have added too many virtual machines to your server.

Much of this would be trial and error, but the primary overriding concept is that you want to have your host so that it contains as many virtual machines as possible while maintaining as little impact to the regular running of all and leaving enough overhead to deal with peak processing loads.

Overprovisioning

In order to achieve the ideal aim of having a large number of virtual machines on a single host with no impact you need to become familiar with a concept called .

Overprovisioning means allocating more resources and (normally) more virtual machines that your host has available to it. This is for many people an odd concept at first. They key is in understanding how servers are loaded - which in and of itself will help you understand your long-term performance. In a server running just an operating system, you should expect to see very low levels and flat graphs - as the usage of the server doesn't change over time, it's just sitting there.

From this basic operating system level you can now add the application - the purpose for us having a server. Now that you have this running, you should see an increase in your base running, but in addition to this you will likely see some periods of higher running or regular spikes.

These indicate periods of higher processing by your application; as an example, times when a larger number of users is connected. From these you should be able to find what would be the normal expected level of usage when your application is under server processing load from high usage.

Once you have an idea what level of resources your server will use while processing, you can use this level as the realistic maximum and then give your server this amount of resources and a small amount of overhead, in case its workload exceeds your expectations (normally this overhead is somewhere between one-third to one-fifth). It is that overhead between your normal workload, peak workload, and the small amount of excess that gives a whole lot of excess resources and is where virtualization shines!

All those slivers of leftover overhead, all that space that is not being used at any one given moment when combined form a significant volume of resources, and all of them when combined are enough to power several virtual machines. This is what you call overprovisioning, adding more servers than you have provisioned for, because you know that you will have spare extra capacity to use with these servers. This is similar to what most airlines do with bookings: to avoid having unfilled seats they book for more people than a plane can carry – assuming that some passengers won't show up!

Working overprovisioning correctly is similar in manner to how you allocate resources to a virtual machine, simply find your "normal" loaded resource consumption and then add virtual machines, while continually checking to ensure you aren't affecting any one virtual machine.

Additionally, this is where resources such as CPU waiting time and memory reclamation come into their own. They can provide real-time indication that your host is in trouble and you can react by shutting down a virtual machine or redistributing resources.

Planning

Much of what is required to make a virtual machine or virtual machine host function correctly is planning. Planning in this context is simply about the collection of data and adapting your systems based on this data.

So to start your planning system, you need to collect data. Most virtual machine platforms have a significant performance history system within them, so take advantage of this and find times when your virtual machines' loads have peaked. Match this with any load or user information you have on your servers, such as times when you were performing backups or times when you had a significantly heavy user volume.

In addition, you can also look at what kind of levels you have when your system is quiet, so between the two you can begin to make comparisons and find commonalities between the loads.

Consider the example illustrated in Figure 13-4.

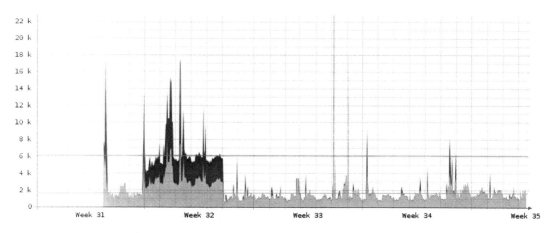

Figure 13-4. Performance graph

In the figure, you can see that you have several high load spikes: one big spike during the first week when the server was being stress tested and big spikes once a week. They occur on Saturday night as this is when you are performing stress and load tests. Knowing this, you could set up systems within our virtual platform to help cope. Before our load is expected to increase (say on Saturday morning), we make a request to our cloud provider (or virtual machine host) to double the capacity of our server, temporarily. This means that when the load comes, our server is ready and will function effectively. Finally, after the peak period we can drop the server off to the lower normal level.

These kinds of changes take full advantage of the cloud; we can dynamically expand our capacity in real time to accommodate a known period of heavy load. In addition, we minimize costs by keeping the allocation of resources to our server low during the periods of lower workload.

Cloud Elasticity

Cloud servers that are virtualized have other advantages to boot. In addition to being able to be scaled, they are portable.

The portable nature of cloud servers comes from the style that their storage takes. In the case of most virtual machines, the storage for them are written to *hard drive files* on disk, which allows them to be easily backed up, allocated per virtual machine, and so on.

The added benefit here is that each file can be treated as one would normally treat a file: it can be moved, renamed, or copied. This is an extremely useful thing since a copy of an existing virtual machine can give you an identical clone of an existing server.

Many cloud providers offer the ability to clone a server from an existing one using this method. This means that if you are aware of an incoming period of excessive usage, you can take advantage of this feature, clone your machine, and set this up to work as a clustered partner with your existing server.

Or if you already have an existing cluster, simply add this server to the load balancer, and it will function. After the load has passed, you can shut down the server, which has dealt with some excessive load and again minimized costs to you by leveraging the flexibility of the cloud.

There is an even greater advantage: if you see the load spike again later, you can simply power the server up again and (assuming you have a high availability cluster, as discussed in Chapter 12) power the server up. It would register with heartbeat and would begin working until the server is no longer needed!

Working with a Cloud Server

So, now that you understand the full power of a cloud server, let's have a look at working with one. All the testing needs were covered by a group of cloud servers provided by serverlove.com, so we will show you how you can configure a virtual cloud server as outlined previously.

So, to begin with let's look at resource renegotiation. To perform this, we needed to log in to the Serverlove management page. From here, you can see a list of the servers you have been using (Figure 13-5).

Your Servers

Server Name	Status	CPU	RAM	Drives	Network	Actions
lb	Started at 2011-08-05 12:25:31	2000 Mhz	2048 MB	lb-eelco	Running at 178.250.53.225 (traffic) Password *: lmf6263	Shutdown Hard power off Hard reset
server2	Started at 2011-08-05 00:27:17	2000 Mhz	1024 MB	server2	Running at 178.250.53.133 (traffic) Password *: Uguu3987	Shutdown Hard power off Hard reset
testbox	Started at 2011-08-05 10:51:27	2000 Mhz	1024 MB	testbox	Running at 178.250.53.132 (traffic) Password *: Jcul4495	Shutdown Hard power off Hard reset
server1	Started at 2011-07-20 14:01:44	2000 Mhz	1024 MB	server1	Running at 178.250.53.142 (traffic) Password *: Evbu3329	Shutdown Hard power off Hard reset
Demo	Stopped	2000 Mhz	1024 MB	Ubuntu 10.04 Desktop Live CD	Dynamic IP	Start Edit Delete
memcache	Stopped	2000 Mhz	2048 MB	memcache	178.250.53.225	Start Edit Delete

* This is the VNC password for console access, and also the default root/administrator password for the server. These passwords are synchronised when the server is first created, however if you change either the VNC or the administrator/root password, the other will not be updated.

Help: FAQs | Configuring your Server | Linux Setup Notes | Windows Setup Notes | Console Access

Figure 13-5. *Server list page*

From the server list page, you can power on or off a server. Unfortunately, just like with a real server, you need to shut down and reboot the server to make a change to the resources allocated it. This is due to the fact that most, if not all, modern operating systems cannot dynamically reconfigure their internal memory allocation from scratch.

Once you have shut the server down, you can press Edit to bring up the server configuration page. The configuration page allows you to edit the available CPU, RAM, Hard Drives, Network Adapter, VNC, and other specific details. From this panel (see Figure 13-6) you can elastically alter the resources as needed (with the altered costs, of course).

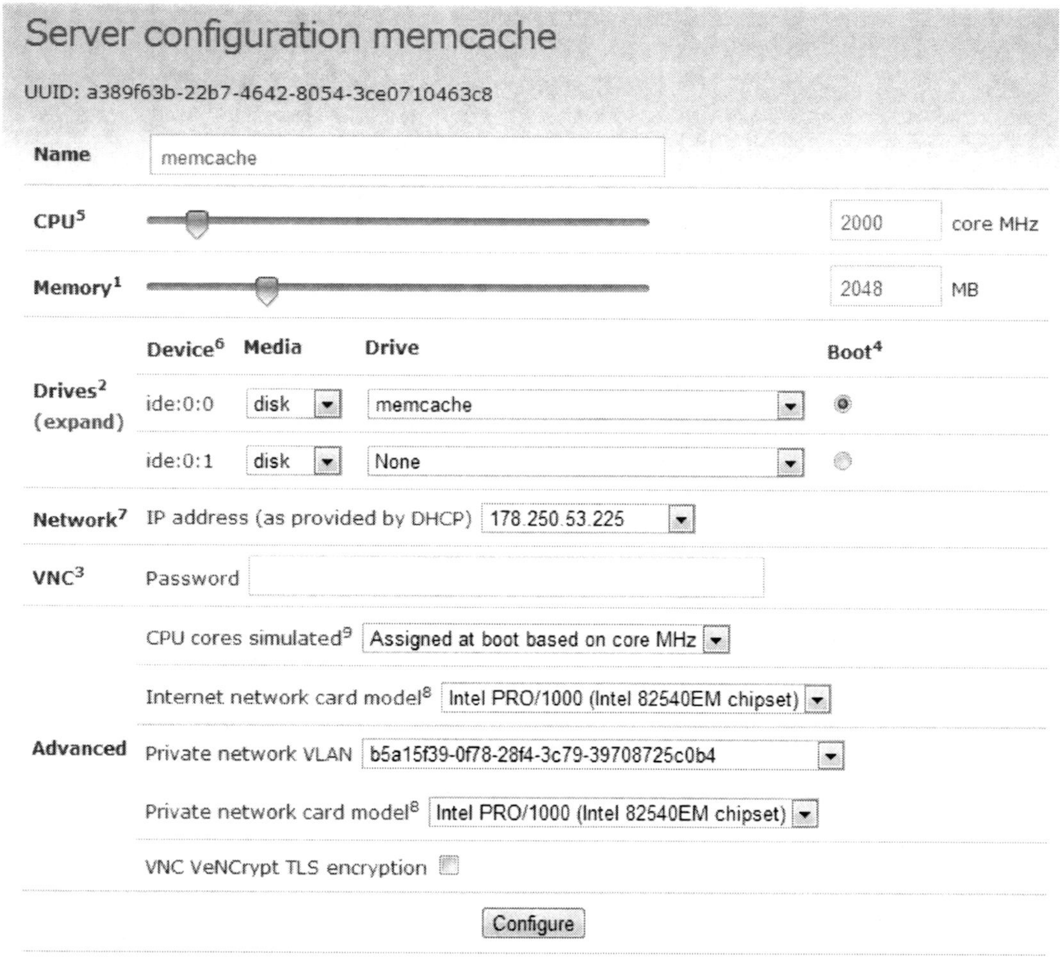

Server configuration memcache

UUID: a389f63b-22b7-4642-8054-3ce0710463c8

Name	memcache

CPU[5] ——————————————————————— 2000 core MHz

Memory[1] ——————————————————————— 2048 MB

	Device[6]	Media	Drive		Boot[4]
Drives[2] (expand)	ide:0:0	disk ▾	memcache	▾	◉
	ide:0:1	disk ▾	None	▾	○

Network[7] IP address (as provided by DHCP) 178.250.53.225 ▾

VNC[3] Password [   ]

CPU cores simulated[9] Assigned at boot based on core MHz ▾

Internet network card model[8] Intel PRO/1000 (Intel 82540EM chipset) ▾

Advanced Private network VLAN b5a15f39-0f78-28f4-3c79-39708725c0b4 ▾

Private network card model[8] Intel PRO/1000 (Intel 82540EM chipset) ▾

VNC VeNCrypt TLS encryption ☐

[Configure]

Figure 13-6. Server config panel

Keeping in mind that the drive selector is a drop-down, you can head back to the main page (see Figure 13-7) to see the hard-drive creation utilities in which you can create virtual hard disks to attach to the virtual machines.

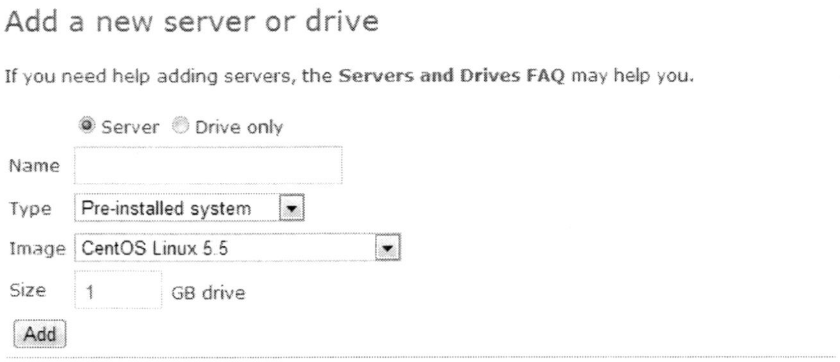

Add a new server or drive

If you need help adding servers, the **Servers and Drives FAQ** may help you.

● Server ○ Drive only

Name	
Type	Pre-installed system ▾
Image	CentOS Linux 5.5 ▾
Size	1 GB drive

Add

Figure 13-7. Adding a new drive

In addition to creating new virtual drives you can also scroll down and modify and clone the drives that already exist with the servers (see Figure 3-8).

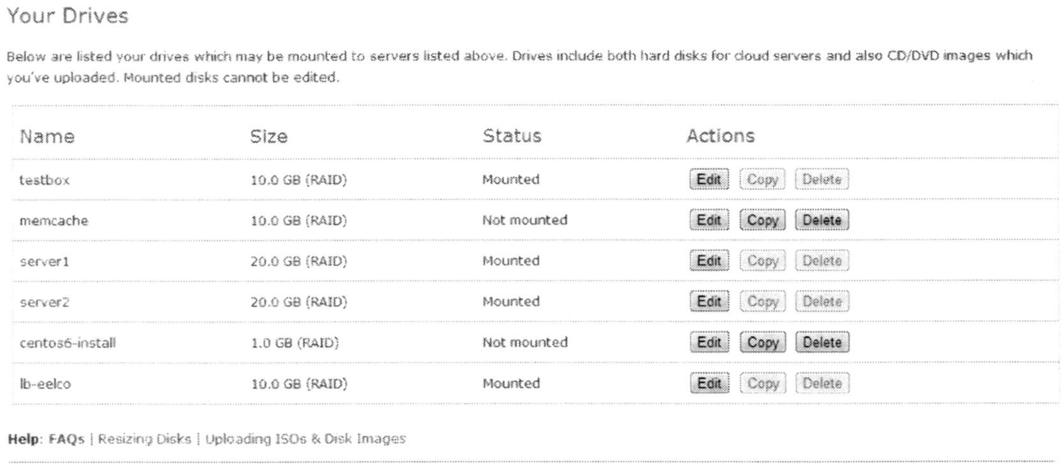

Your Drives

Below are listed your drives which may be mounted to servers listed above. Drives include both hard disks for cloud servers and also CD/DVD images which you've uploaded. Mounted disks cannot be edited.

Name	Size	Status	Actions
testbox	10.0 GB (RAID)	Mounted	Edit Copy Delete
memcache	10.0 GB (RAID)	Not mounted	Edit Copy Delete
server1	20.0 GB (RAID)	Mounted	Edit Copy Delete
server2	20.0 GB (RAID)	Mounted	Edit Copy Delete
centos6-install	1.0 GB (RAID)	Not mounted	Edit Copy Delete
lb-eelco	10.0 GB (RAID)	Mounted	Edit Copy Delete

Help: FAQs | Resizing Disks | Uploading ISOs & Disk Images

Figure 13-8. Modify drives

From the preceding examples, you should be now be aware of exactly how flexible a cloud server can be and how easy it is to expand the power and capacity of your servers – as needed.

Summary

Having been through this chapter, you should now be familiar with the real benefits offered by the new cloud technologies emerging all over the planet. You learned about cloud services – how they are built and run. The chapter also discussed virtualization, one of the key technologies that work with cloud. Finally, you should now have some of the basic strategies with which to take advantage of cloud servers to increase your server performance and minimize costs.

## CHAPTER 14

IPv6: Implications and Concepts

IPv6 is the current standard for Internet communications replacing the currently used and outdated IPv4 protocol.

The aim of this chapter is to:

- Provide an overview of IPv6

- Provide an understanding of the reasons why IPv6 is replacing IPv4

- Explain the implications of changing from IPv4 to IPv6

- Show how to modify the applications you have been working with to use IPv6

IPv6

IPv6 is the next generation Internet addressing and routing protocol. IPv6 has been in development since the mid-1990s as a replacement for the existing and increasingly limited IPv4.IPv4 began its life as a protocol that formed the basis of the Internet and was standardized in 1980.

IPv6 allows the addressing of Internet-capable devices with addresses 64 bits long. These are normally written as eight groups of four hexadecimal digits, separated by colons. This gives the addresses the following appearance:

OOFF:OOFF:OOFF:OOFF:OOFF:OOFF:OOFF:OOFF

Given the large size of these numbers, IPv6 provides addressing for approximately 340 undecillion (3.4×10^{38}) systems. The reason for this large number is to avoid the issues currently present in most modern computer systems due to the limited availability of IPv4 addresses.

Hexadecimal Notation

IPv6 addresses contain both letters and numbers. This format is called *hexadecimal* (*hex* for short) notation because it represents a base 16 counting system. This means you count 1 to 16 bits; then increment your units. Each hex digit represents 4 bits, using the letters A to F to supplement the familiar decimal digits 0-9 (see Table 14-1).

Table 14-1. *Hexadecimal Numbers*

Decimal	1	2	3	4	5	6	7	8	9	10	11	12	13	14	15	16	17	...
Hexadecimal	1	2	3	4	5	6	7	8	9	A	B	C	D	E	F	10	11	...

From Table 14-1 you should be able to get a much better idea of how hexadecimal notation works, which numbers are represented, and how they fall in sequence.

Truncation

IPv6 addresses are very long, and you can get quite exhausted looking at one. There are two things you can do to make them more readable:

- Leading zeroes for each set (between colons) can be removed.

- Sets of consecutive zeroes can be replaced by a double colon.

For example, (192.168.0.0.0.0.0.1 in decimal format):

1. Start with `00c0:00a8:0000:0000:0000:0000:0000:0001`.

2. Apply rule one becomes `c0:a8:0:0:0:0:0:1`.

3. Apply rule two becomes `c0:a8::1`.

This standard part of IPv6 notation allows you to make these addresses much more simple and human readable.

IPv4 Exhaustion

As Internet growth has grown and then exploded over the past 30 years, IPv4 has faced a problem. It could only provide addresses for 2^{32} addresses (4,294,967,296). This limit is decreased, however, as 288 million of these addresses are unavailable for regular public use - they are special-purpose addresses.

It has been known that the world will run out of addresses since the early to mid-1990s, so a number of technologies have come along to help address these issues. Network Address Translation (NAT) is the best example as it meant that larger companies were able to rely on a single or small pool of addresses. However, as of January 31 2011, there are no more IPv4 addresses available for public usage.

As there are no more IPv4 addresses available, the need for Internet users to understand, embrace, and transition to IPv6 is pressing and urgent. The reason for this is that the Internet has expanded so far that it is no longer possible for every computer to switch to IPv6 at once. This was the transition method that led to the use of IPv4: on January 1 1983, the collection of networks that formed the then-fledgling Internet (then called ARPANET) switched over to IP.

This switch would have meant software changes as all the devices attached to the network needed to be changed over to use the new IP protocol. This meant changes to several thousand systems across the continental USA and was considered a major feat in its time.

What if the same change needed to be made today? It would mean that more than 4 billion devices would need to be changed over in one day. Moreover, the diversity of devices and the age of others make this impractical if not impossible. This has lead to a more mixed approach to the rollout of IPv6.

Approach to IPv6

The current approached is very phased, with the policy being "adopt when you can." However, with the increasing urgency that comes from the world having run out of IP addresses, it is more prudent that you be able to have your servers use IPv6.

In addition to adopting wherever possible, many people have taken up using IPv6–capable NAT devices to fulfill the basic requirements. This means that an IPv6 router acts as the front end of a network and provides an IPv6 Internet address, while behind the router an IPv4 network exists. This solution provides the best of both worlds, bringing forward compatibility while minimizing the volume of changes that need to be made.

Advantages of IPv6

While simply having an IPv6 gateway may seem ideal, it does not provide you with the full volume of benefits offered by the IPv6 suite. In addition to the increased address space available to IPv6 users and the future proofing this entails, there are a number of other benefits of IPv6.

The first advantage is a decrease in the amount of processing needed by routers to forward IPv6 packets. This is due to a reorganization in the way that IPv6 packets are structured. With hindsight, the less-used options of the packet are placed in a trailing optional section. This means that routers can find the information they need much more readily.

The second advantage is in the processing of message sub-blocks. When transmitting an IP packet (v4 or v6), the packet can be split up into smaller chunks called fragments for easier transmission over a network. For IPv4, these packets are then reassembled again between routers, which can add delay - especially if a packet is lost. In IPv6, only the destination is responsible for the reassembly of packets, which cuts down considerably on the trip time over networks that fragment packets.

The third advantage is Internet Protocol Security (IPSec) support. IPSec is the security protocol that functions as part of the Internet Protocol. IPSec works in the same manner as SSL: it creates an end-to-end encrypted tunnel with the sender and receiver negotiating keys between them to ensure a secure communications channel is established. From this, each packet transferred is encrypted at one end and decrypted at the other. IPSec is not the specific domain of IPv6, but was developed as part of IPv6 and then later transferred back to IPv6.

The advantage in this case is that all IPv6 devices must support IPSec, whereas IPv4 does not require that all devices using it be capable of using IPsec. This is a distinct advantage when security is tantamount, as it means that clients can be required to use IPSec to ensure that data being transfer is more secure.

Implementation

Now that we have touted the benefits of IPv6, you need to examine a couple of methods for deploying IPv6 to your environment. There are a number of different ways that you can go about accomplishing this, and we cannot cover every single case with an example. What we will do is to provide some base concepts and then a few select examples covering some of the more broad situations you could encounter.

The goal is that you should understand how an IPv6 implementation should work and adapt from this because no two installations are alike, and it's not possible for us to cover every single permutation. To begin, let's cover the basic directions you will take.

The basic concept is that you will have any Internet facing devices using IPv6, all internal network devices using IPv6, and whichever applications possible using IPv6; and any remaining traffic will use IPv4. For this to occur, you will basically be creating two networks: a "base" IPv6 network with an IPv4 network overlaid for specific traffic. This means that you will need to have two completely separate sets of networking information for each system and will need to maintain any routing or network address information twice. This network layout is detailed in Figure 14-1.

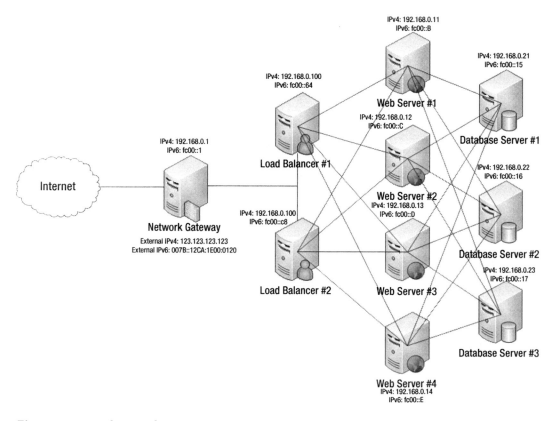

Figure 14-1. Dual networks

The second method is simply having one IPv6 forward-facing interface. This is much easier to accomplish because it only involves having only one network and having an application or router function as an IPv6 gateway. However, this means that you will need to provide the gateway with multiple network adapters and will lose some of the benefits given by IPv6. This network layout is detailed in Figure 14-2.

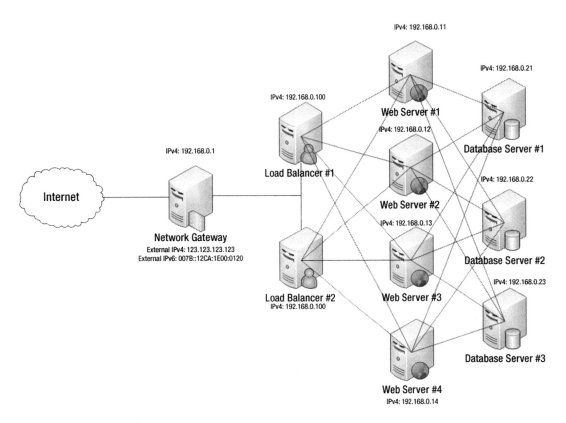

Figure 14-2. IPv4 with IPv6 gateway

Now that you have seen the two examples, let's begin.

Internet Connection

The first thing you will need to do is make sure that your Internet connection is IPv6, which requires that you are going through an ISP that will provide you with an IPv6 IP and connection to the wider Internet. Not all ISPs currently support IPv6, so it is important to check with an ISP before signing up to see that you will be able to get an IPv6 address and that it is routable to the Internet.

We cannot recommend specific ISPs for you as we cannot speak to availability or any of the many factors that would go into signing an ISP contract; what we can suggest is that you shop around and ensure you understand any contract you sign. Once you have established that your Internet connection is an IPv6 connection, you can begin configuring your network.

DNS

Once you have sorted out an IPv6 IP address, the first thing you should do is to add your new IPv6 address to your existing DNS entries. If you are using a hosted DNS provider you will need to check the capability to support IPv6 addresses and then work with your provider to update your DNS listing. If you are hosting your own DNS server, you will need to make changes to your DNS system to add your IPv6 address.

Just as with the provider, you will need to validate that your DNS server software supports IPv6 DNS addressing. After you have validated that your software supports IPv6, the changes you will need to make are rather simple. You simply need to add an AAAA record to your DNS file that links your URL to the new IPv6 address you have been given. This AAAA record will work in the same manner as a normal A record and is used to signify an IPv6 entry.

■ **Tip**   Don't forget to update the Serial field after each DNS change.

Operating System

As with all the parts of your system, you should ensure that your operating systems support IPv6. While most operating systems released in the past 10 years should support IPv6 out of the box, it is important to be sure whether they do or do not. You should also be aware of any specific caveats to the functioning of IPv6 on that system that may dictate small changes to your implementation.

As it stands, you have used two operating systems within this book, both Centos 6 and Ubuntu 10.04, and both of these operating systems support IPv6. However, any modern Linux that is running any kernel since 2.6 should be capable of running IPv6. Moving beyond Linux, we can confirm that Windows supports IPv6 from Windows XP Service Pack 1 onward. Given the number of operating systems available, we can't go over each of them. All we can recommend is to check the documentation of your OS.

Networking

Now that you have completed the first step in moving toward IPv6, you will need to begin attaching it to our network. From this point, you can begin taking different directions as to how you want to accomplish the task of adding IPv6 support for your website.

Single Gateway Network

Given that you now have an IPv6 address and have configured the DNS for it, all that remains is to add IPv6 support to your network gateway. This gateway is the point in your network that your DNS settings point to as being the face your network presents to the outside world. These gateways normally take requests and forward them back into your network for processing. For this, your gateway device will need at least two device ports and IP addresses. This means that it is in effect multi-homed and lives both in your network and on the Internet.

This means that only your gateway device needs to be capable of working with IPv6. This device can be a router or even be an Internet facing server. If you are using a server rather than a router as your gateway device you will need to ensure that it and all the software you plan to run on the server support IPv6.

Dual Network

This is the much more involved of the two options. For this, you will begin by establishing the layout and addressing for both your networks. The order won't matter as you will need to overlay both networks. To begin, start establishing which devices you have that will support IPv6. From this point you need to establish whether each system is to support IPv4 or both IPv4 and IPv6.

The criteria for establishing these are as follows:

- Will the OS support IPv6?

- Will all the applications that are to contact this system use IPv6?

- Will all applications that are to communicate with this server use IPv6?

From this point, you need to create both the networks by establishing IP addresses for each server (both IPv4 and IPv6 when appropriate). Remember, the aim is to have IPv6 wherever possible and have IPv4 as the fallback for those applications that cannot support IPv6. Once you have established and laid out your network, you should perform connectivity tests on both networks to ensure that your servers can communicate over both protocols.

Application Support

Once you have established connectivity, it's time to begin changing your applications. We will cover the applications that you have been using thus far and how specifically IPv6 affects these applications. For more specific information on the applications, you should visit the earlier chapters in this book that cover each application.

Apache

Apache has built-in support for IPv6, can function in either IPv4 or IPv6 modes, and has two modes for operating the two together. This is handled by an Apache build configuration option that needs to be specified at compile time. These configuration flags are '--enable-v4-mapped' and '--disable-v4-mapped'; and they need to be specified when executing the 'configure' command to compile Apache.

The default for Linux systems is to have v4 mapping enabled. This means that whenever possible, Apache will attempt to map between the IPv6 and IPv4 addresses. This means that adding a basic directive such as 'Listen 80' will make Apache listen on both IPv4 and IPv6 interfaces on port 80. In this instance, Apache keeps both connections within the same sockets and uses all its sub processes for IPv4 and IPv6 connections.

If you want to specify an IPv6 address to your Apache server, it can be done using the same Listen directive. It functions exactly the same way as normal, but the IPv6 address must be wrapped in square braces [...] giving the appearance "Listen [00FF:00FF:00FF:00FF:00FF:00FF:00FF:00FF]:80".

At this point, you might want to have your IPv4 and IPv6 running on separate processes – if, say, you are experiencing slowdown across the board when an IPv6 connection occurs. Then you will need to set the --disable-v4-mapped flag, which means that any socket that is accepting IPv4 connections can't accept IPv6 connections. Then you will need to add the following Listen directives:

```
Listen [::]:80
Listen 0.0.0.0:80
```

These two directives will tell Apache that it needs to read from any port 80 connection via IPv4 and separately any IPv6 connection on port 80. With these two methods, you should be able to tailor the way that Apache deals with IPv6.

Nginx

Nginx leverages part of the Linux operating system to configure whether or not it will need to use the IPv4 to IPv6 mapping. This feature is controlled via the file /etc/sysctl.conf. To modify, you will need to set the following entry so that its value is 1.

```
net.ipv6.bindv6only = 1
```

After this, you will need to reload your config with the following:

```
sysctl -p
```

This change means that IPv6 addresses will never be bound into IPv4 addresses for processing by *any* application! The same as using the --disable-v4-mapped parameter in Apache. From this point, you can modify the listen parameters, just as with Apache IPv6, entries need to be in square brackets.

The key difference is that with bindv6only = 1 set, if you attempt a listen with only the IPv6 entry, you will receive errors. To negate this, you will need to use the ipv6only=on; parameter.

This will cause errors in 'bind socket':

```
listen [::]:80;
```

This will not cause errors as it specifies only IPv6 connections:

```
listen [::]:80 ipv6only=on;
```

However, in contrast to this, if the net.ipv6.bindv6only is set to 0, adding a statement such as listen [::]:80; will allow you to listen on both IPv6 and IPv4.

Varnish Cache

Varnish cache needs to be above version 1.0 and it will accept IPv6 addresses. As with the previous applications, simply replace IPv4 addresses with IPv6 addresses inside square brackets. If only a port is specified within its config then Varnish will listen on both IPv4 and IPv6 interfaces.

Memcached

Memcached simply needs to be above version 1.2.5 to function with IPv6 addresses. In this instance, as with previous ones, you simply need to replace IPv4 addresses with IPv6 addresses inside square brackets.

IPVS

IPVS has limited support for IPv6. The requirement for this is that your kernel version be greater than 2.6.28-rc3 (as this kernel was the one that included the new IPVS IPv6 features). In addition, you should have the latest version of IPVS possible. Once you have IPv6, support is fairly straightforward, the IPv6 entries just need to be made as normal with IPv6 addresses being in square brackets. An IPVS entry can be worked like the following example:

```
ipvsadm -A -t [c0:a8::1]:80
ipvsadm -a -t [c0:a8::1]:80 -r [c0:a8::2]:80 -m
ipvsadm -a -t [c0:a8::1]:80 -r [c0:a8::2]:80 -m
```

In addition, the IPVS team has published the following list of what is supported and what is not supported with regard to IPv6:

What Works with IPv6

- Forwarding mechanisms: NAT, Direct Routing(DR), maybe Tunnel (not fully tested yet)

- Protocols: TCP, UDP, Encapsulated Security Payload (ESP), Authentication Header (AH) (last two not tested)

- Manipulation and inspection of both IPv4 and IPv6 entries with ipvsadm

- Six out of ten schedulers (10/10 in latest net-next dev tree)

- ping6 monitor in heartbeat

- ldirectord using external commands for monitoring

What Is Not Supported with IPv6

- Handling fragmentation or other extension headers

- FTP application helper (can be loaded, but only operates on v4)

- sync daemon (can be started, but only operates on v4)

- Probably some incorrect handling of ICMPv6 or other corner cases

- Most built-in probes in ldirectord - use checkcommand

- Real servers must be specified individually in ldirectord, address ranges are not supported

Ldirectord

As with IPVS, ldirectord is simply a static replace of IPv4 addresses with IPv6 ones. The following is an example config for Ldirectord.cf:

```
virtual = [c0:a8::1]:80
        protocol = tcp
        scheduler = wlc
        real = [c0:a8::2]:80 gate 1000
        real = [c0:a8::3]:80 gate 1000
        service = http
```

Heartbeat

Like Ldirectord, heartbeat involves a static replacement of IPv4 addresses with IPv6 addresses. The only differences between the two this time is that support is limited to 'full' addresses only - meaning that you cannot shortcut the addresses with step two of IPv6 truncation.

Summary

Throughout the course of this chapter, you have covered the implications of IPv6 and the changes it is bringing about to the Internet and world. This chapter has covered what IPv6 is and how IPv6 addresses look and the benefits it provides. You have covered the basic methods for adding IPv6 to an existing system and you have covered the implications of doing this. Finally, you covered the configuration changes needed over a number of applications to establish IPv6 connectivity with them.

CHAPTER 15

Where to Go Next...

Over the course of this book, we have covered a large number of topics in a considerable amount of depth. We have looked at load balancing from almost every conceivable angle. We have examined the following:

- Content cacheing
- DNS load balancing
- HTTP load balancing
- Database load balancing
- SSL load balancing
- Clustering for higher performance
- Load balancing in the cloud
- IPv6

This is quite a large amount of content to have covered, but this list is by no means exhaustive. Load balancing as you are well aware by now is a method for getting the best performance out of a system for your money. It maximizes the return you get on the investments you have made to your systems.

This, of course, means load balancing will never die. There will always be more of a drive to extend the performance and capabilities of systems, and this means there is always more to learn. So from here, we need to discuss some of the many other avenues you can look at to further increase performance. Many of these areas are highly specialized and would take more space than we have to go over them in any reasonable amount of depth.

In this chapter, you will look at the following:

- Monitoring
- Security
- Operating System Performance
- Planning

Recap

Over the course of this book we have covered quite a lot of stuff! We opened to an introduction on web servers: what they are, what they do, and what can cause them to have lower performance than expected. Following this we went through some of the many ways that people can improve the performance of their web server's through the use of things like cacheing. You also looked at content delivery networks and DNS load balancing, and learned the methods for planning performance and reliability.

The second part of the book covered load balancing for HTTP, databases, and SSL servers. Load balancing throughout these chapters was to find ways to not only improve the performance of your web servers but also all the other components that it depends on.

Finally, we covered some specific load balancing situations, including the creation of a clustered environment. We also went further to cover load balancing within a cloud environment and finally the implications of IPv6 on a clustered environment.

Monitoring

Over the course of most of the book, one of the few running themes that cropped up was watching your system's performance and its resource consumption. This can be quite time-consuming, especially in the case of a large clustered environment; moreover, when you are trying to collect and compare for a dozen devices, it can become a little overwhelming. This is where monitoring solutions come into play.

Monitoring solutions are systems that are designed to collect performance statistics for servers and applications and often to collect performance statistics and alert end users when certain events occur on these monitored devices. This can be really beneficial when you want to look at the impacts of one or more changes to your system, as you can compare its current performance with historic performance and continue trending.

There are a large number of free open-source solutions to monitoring your applications, and within them a plethora of configuration and monitoring options. Some of the more common open-source monitoring solutions are these:

- Nagios
- Cacti
- Zabbix
- Zenoss
- GroundWork
- Munin

In addition to these solutions, there are a number of options for what kind of monitoring you will do. At a high level, there are two basic types: agent-based and agentless. These two are simply for differentiating which type of monitoring you are using. *Agent-based* monitoring involves installing a specific piece of monitoring software onto your server; this software is called the *agent*.

Agentless is the opposite; it involves using common features within the system it is monitoring to collect data, without the need to invoke a specific application to do this. The trade-off is in resource usage and availability. Agent-based systems require the installation of an agent, and the agent must be running and working at all times to allow monitoring to function. This consumes system resources.

Agentless systems will still use resources and can use more, fewer, or similar resources. The level of resources used comes down to how broad the scope of the monitoring is and which tools from the OS it invokes to help accomplish this.

Given that agents are specific to the systems that require them, we cannot go into much detail about how they work without going into very specific detail. If you want to know more about agent-based monitoring, you should investigate some of the tools mentioned (Nagios has some very powerful plugins and Zabbix has its own agent). Beyond the agents, there are several very common agentless systems that allow you to monitor your system without installing specialist software.

For all systems and devices, the most common is Simple Network Management protocol (SNMP for short). SNMP provides a Management Information Base (MIB) that provides a collection of references to pieces of data related to the server. This means that vendors can create MIB, which can be used over all their devices (say a Cisco MIB). This means that one reference can be used to query the same data for all devices in a collection. The one grey area with regard to SNMP is that often your servers will need to have SNMP software installed in order to provide the ability for it to respond correctly to SNMP requests.

Within most Linux systems, the most common implementation of SNMP is net-snmp, which should be able to be installed via your package management system. In addition to SNMP, the next most common monitoring solution is monitoring via SSH. This means that the monitoring system logs into the monitored system and then performs any checks it needs to on the loacl system via SSH taking the collected information with it.

The advantage is that only built-in operating system functions would be used to perform checks, but the problem is that you need to configure a static form of remote access to perform the queries. And your queries can be limited by the availability of commands on the operating system, which means that if commands are missing or output different between versions, output can differ and cause issues between systems!

As you can guess, there is no one-size-fits-all solution. It has been our experience to simply do things depending on the situation. Even if you have a group of similar servers, the same monitoring may not work for all. Some may have limited access and only need to be monitored infrequently and be a good case for using SNMP. User machines may have ready remote access and a large toolset, making monitoring via SSH the best solution there.

Finally, heavy load production machines may need very specialized monitoring requirements and limited access making them ideal for a specialist agent service. It is simply a matter of finding what works with the system you are monitoring and tailoring your system to work best with the device to be monitored.

Security

While it is almost never something that is associated with performance systems, security is something that almost always needs to be considered in high-performance systems. It is an unfortunate truth that security is often considered an impediment to high performance as the two often have competing goals.

The state aim of many security systems is to prevent or limit access to systems, which often means imposing checks and enforcing encryption measures. These checks can take time, and encryption (as you will recall from the SSL chapter) can be costly due to the increased processing overhead. This is not to say that you should take security lightly. In the environment online, it is more and more important to consider security. It can even be used to increase performance.

Access Control

Probably one of the easiest ways to increase security on your system with a minimal performance impact is to limit access to your systems. This means that fewer users can log in, and you can save a small number of resources that could be used to deal with false logins. If you have enabled SSH on your system, you can often do small changes to stop users constantly attempting to brute force access to your server.

The easiest methods we have found to control access are discussed in the following two sections.

Limit Root Login

If you want to be root on your server, you can log in via a normal account and escalate with 'su -' and the root password or 'sudo su -' and your password (assuming you're a sudo-er). To limit root, you need to edit the /etc/sshd/ssh_config file and change the entry for PermitRootLogin to no. This means that nobody can log in to your server by root, which means that the majority of external attempts to login are automatically bounced.

Block Known Attackers

Almost all Linux systems keep a track of who has attempted to login to a given server. This file is normally /var/log/auth.log and will list every attempt. Often users will fire attempt after attempt to try and gain access to your server by guessing passwords. This can be a real problem as you may wind up with lots and lots of connection attempts, each taking up a small amount of resources to be dealt with.

The solution we have found most effective is to use software such as DenyHosts, which simply parses the /var/log/auth.log file for users that make more than a certain number of attempts and then adds the IP addresses of these people to the hosts.deny file. This means that any further attempts from these addresses will be blocked.

■ **Warning**   This can 100% lock you out of your server if you are not cautious.

Views

One of the best security measures that can increase performance are views within databases. As it stands, attacks on databases are some of the most common attacks on the Internet, and views not only provide an effective measure for mitigating a lot of the risk but also increase performance.

The basic concept behind the view is to create a specialized "subset" of your whole database that you will be used on queries instead of using the whole database. Using this cut down subset can significantly reduce the time taken to execute queries, which improves the time required to process a transaction.

From a security standpoint, views provide the benefit of limited exposure. Meaning that if by some means a malicious entity gains access to your database to read from the tables or write to them, they are limited in the damage they can cause. Moreover, you can create read-only views that provide you with a further layer of security - denying the ability to write. Making read-only views of common portions of tables that are regularly queries becomes a real performance and security benefit.

Common Exploit Prevention

In addition to the security changes outlined previously, a significant amount of work can be done to secure your website from the inside as well. As it stands, the most common attacks against websites are these:

- Remote code execution exploits
- SQL injection
- Cross site scripting (XSS)

Remote Code Execution

Remote code execution means feeding data into the webpage so it will execute a command on the server it is hosted with the aim of gaining access to the server. These exploits take advantage of points in the system that take leverage server command-line functions to process data. These kinds of exploits pose a severe risk to servers as remote execution of code can allow a remote user to modify, read, or delete files. This exploit is also commonly used to allow remote users to gain access to the server via SSH - if the SSH access isn't controlled.

SQL Injection

SQL injection works in a similar manner to remote code execution. A normal website input is modified to perform additional functions against a database. While this is often not as dangerous as remote code execution, it can still be used to collect or destroy potentially any user data still held in the database. SQL injection works by malicious parties appending extra SQL to data in data entry fields in the hope that they will be executed in addition to or as part of a normal query. This piggybacking can be used to delete an entire database or dump all the usernames and passwords used by the website's users.

Cross Site Scripting

Cross site scripting represents less of a danger than both of the above, but it is still a big issue for the users of a website. Cross site scripting involves introducing content to a website in such a manner that when this content is displayed, it will cause the webpage the viewer is displaying to perform unwanted functions.

The most common example is a simple hijack, as happened to YouTube in 2010. Someone found that if you made comments in certain formats, you could actually introduce additional web code into the web page. This new web code was used to alter content and provided people with the ability to redirect from one page to another and disable links. Through the use of comment systems or other systems that accept user input, malicious parties are able to introduce content into your web system that can cause users problems.

Mitigation

These three attack vectors are all due to the way that web developers implement their code. There are a number of ways to prevent against these things and numerous works that provide a significantly larger amount of detail and method for these. But the common theme that all these exploits have is to never trust any information that your website loads from anywhere or put more succinctly "always sanitize your variables." When you are doing development work, you will almost always trust that any data loaded into your running webpage will come in a certain format. This is not the case and is the reason why so many websites are susceptible and attacked using these vulnerabilities.

Operating System Performance

We have focused on a significant amount of performance improvements and optimizations for applications and examined methods for offloading processing to other servers and hardware. We have not examined one key piece of any server system: the operating system. It is not hard to derive further performance from operating systems and there are many tweaks and changes you can make to get more.

The problem is that these tweaks can have flow-on effects and can cause problems for certain applications. More to the point, however, many of the specific performance increases for one OS may not work on another and can even have negative impacts. This can also affect performance between two identical servers that have the same operating system yet have different purposes. No small amount of advice from us would replace good research into the specific needs of your system, its operating system, and its function. However, with this all in mind we can provide some general advice.

Compile Yourself

For most of these applications we have been recommending the use of tools like yum and apt-get to install software.

However, these installations are configured to work with a generic system build. This means that if you compile yourself, you can increase the performance of the application by configuring it to your particular system. The downside here is that compiling takes time; and to get more performance out of your application, you will need to become familiar with how the application is compiled and build increasing the complexity. In addition, you will need to keep a full suite of compiling tools on your system, which can consume space.

Note   In the following section there are suggestions for additional Linux distributions that can be used to achieve higher performance.

This may not always be the correct thing for any particular circumstance and makes no account for the advantages of a sysadmin working with a familiar distribution. The following suggestions are intended, like this entire chapter, to be a guide and a suggestion of areas to consider next to increase the performance of the server.

Cut Down

For the most part, installing an operating system comes down to clicking through the installer and getting the OS to boot. However, there are ways to drastically increase performance of servers by cutting down the amount of software installed. The best way to accomplish this is to perform the smallest install possible of your OS and build up from there as needed. Both Ubuntu and Centos offer cut down "core" installs. In addition to these two, distributions such as Arch Linux focus heavily on having a highly customizable operating system.

This means more resources free to be used where they are needed: powering your applications.

▧ **Note** If you can avoid it, *don't* install X. Graphical displays are costly and using only command line can save a lot of resources.

High-Performance OS

We have used Centos and Ubuntu throughout this book, and they are great distributions of Linux with a large support base and ready availability of precompiled software. However, there are distributions designed to significantly increase performance through heavy customization. The most popular and widely used high-performance distribution of Linux is Gentoo.

Gentoo provides no precompiled packages and requires that everything that is to be installed on the operating system be compiled from scratch. Moreover, to begin compiling you need to be familiar with the architecture of the server that is to run the operating system, and will go through and configure the compiler to take advantage of this hardware.

In addition, most high-performance Linux distributions require that you compile the Linux kernel yourself and configure all the components it will use. This can be daunting at first and is quite a lot to take on board the first time you do it, but in the end it can become quite addictive to tweak your system for higher performance.

Planning

We have discussed planning at length in other chapters, but we cannot stress how important it becomes. Planning in this context is simply an extension of everything mentioned before. Using tools such as monitoring solutions discussed earlier to model your server's load patterns and respond accordingly. We stress this because no system is static; you will always have users coming and going, and will almost always see load changes.

Given all this, no load will ever be static, and you will likely wind up consuming more resources than you have available. This makes planning the most valuable thing you can do; a regular examination can show that you are running low, and you can add new resources or shuffle loads to compensate. The management of system performance is two components: getting them to initially perform well and ensuring that this continues into the future. Much of the work that has been laid out throughout this book has been toward creating a good system that allows for an increase in performance.

Summary

By this point, you should have a significant amount of material to consider and plenty of direction to move forward. The material in this chapter should have provided you with a number of stepping stones to build upon the concepts covered throughout the book. As with everything in this book, there is no substitute for understanding your system. What is provided here are guides that provide examples and concepts that will allow you to load balance your servers over any number of situations.

Following the guides and concepts in this book is not a guaranteed method to make your servers perform better as there is no way to cover every iteration and the millions of little things that make your servers unique. We have tried to provide as generic examples as we can that can be adapted to the particulars of a situation. So, with all this in mind, all we can say is good luck and thank you for reading.

Index

CPSIA information can be obtained at www.ICGtesting.com
Printed in the USA
LVOW050028300412

279634LV00004B/51/P